AF841767

...entre
...vay Road
...P
LOND...
metropo...
unive...

Chapter Three is missing from this book
it can be found in
Offprints in Holloway Road Library
Ask for Offprint by Claudio Morana

40 0068780 4

TRENDS IN INFLATION RESEARCH

TRENDS IN INFLATION RESEARCH

BARBARA T. CREDAN
EDITOR

The Learning Centre
Library
236-250 Holloway Road
London N7 6PP
LONDON metropolitan university

Nova Science Publishers, Inc.
New York

Copyright © 2006 by Nova Science Publishers, Inc.

All rights reserved. No part of this book may be reproduced, stored in a retrieval system or transmitted in any form or by any means: electronic, electrostatic, magnetic, tape, mechanical photocopying, recording or otherwise without the written permission of the Publisher.

For permission to use material from this book please contact us:
Telephone 631-231-7269; Fax 631-231-8175
Web Site: http://www.novapublishers.com

NOTICE TO THE READER

The Publisher has taken reasonable care in the preparation of this book, but makes no expressed or implied warranty of any kind and assumes no responsibility for any errors or omissions. No liability is assumed for incidental or consequential damages in connection with or arising out of information contained in this book. The Publisher shall not be liable for any special, consequential, or exemplary damages resulting, in whole or in part, from the readers' use of, or reliance upon, this material.

This publication is designed to provide accurate and authoritative information with regard to the subject matter covered herein. It is sold with the clear understanding that the Publisher is not engaged in rendering legal or any other professional services. If legal or any other expert assistance is required, the services of a competent person should be sought. FROM A DECLARATION OF PARTICIPANTS JOINTLY ADOPTED BY A COMMITTEE OF THE AMERICAN BAR ASSOCIATION AND A COMMITTEE OF PUBLISHERS.

LIBRARY OF CONGRESS CATALOGING-IN-PUBLICATION DATA
Available upon request

ISBN 1-59454-825-0

Published by Nova Science Publishers, Inc. ✢ New York

WITHDRAWN

Date	3.1.08 JS
Fund	635IN
Control no	
Collection/ Loan type	HR Loan.
Class no	332.41 TRE
Accession no	4000687804

Chapter Three:Structural Core Inflation Estimation
can be found in
Offprints in Holloway Road Library
Ask for Offprint by Claudio Morana

CONTENTS

PREFACE

In modern economics, inflation refers to the increase in the general level of prices of a given kind. General inflation is caused by a fall in the market value or purchasing power of money within an economy, as compared to currency devaluation which is the fall of the market value of a currency between economies. General inflation is referred to as a rise in the general level of prices. The former applies to the value of the currency within the national region of use, whereas the latter applies to the external value on international markets. The extent to which these two phenomena are related is open to economic debate. Inflation may also be caused by supply disruptions. For example, climatic changes may cause crop failures, pushing up food prices, or a war or another natural disaster may restrict the supply of crude oil, thus pushing up energy prices. These events may cause inflation within the modern meaning of the word, but are not the result of a fall in the value of the currency. This new book presents new and important research on inflation.

The aim of chapter 1 is to fill this gap by carrying out an analysis that helps explain recent U.K. developments, yet focuses on past policies rather than current arrangements. As one study observed, "The British experience is one that is full of experiments in monetary regimes and switches in regimes." And that statement was written in 1982, prior to the variety of experiments undertaken in the last two decades: a switch of emphasis of monetary targeting from broad money to the monetary base; a subsequent period of informal and then formal pegging of the pound to the Deutschmark; and inflation targeting from 1992. We will provide an up-to-date account of U.K. experiences under different policy regimes, with the emphasis on sources of policy mistakes (both in specific policy decisions and, more fundamentally, in the underlying economic analysis). Thus, our objective is not to provide yet another review of inflation targeting in the United Kingdom, but rather, a critical analysis of U.K. monetary policy developments over 1955-2004, focusing on the confusions, misconceptions, and theoretical mistakes in the economic analysis that guided U.K. macroeconomic policy over that period, and how current arrangements have shaken off the earlier sources of error.

Chapter 2 shows that when valuating cash flows they should be based on estimates of free cash flows at nominal prices. In particular, the authors show that results from the valuation of cash flows with the constant and real price methods are biased upwards and there is a risk that in practice, bad projects will be accepted as good projects or that the valuation of free cash flows for valuing firms is overstated. Generally speaking, inflation has a negative impact on the Net Present Value, NPV of a project. When expected inflation rates over the cash flow horizon are high, which is a typically case in emerging and transitional markets, the use of the real and constant prices methodology could lead to serious mistakes in valuation. There is no doubt that some decades ago, before the advent of the powerful computing capacity of personal computers, modeling the impacts of inflation in investment appraisal was an insurmountable task. Today, conducting investment appraisal by constructing financial statements with nominal prices is a simple and straightforward task. In this chapter, we would like to persuade the reader (if indeed there is need for persuasion) that conducting investment appraisal based on financial statements with real or constant prices is potentially misleading and under some conditions, the adverse effects of inflation could result in the selection of the "wrong" projects. Estimated financial statements (i.e. Income Statement, Balance Sheet, cash budgets and free cash flows) are managerial tools that help the manager to control and follow up any activity. Financial statements at constant or real prices will be of no use when the project is implemented because what occurs in reality (that is what we are interested in) is very different from what is written in the final report of a project evaluation. Some items are deflated while others (say depreciation charges and interest payments) are in nominal prices. Hence, for managerial purposes, it is useless to have this mixed information in the financial statements. The authors present some examples where we show that the value of a cash flow should be based on estimates of free cash flows at nominal prices. It is an accepted practice to evaluate projects at constant or real prices. These days, the use of constant or real prices is an unnecessary oversimplification of reality. In particular, they present an example where the results from the constant and real price methodologies are biased upwards and there is a risk that in practice, bad projects will be accepted as good projects. It is a third party and near real life example (an example presented in the training material on economic regulation of public utilities developed by the World Bank Institute) we compare the results of the constant prices methodology with results of the nominal prices methodology. World Bank (WB) has played a crucial role in the development of the economies of the world, especially in the emerging countries. They recognize the leadership it has shown and the intellectual authority it has on planning offices, practitioners and consultants. For this reason it is critical whatever improvements made in the methodologies it uses in assessing the feasibility of infrastructure projects. This influence affects private practice in valuation and project appraisal as well. Vélez-Pareja in 1999 warned: "constant price methodology implies some assumptions and a mixture of items, some deflated, and some others not deflated". Vélez-Pareja 1999 and Vélez Pareja and Tham, 2002, warn about the overvaluation of a project when appraised at constant prices. On the other hand Tham and Vélez-Pareja 2004 mentioned the most frequent (and avoidable) mistakes when valuing cash flows. The authors show how in the case based on the example from WB where they use some current practices several improvements to some areas of the model can be made, such as valuation at constant prices, mixing deflated and non-deflated items in a financial statements, using constant leverage when in the forecasted financial statements it is not constant, inconsistency in the cash flow and value calculations and some other irregularities that will be described in the body of the chapter. This analysis shows an overvaluation of more than 21% when the constant prices methodology is compared with the current prices methodology and using market values to calculate the WACC. This is a dramatic number.

Chapter 3 proposes a new structural approach to core inflation estimation, based on the linkage between inflation and excess nominal money growth postulated by the quantity theory of money. The proposed core inflation measure bears the interpretation of monetary inflation rate and is characterised by all the properties that an ``ideal" core inflation process should show.

Using the *Johansen* test for cointegration, chapter 4 examines to which extent inflation rates in the Euro area have converged after the introduction of a single currency. Since the assumption of non-stationary variables represents the pivotal point in cointegration analyses we pay special attention to the appropriate identification of non-stationary inflation rates by the application of six different unit root tests. The authors compare two periods, the first ranging from 1993 to 1998 and the second from 1993 to 2003 with monthly observations. The *Johansen* test only finds partial convergence for the former period and no convergence for the latter.

Chapter 5 analyzes the interaction between the inflation and growth within the Mankiw-Romer-Weil (1992) framework. The results indicate that the inflation level has a significant negative effect on output in advanced capitalist economies, whereas inflation variability has a negative and significant effect on output in the long-run for all sub-samples. The results also show that the variability effects are larger in terms of significance.

Domestic inflation appears to have declined since the mid-1980s in many countries, including those that switched to inflation-targeting regimes. In theory, when a central bank establishes a credible inflation-targeting regime, this anchors inflation expectations and helps ward off inflationary impetus. In Chapter 6 the authors ask whether this has been the case in 5 industrial countries: Australia, Canada, New Zealand, Sweden, and the United Kingdom. They model inflation before the adoption of inflation targets with a modified Phillips curve, which incorporates multiple factors, such as capacity utilization, commodity prices and exchange rates. From this model we control for how much each of these standard variables affects inflation. In addition, they measure the effects of a credible inflation-targeting regime in two ways. First, they estimate the Phillips curve model pre-target adoption, and then forecast inflation in recent history, comparing the forecasts to actual values to see how much the pre-inflation target model over-predicts inflation in the targeting-regime. Second, they conduct rolling Phillips curve regressions in order to see whether: 1) the utilization coefficient shifts toward zero around the time of target adoption, signifying that central bank credibility has dampened the effects of capacity constraints on inflation; and/or 2) the model's intercept moves toward the inflation target range.

Inflation is widely regarded as a monetary phenomenon. The long run relationship between money and prices has been confirmed by a large number of empirical studies across countries and across time. Nevertheless, the *"science of monetary policy"* largely neglects money. In the now popular New Keynesian type models money plays no active role. Analysing monetary policy without money is so widely accepted that it is now standard in macroeconomics textbooks. In contrast, some authors question the redundancy of money and argue that an independent role for money in the transmission mechanism should be taken seriously. The P-Star model offers a convenient framework of *"putting 'M' back in monetary policy."* In this model money plays an active role in the transmission process and monetary policy affects inflation through two channels, output and liquidity. It is shown that New Keynesian models are special cases of the P-Star-model. Chapter 7 analyses alternative monetary policy rules in the P-Star model. The authors find that inflation targeting is not a robust strategy for monetary policy. If the central bank does not solely care about inflation, a Taylor rule, monetary targeting or a two pillar strategy, combining monetary and inflation targeting, are clearly superior to inflation targeting. This holds if there is model uncertainty.

Moreover, under asymmetric information, monetary targeting outperforms inflation targeting and a Taylor rule even if the central bank is geared to stabilising inflation and output.

In: Trends in Inflation Research
Editor: Barbara T. Credan, pp. 1-86

ISBN: 1-59454-825-0
© 2006 Nova Science Publishers, Inc.

Chapter 1

THE U.K.'S ROCKY ROAD TO STABILITY

Nicoletta Batini and Edward Nelson
Centre for Economic Policy Research (CEPR), London, United Kingdom

ABSTRACT

The aim of this paper is to fill this gap by carrying out an analysis that helps explain recent U.K. developments, yet focuses on past policies rather than current arrangements. As one study observed, "The British experience is one that is full of experiments in monetary regimes and switches in regimes." And that statement was written in 1982, prior to the variety of experiments undertaken in the last two decades: a switch of emphasis of monetary targeting from broad money to the monetary base; a subsequent period of informal and then formal pegging of the pound to the Deutschmark; and inflation targeting from 1992. We will provide an up-to-date account of U.K. experiences under different policy regimes, with the emphasis on sources of policy mistakes (both in specific policy decisions and, more fundamentally, in the underlying economic analysis). Thus, our objective is not to provide yet another review of inflation targeting in the United Kingdom, but rather, a critical analysis of U.K. monetary policy developments over 1955-2004, focusing on the confusions, misconceptions, and theoretical mistakes in the economic analysis that guided U.K. macroeconomic policy over that period, and how current arrangements have shaken off the earlier sources of error.

1 INTRODUCTION

With the end of 2004, the United Kingdom has had positive economic growth for 50 consecutive quarters, a record unmatched in its half-century of quarterly GDP data. Figure 1, showing a 50-quarter moving average of U.K. growth since the mid-1960s, and Figure 2, showing corresponding moving standard deviations, illustrate this achievement.

Over the same period, unemployment has declined, while inflation has been low and stable. Indices of inflation performance depend on the precise price index used; in addition, they depend on how the price index is extended back in time and how seasonality is removed, since official seasonally adjusted inflation series are not available over a long sample. But because the improvement in performance has been so marked, such choices have a relatively minor effect on the comparison. Estimates using a series for U.K. consumer price inflation[1] that we constructed give annualized mean and standard deviation of 2.7% and 2.2% respectively for October 1992-August 2001, compared to 8.8% and 8.6% for January 1965-September 1992.[2] Similar (indeed, better) results hold if the 1992-2001 sample is extended to 2004, while the inflation record still registers a pronounced improvement after 1992 if a different sample period is chosen to represent pre-1992 behavior.[3]

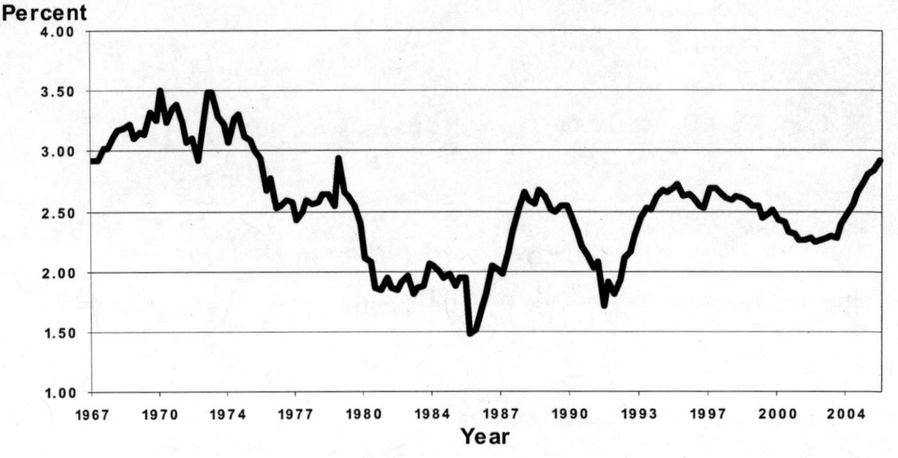

Figure 1: U.K. real GDP growth: 50-quarter moving average

Figure 2: U.K real GDP growth: 50-quarter moving standard deviation

The reason that springs to mind for this improved record is the overhaul of the macroeconomic policy framework in the U.K. over the last 25 years. True, the decline in output volatility, the achievement of longer economic expansions, and the fall in the mean

[1] Defined in Section 2 below.
[2] Batini and Nelson (2001), Table 1.
[3] As we stress below, it is desirable to break the pre-inflation targeting period into several regimes rather than treat it monolithically.

and variance of inflation are by no means phenomena unique to the U.K. Increased macroeconomic stability has been a development present in the United States and several other economies, as discussed by McConnell and Perez-Quiroz (2000) and Blanchard and Simon (2001), among others. But greater stability at a global level does not preclude the possibility that the dominant sources of U.K improvement are the changes rung in domestic macroeconomic policy. For one thing, as emphasized in Bernanke's (2004) discussion of the "Great Moderation," just as there are parallels between different economies' improvements, there are parallels between the shifts in policy regime that took place in each country over the same period—particularly in the exclusive responsibility assigned to monetary policy for inflation control. For another, the improvement in the U.K. economy has been *especially* drastic: from double-digit inflation rates in the 1970s far exceeding those in the U.S. and many other countries, and poor inflation outcomes as late as 1990, to a high level of stability in inflation from 1992; and from several episodes of negative economic growth to the complete absence of negative growth in the last decade (unlike, for example, Australia and the U.S., which had at least one quarter of negative growth during 2000-2001).

It is from that perspective that we provide in this paper an analysis of U.K. macroeconomic policy developments. At first blush, a study of changes in U.K. macroeconomic arrangements would appear to be a redundant exercise, given the vast amount of research that has already been undertaken on inflation targeting. The existing literature does provide many useful comparisons of the U.K.'s recent record with other countries (see especially Bernanke, Laubach, Mishkin, and Posen, 1999, Mishkin and Schmidt-Hebbel, 2001, and Levin, Piger, and Natalucci, 2004), which we do not provide here. But equally, it does not go to the heart of the issues that we are interested in.

A shortcoming of what has been written in recent years is that the focus on the effects of U.K. inflation targeting naturally leads to the pre-inflation targeting period being treated monolithically. In this category one can include quantitative studies such as that of Ball and Sheridan (2005), which compresses the entire pre-inflation targeting period into a single regime (albeit one with a shifting steady-state inflation rate). Discussions by U.K. commentators which group the 1970s and 1980s together as a "high inflation" period, failing to note the differences in both policy and performance across the two decades, are guilty of a similar oversimplification. Other recent analyses, such as Balls and O'Donnell (2001), emphasize the post-1997 macroeconomic arrangements—i.e., the independence conferred on the Bank of England as well as other reforms by the Blair Government—and contrast the macroeconomic results with those of earlier in the 1990s. Though important in consolidating the period of stability since 1992, these reforms are evidently minor in effect relative to the changes in arrangements introduced in 1992, since low inflation and continuous economic growth were achieved over 1992-97. Existing accounts, on the whole, give insufficient detail on the initial conditions leading to inflation targeting in the United Kingdom or on the developments that made the U.K. pre-1990s record exceptionally poor.

The aim of this paper is to fill this gap by carrying out an analysis that helps explain recent U.K. developments, yet focuses on past policies rather than current arrangements. As one study observed, "The British experience is one that is full of experiments in monetary regimes and switches in regimes."[4] And that statement was written in 1982, prior to the variety of experiments undertaken in the last two decades: a switch of emphasis of monetary

[4] Howard and Johnson (1982, p. 161).

targeting from broad money to the monetary base; a subsequent period of informal and then formal pegging of the pound to the Deutschmark; and inflation targeting from 1992. We will provide an up-to-date account of U.K. experiences under different policy regimes, with the emphasis on sources of policy mistakes (both in specific policy decisions and, more fundamentally, in the underlying economic analysis). Thus, our objective is not to provide yet another review of inflation targeting in the United Kingdom, but rather, a critical analysis of U.K. monetary policy developments over 1955-2004, focusing on the confusions, misconceptions, and theoretical mistakes in the economic analysis that guided U.K. macroeconomic policy over that period, and how current arrangements have shaken off the earlier sources of error.

In carrying out this analysis, we have found it useful to draw heavily of archival material. Our analysis will make use of information about changes in policymakers' views of the role of monetary policy, as recorded in contemporaneous records such as newspaper reports, publications of policy agencies and financial institutions, policymakers' speeches, and transcripts of television interviews. We also will draw critically on memoirs of several of the relevant policymakers. Again, it is tempting to conclude that this exercise is unnecessary, on the grounds that the relevant information is already provided in the existing retrospective accounts of U.K. monetary policy. We have found, however, that this is in fact not the case, and that our own consultation of the archival record has been essential both in obtaining factual information and in guiding our interpretation of policy developments. An example of where our analysis differs from the existing literature on U.K. policy produces not simply in interpretation but, instead, on the factual record, is brought out by the statement in a recent study of U.K. monetary policy over 1975-2000 by Cobham (2002, p. 29): "A remarkable feature of U.K. monetary targeting is the almost complete lack of official explanation for (and non-official comment on) the numbers selected for the target ranges," a situation that Cobham claims changed only in 1985. But in fact an official memorandum was published in 1980 by the U.K. Treasury (which had authority over monetary policy until 1997), providing its estimates of the velocity trend in the targeted monetary aggregate (Sterling M3). So further examination of documentary material establishes that an alleged "remarkable feature" of U.K. monetary targeting was not in fact a feature of monetary targeting at all.[5] Our discussion will bring out further differences from the existing literature that arise from our own consultation of archival material.

In studying the monetary policy record of the U.K., there are two pitfalls to be kept in mind. The first is the danger of assuming that a policy analysis appropriate for other countries—particularly the U.S.—can be transplanted without modification to the U.K, without regard to institutional differences. This danger has meant that U.K. policy officials have understandably been wary of analyses of their economy by non-U.K. economists; in the words of an internal Treasury memorandum in 1981, a flawed analysis should "not [be] surprising from someone unfamiliar with our institutions."[6] And whether the analysis is by U.K. or non-U.K. economists,[7] the degree of attention given to U.K. institutional detail can

[5] See HM Treasury (1980). We discussed this memorandum in Batini and Nelson (2000). The velocity assumptions in the 1980 Treasury memorandum were also mentioned by Budd and Holly (1986, p. 17).

[6] Quoted in Howe (1994, p. 186). The memorandum was from Peter Middleton (the Permanent Head of the Treasury) to Geoffrey Howe, the Chancellor of the Exchequer (the Cabinet minister responsible for economic policy).

[7] The reader is forewarned that the present authors are in the second category, although we have worked in the U.K.

make a crucial difference. One example that illustrates this is the study of Haldane and Quah (1999), whose explanation for the U.K.'s inflation experience rests on the assumption that the Phillips curve was the model guiding U.K monetary policy between the late 1950s and the mid-1970s. But U.K. policymakers in fact subscribed to a nonmonetary view of inflation throughout this period, immediately ruling out the hypothesis advanced, even as a partial explanation. To avoid this pitfall, the explanations for policy behavior that we provide will be documented by statements of policy officials.

The opposite pitfall is to accept too readily a position of "U.K. exceptionalism." Under such an approach, U.K. policy arrangements that appear suboptimal, and economic analysis by policy officials that appears flawed, might be too readily excused by the claim that the U.K. is "different," hence the nonstandard approach. Acceptance of U.K. exceptionalism can imply that even what is intended as a critical analysis of U.K. monetary policy might unwittingly repeat the omissions, analytical errors, and talking points of the U.K. policymakers themselves. One class of studies that falls into this category consists of the outside analyses of 1970s economic policy that criticized U.K. governments for adopting the "wrong" type of incomes policy—e.g. a compulsory wage freeze instead of a tax-based incomes policy. Such critiques accepted the governments' nonmonetary diagnosis of inflation, and therefore shared with policymakers a major misconception. A second and more recent class of studies that suffer from this pitfall are those that accepted the validity of the authorities' "credit counterparts" approach to analyzing money growth determination, and criticized policy from within that framework.[8] As we discuss below, this framework should itself be regarded as flawed. Conscious of this second pitfall, we will take a critical view of the analysis *both* of the policymakers *and* of many of their outside critics.

Our discussion will draw on our own prior research on U.K. macroeconomic policy. We will not, however, reproduce that research here; instead, our prior work will allow us to give relatively brief treatment of topics that are usually prominent in discussions of the U.K. experience. For example, the extensive analysis of the U.K.'s 1970s inflation in Nelson and Nikolov (2004) and Nelson (2004) allows a short treatment of that episode here. Another example is the low emphasis we put on openness and exchange-rate issues. Our prior work suggests that imports should be treated as an intermediate good rather than a final consumer good. This implies that the Phillips curve describing CPI inflation involves only the output gap and expected-inflation terms, just as in the closed-economy case (see e.g. Kara and Nelson, 2003; and Batini, Jackson, and Nickell, 2005).

The plan of the paper is as follows. Section 2 lays out some terminological rules we follow in discussing U.K. economic variables. Section 3 discusses the nonmonetary approach to macroeconomic policy that prevailed in the U.K. in the 1950s and the 1960s. Section 4 discusses the era of broad money targeting, while Section 5 discusses several problems with U.K. monetary policy conduct from the 1950s to the 1980s. Section 6 discusses monetary policy developments in the final 15 years of the period under study—1990 to 2004. Fiscal policy is taken up in Section 8, followed by a discussion of economic growth in Section 9. Some conclusions (Section 10) complete the discussion.

---

[8] For example, the book by Congdon (1992), though described on the back cover as "critic[al] of successive governments' failures in economic policy," accepts many of the authorities' premises that we criticize, including the counterparts approach to money supply determination, the advantages of targeting broad money over narrow money, and the effectiveness of "overfunding" as a means of altering broad money growth.

2 Terminological Preliminaries

Due to the frequency of changing terminology and U.K.-specific terminology in policy discussions over the period we are studying, it is useful to lay out some conventions that we will be following regarding terminology. We start with the country name (Sect. 2A), then consider financial variables (Sect. 2B), and consumer prices (Sect. 2C).

2A United Kingdom

We will use "United Kingdom" or "U.K." throughout as the abbreviation for the full name of the country (i.e., The United Kingdom of Great Britain and Northern Ireland). This convention is in line with most official U.K. publications on monetary policy, as well as the IMF's *International Financial Statistics* and the OECD's *Economic Outlook*. Many U.S. writers in monetary economics, including Friedman and Schwartz (1963), have used "Great Britain," as have some U.K. authors such as Carter (1960) and Griffiths (1974). During the period studied in this paper, many U.K. citizens and policymakers did give the impression that "Great Britain" was the term to use in formal discussions,[9] although this view seems to have tapered off during the 1960s and 1970s, and "U.K." is now standard.

U.K. government publications have occasionally given the term "Britain" some official status, as in a 1987 publication by the U.K. Central Office of Information entitled *Britain* which stated that Britain was "the same as" the U.K.,[10] and a 2001 book by the U.K. Treasury entitled *Reforming Britain's Economic and Financial Policy*.[11] However, as Crick (1988, p. 2) notes, "Britain" is "the name of a former Roman province, [with] no modern legal or precise geographical meaning." In light of this, it seems preferable to use "U.K.," which is already an abbreviation, in macroeconomic discussions, rather than adopt the further shorthand of "Britain."

For economic data, an important qualification should be made. Some aggregate data, most notably those for the labor market, are available historically only for the Great Britain portion of the U.K. Aggregate estimates of U.K. productivity require aggregate real GDP data (which are available for the U.K.) as well as data on employment and/or hours (generally available for Great Britain alone). In our discussion, we refer to the implied output-per-

---

[9] For example, James Callaghan, who later served as Chancellor of the Exchequer and Prime Minister, opened a House of Commons debate in 1962 with the criticism that the government "proposes no adequate policies for lifting Great Britain out of the prolonged industrial stagnation from which the country is still suffering… especially in Scotland, the North of England, Wales, and Northern Ireland." *House of Commons Debates*, November 5, 1962, page 604. (For speeches and unsigned articles in official U.K. government publications, as well as for newspaper articles and financial circulars, we provide full bibliographical details in footnotes. The details for other articles we cite are provided in the references.)

[10] Quoted in Crick (1988, p. 2).

[11] Balls and O'Donnell (2001). The usage of "U.K." vs. "Britain" evidently differs across institutions within the U.K. government. This was illustrated by the annual "Mansion House" speeches for 2004 by the Chancellor of the Exchequer (Gordon Brown) and the Governor of the Bank of England (Mervyn King). Chancellor Brown's speech referred to the U.K. as "Britain" 34 times, as "Great Britain" twice, and "U.K." three times; Governor King's speech used "U.K." six times, and did not use the alternative terms. Gordon Brown, "Speech Given by the Chancellor of the Exchequer Gordon Brown at the Mansion House, London," June 16, 2004, U.K. Treasury website; Mervyn King, "The Governor's Speech at the Mansion House," June 16, 2004, Bank of England website.

worker series as "U.K. productivity," although, in fact, series such as this are derived from a combination of U.K. and Great Britain aggregates.

2B Interest Rates, Money, and Credit

Because of the close historical and geographical connections between U.K. policy officials and the "City of London" (i.e., the U.K. financial markets), macroeconomic discussion in the U.K., especially that in the 1950s and 1960s, has been dominated by "City" terminology. This terminology sometimes dates from the nineteenth century and typically differs from that used in macroeconomic discussion. For example, what the City calls "gilt-edged Government stock" are simply long-term government securities. In this paper, we will eschew "City" jargon and will instead use standard macroeconomic terminology.

This will include the terminology we use for monetary and credit aggregates. Particularly in the era of official quantitative controls on banks, the term "advances" was commonly used in the U.K. to refer to (the increase in) commercial banks' loans to the private sector. We will avoid this terminology and make clear in the context whether we are referring to commercial bank loans to the private sector, bank lending to the private plus public sectors (i.e. total bank credit), or total credit (i.e. the aggregate of bank and nonbank credit). "Lending" and "credit" will thus refer to stocks of loans, and not to the absolute or percentage changes in those stocks.

For money, a glossary of terms in a book by a U.K. financial journalist contains the puzzling statement: "The money supply is the increase in the stock [of money]" (Smith, 1987, p. 174). This definition is clearly not that used in macroeconomics, where "money supply" and "money stock" are used interchangeably. As far as we can tell, Smith's terminology was not widely used in the U.K. at any point, even in the City. His definition seems to arise out of tentative moves to change official terminology in the early 1970s. For example, the *Midland Bank Review* in 1970 observed that a recent Bank of England publication had started to show a preference for the term "stock of money," which the Review applauded "since ['money supply'] contains implicit suggestions of a flow rather than a stock."[12] In the event, this switch in terminology never came to pass, and the continued use of "money supply" to refer to the money stock was acknowledged by the Governor of the Bank of England's reference in May 1971 to the "money supply" as an "inelegant but apparently unavoidable term."[13] In our own discussion we will use "money supply" synonymously with "money stock."

In referring to specific monetary aggregates (M0, M1, Sterling M3, M4, etc.), we use the definitions used by the U.K. authorities. However, in referring to different categories of money within each aggregate, we use standard macroeconomic terminology. For example, the standard terminology for the non-reserves component of outside or base money is "currency," and we will use that in preference to the U.K. terminology of "notes and coin." We will refer to the non-currency component of (the former) M1 as "demand deposits," rather than the U.K. labels of "current accounts" or "sight deposits."

---

[12] "Another Look at Money Supply," *Midland Bank Review* (November, 1970), reprinted in Wadsworth (1973, pp. 93–98); quotation from page 97.

[13] Leslie O'Brien, "Key Issues in Monetary and Credit Policy," May 28, 1971, speech, *Bank of England Quarterly Bulletin* (June, 1971), Vol. 11(2), pp. 195–198; quotation from page 195.

2C Consumer Prices

Traditionally, the cost-of-living index of consumer prices used in U.K. discussions has been the Retail Price Index (RPI). This was frequently referred to as an index of "consumer prices," for example in speeches by U.K. Chancellors of the Exchequer[14] and in statistical publications by agencies such as the IMF and the OECD, as well as in research, such as Artis and Kontolemis' (1996, p. 68) reference to the RPI as the "consumer price level." With inflation targeting in the 1990s, the RPIX (the RPI excluding mortgage interest payments) acquired prominence,[15] with official inflation targets from 1992 to 2003 given in terms of the RPIX. Recently, however, an official "Consumer Prices Index" or CPI series, distinct from the RPIX, has been advanced by the U.K. government, and since December 2003 its inflation rate has served as the rate targeted by monetary policy.

In this paper, "consumer price inflation" will refer to inflation in an RPI/RPIX series. The specific price series we use is the RPIX as far back as that series is available, spliced into the RPI to obtain observations earlier than 1975. As the official RPI/RPIX series are not seasonally adjusted, we have applied our own seasonal adjustment in generating inflation rates from our consumer price series.[16]

3 The Nonmonetary Approach to Macroeconomic Policy (1955-79)

In this section we cover U.K. macroeconomic policy developments over the first half of the 1955-2004 period—that is, the years to 1979. As well as splitting the period evenly, this division is convenient because 1979 represented the clear break away from a nonmonetary approach to inflation control. By 1979, U.K. policymakers had also turned away from using devices other than monetary policy as their main tools for manipulating aggregate demand. The nonmonetary approach to aggregate demand control had dissipated earlier than the nonmonetary approach to inflation control, which is why in Section 3A we consider the block of years from 1955 to 1970—the heyday of U.K. policymakers' nonmonetary outlook toward demand management. We follow this with a discussion in Section 3B of the nonmonetary approach to inflation control that was dominant from 1955 to 1979.

3A The Nonmonetary Approach to Demand Management (1955-70)

We consider first developments in demand management and monetary policy in the 1950s (Section 3A.1) then subsequent developments to 1970 (Section 3A.2).

---

[14] E.g. Chancellor Selwyn Lloyd, *House of Commons Debates*, November 7, 1961, page 833; and Chancellor Iain Macleod, *House of Commons Debates*, July 7, 1970, page 504.

[15] As early as November 1989, the U.K. Treasury had stated: "A better indicator of underlying inflation is provided by the RPI excluding mortgage interest payments" (quoted in Craven and Gausden, 1991, p. 30).

[16] The adjustment procedure, described in Nelson and Nikolov (2004), uses seasonal effects estimated on those sample periods where price controls were not in effect.

3A.1 U.K. Monetary Policy in the 1950s

Milton Friedman and the Romers have argued that U.S. monetary policy in the 1950s was guided by an emphasis on aggregate demand and inflation control that was more enlightened than the policies that followed in the 1960s and 1970s—indeed, by "a relatively modern view" in the Romers' evaluation.[17] On the surface, the same judgment would appear appropriate for the U.K.: U.K. consumer price inflation averaged only 3.4% for 1955-59, while the real ex-post Treasury bill rate averaged 1.1% over the same period,[18] certainly low but far from the negative values observed in the 1970s. In addition, Congdon (1980, p. 28) describes the 1950s as "the only prolonged period since the war… [where] conscious and deliberate use was made of monetary policy" to control inflation in the U.K.[19]

Despite these similarities, the parallels between U.K. policy in the 1950s and either U.S. policy in the 1950s, or modern U.K. inflation targeting, are not very close. The key differences are that nonmonetary views of inflation, on the one hand, and skepticism about the effectiveness of monetary policy in controlling aggregate demand, on the other, remained prevalent in official circles throughout the 1950s. The relatively tight monetary policy that took place occurred in part because official advice was resisted by policymakers, and in part because the U.K.'s fixed exchange rate obligations under Bretton Woods limited the extent to which the authorities could disregard monetary policy. Most importantly, despite what in retrospect was a successful decade for the use of monetary policy in demand management, the skepticism in policy circles about such use intensified in the 1950s, and led to a strongly nonmonetary perspective coming into force in 1958-59.

The doubtful attitude toward monetary policy among 1950s U.K. officials reflected their acceptance of what was regarded as a major message of the Keynesian revolution. Blinder (1984) and Gordon (1984) dispute the claim of monetarists that skepticism regarding monetary policy was prevalent in the 1950s. Instead, they suggest that what Blinder calls "the bad old days in which Neanderthal Keynesians roamed the land, spreading the false word that money does not matter" (1984, p. 118) were essentially over by the early 1950s. But the "land" Blinder refers to was of course the U.S. What monetarists thought they saw in the U.S. was a reality in the U.K.: the majority of both policy advisers and academics adhered closely to the "Neanderthal Keynesian" view.[20]

The climate of 1950s academic opinion on monetary policy in the U.K. is reflected, though not endorsed, in Meade's (1951) *Theory of International Economic Policy*, the only U.K. contribution to monetary economics to be the basis for a Nobel Prize. Since Meade's focus was on stabilization policy for an open economy, he could hardly ignore monetary policy. On the contrary, in addition to emphasizing the link between exchange-rate movements and interest rates, he actually proposed using monetary policy to stabilize the

---

[17] Romer and Romer (2002b, p. 19); see also Romer and Romer (2002a) and Milton Friedman, "To Jimmy from James," *Newsweek*, December 6, 1976, page 45. Friedman argues that the 1950s monetary policy proceeded as it did "only because… [President] Eisenhower was willing to flout the reigning temper of the time" and tolerate two recessions to subdue inflation. Romer and Romer, on the other hand, argue that the successful policy reflected a generally coherent framework on the part of the Federal Reserve.

[18] As we discuss in Section 4, we use the U.K. Treasury bill rate since it has always been closely related to the official policy rate.

[19] As Congdon was writing in 1980, when it was not yet clear that the shift to an inflation-oriented monetary policy in 1979 would be "prolonged." See our discussion of this shift in Section 6 below.

[20] As Cobham (1984, p. 160), observes, "British Keynesianism has traditionally been more 'extreme,' more 'hard-line' than that prevalent for example in North America."

price index for domestically produced goods (Meade, 1951, p. 106). But just before making this prescription, Meade gave credence to the possibility that "domestic expenditure is not in fact very sensitive to changes in the rate of interest," while expressing no corresponding doubt about the effectiveness of fiscal policy (1951, p. 104). Essentially, Meade was making a concession to the "Neanderthal Keynesian" body of opinion in the U.K. that monetary policy was ineffective.

The "Neanderthal Keynesian" position implied extremely interest-inelastic aggregate demand. One example of this view was the judgment of Thomas Balogh—a 1950s academic in the U.K. who became a senior Treasury adviser during the 1960s—on the U.K. evidence: "Monetary policy seems to have no systematic impact on either fixed or liquid capital investment."[21] Nevertheless, there had to be some adaptation of this position to recognize the open-economy contribution to U.K. aggregate demand. Even extreme Keynesians did not deny that policy choices for the interest rate mattered for maintenance of a fixed exchange rate, and that the exchange rate mattered for net exports. The position that emerged from this acknowledgement was the view that consumption and investment were quite insensitive to monetary policy actions, so that monetary policy mattered *only* via its influence on the exchange rate. This position continued into the 1960s, enshrined in the Chancellor of the Exchequer's accompaniment of a 1964 increase in the policy rate (Bank Rate) with the statement that the action was intended to support the exchange rate and that he "hoped it would not work through to the domestic economy."[22]

The skepticism about monetary policy was not always apparent from public statements. When, for example, the authorities increased short-term interest rates twice in early 1955, a wire report recorded: "A Bank of England spokesman said Thursday morning that the second increase, like the first, was imposed as an anti-inflation measure."[23] The same Thursday of the increase, however, the Governor of the Bank of England wrote to the Chancellor of the Exchequer expressing doubts about the measure: stating that "the contribution of credit policy to a balanced economy should not be overestimated," he added that "the inflationary pressures which have threatened to develop in recent months have their origins much less in the monetary than in the cost and wages structure" (quoted in Dell, 1996, p. 198). Reflecting the U.K. consensus, the Governor's concerns combined an elasticity pessimism that implied a nonmonetary view of aggregate demand determination, with a nonmonetary (cost-push) view of inflation that discounted the role for demand restriction.

It was, however, a monetary policy tightening in 1957 that saw the greatest departure of policymakers from the prevailing skepticism about monetary policy. In announcing an increase in the short-term policy rate (Bank Rate) to 7%, Chancellor Thorneycroft said: "There can be no remedy for inflation and the steadily rising prices which go with it which does not include, and indeed is not founded upon, a control of the money supply."[24] *The Economist* noted accurately that this "resort to a classical monetary policy" by the government was a major break from its practice in the 1950s of attempting demand

---

[21] Balogh (1958, p. 226).

[22] James Callaghan, November 23, 1964 statement, quoted in Iain Macleod, "Iain Macleod" column, *Daily Mail* (London), March 29, 1966, page 8.

[23] "Bank of England Again Increases Its Interest Rates," *The Daily Oklahoman*, February 25, 1955, page 2.

[24] Peter Thorneycroft, September 19, 1957 statement, quoted in the November 1957 *Midland Bank Review* article "Bank Deposits and Currency," reprinted in Wadsworth (1973, pp. 77–81). The quotation also appears in Dacey (1960, p. 130) and "Mr. Thorneycroft Rejects 'Mere £50m' Argument," *The Times* (London), January 15, 1958, page 13.

management by "nonmonetary means."[25] The shift in priorities did not, however, reflect a major change in thinking among policy advisers: indeed, according to Dell (1996, p. 233), Thorneycroft's statement "horrified Treasury economists."[26] Roy Harrod, an economist who became a major influence on members of the government, criticized the fact that "remedies for a demand-pull inflation have been applied" when, he claimed, "there has been no demand-pull inflation… there has [instead] been a moderate cost-push inflation."[27]

Lacking deep support in official circles, the 1957 shift toward greater reliance on monetary policy was therefore vulnerable. In the event, a successful backlash of opinion against monetary policy did occur, in the form of widespread misinterpretations of the effects of the 1957 tightening. The lag in reaction of aggregate spending to the monetary tightening appeared to reaffirm the view that demand was interest-elastic. By the late 1960s, with greater acknowledgment of the effects of monetary actions on aggregate demand, the verdict on the 1957 tightening remained negative, but stressed instead the lack of reaction of inflation rather than of aggregate demand to the tightening measures. For example, Peter Jay, Economics Editor of the London *Times*, wrote in 1968 of "the failure of Mr. Thorneycroft's policies, which caused high unemployment without stopping inflation,"[28] while *The Guardian*'s Financial Editor said in 1969 that the 1955-58 experience had established that "dear money will drive up prices… [producing] stagnation accompanied by price inflation"—an interpretation apparently relying on an interest-cost-push and unit-cost-push view of inflation.[29]

In fact, the judgment that monetary tightening did not reduce inflation is based on an analysis that fails to take into account the importance of lags. Artis (1961), for example, found that money had a low contemporaneous correlation with prices over 1956 Q1-1960 Q3, and that the correlations between prices and money 1-2 quarters earlier were even smaller. In Batini and Nelson (2001), however, we found that there were significant correlations of money growth with U.K. inflation over 1953-69 when money growth behavior of about a year earlier was considered.[30] This pattern appears to describe well the response of inflation following the 1957 monetary tightening,[31] since, as Hanson (1962, p. 345) observed, "Great Britain [i.e. the U.K.], helped to some extent by the fall in world prices of primary products, enjoyed its longest period of stable prices for a quarter of a century, the Index of Retail Prices rising little more than one point in the three years 1958-60." The fact that Hanson's account of this success made use of a cost-push explanation (i.e., his reference to primary goods prices) again shows that monetary policy got little credit for the late 1950s price stability.

Over this same period, as it happened, monetary policy was being critically examined by an official inquiry, the Radcliffe Committee, whose Report arrived in 1959. Laidler (1989) characterizes the Report as painting interest rates as the center of the transmission

[25] Editorial, "Putting On the Brakes," *The Economist*, September 28, 1957, pp. 997–999; quotations from page 998.

[26] Similarly, Goodhart (1973, p. 502) says that Thorneycroft's views were not shared by his officials.

[27] Harrod (1958, p. 67).

[28] Peter Jay, "Inflation: Is the Money Supply Crucial?," *The Times* (London), May 31, 1968, page 31.

[29] Anthony Harris, "Help Stamp Out Friedmanism," *The Guardian* (London), November 18, 1969.

[30] We found (2001, Table 3) for 1953–69 a peak correlation between 12-month inflation and 12-month money growth of 0.42, with money growth leading inflation by 11 months. If we use that dataset to consider the 1950s subsample alone (January 1953–December 1959), the peak correlation is again with money growth 11 months earlier, now with a correlation of 0.41; while a reduced-form regression of 12-month inflation on lags 1–12 of 12-month money growth delivers a coefficient sum on money growth of 0.98.

[31] Griffiths and Wood (1984, p. 4) also attribute price stability in 1959 to the 1957 monetary tightening.

mechanism, at the expense of focus on the money stock; Goodhart (1999, p. 64), on the other hand, argues that the "focus, and heart" of the Radcliffe Report was its emphasis on liquidity, a quantity covering both monetary and nonmonetary assets,[32] as the variable that mattered for aggregate demand. The two characterizations can be reconciled: from the Radcliffian perspective, it is asset prices that matter for aggregate demand, while the quantity of liquidity matters for asset-price determination. And regardless of whether the Radcliffian view is seen as emphasizing liquidity or interest rates, the common element is a negative conclusion for monetary policy. The Radcliffe Committee specifically concluded that aggregate demand was insensitive to securities-market interest rates, especially the short-term rates on which the authorities had most influence.[33] The key asset prices that mattered for aggregate demand could not, the Committee believed, be appreciably influenced by monetary policy actions; likewise, central bank actions could not hope to have an appreciable impact on the key liquidity variable because open market operations affected only the composition of liquidity and not its aggregate quantity.

Many of the analyses of the Radcliffe Report have emphasized its negative conclusions about the role of monetary aggregates in monetary policy.[34] It should be stressed, however, that the Report's view of the transmission mechanism was inconsistent with assigning *any* important macroeconomic role for monetary policy, not just a framework that emphasizes monetary aggregates. Thus the implication of its analysis was not a preference for a Wicksellian analysis of price-level determination over a quantity-oriented approach, but a rejection of *both* these perspectives due to its conclusion that aggregate demand (let alone the price level) was out of reach of monetary policy actions.[35]

In 1970 testimony, Lord (or, more precisely, Viscount) Radcliffe explained that "I have rather turned away, and not tried to keep *au fait* with what has gone on."[36] *Au fait* or not *au fait*, Radcliffe had played a pivotal role in "what [had] gone on" in 1960s policy: his Report was "extremely influential," as Allsopp and Mayes (1985, p. 401) observe.[37] It did not, as noted, contradict the *status quo* majority view of policy advisers and academics regarding monetary policy—on the contrary, Goodhart (1999, p. 66) reported that Bank and Treasury officials' evidence "formed much of [the] basis" for the *Report*'s outlook.[38] Instead, the Report ratified the disapproval officials had voiced of the use of monetary policy to fight

---

[32] As Dacey (1960, p. 133) observed, the Radcliffe Report was ambiguous on the issue of whether its "liquidity" concept referred to an aggregate of assets or of credit. There is support in the Report for Artis' (1974, p. 524) interpretation that its "emphasis [was] on total credit flows," just as other passages suggest that a broad assets aggregate was the crucial quantity.

[33] See Radcliffe Committee (1959, e.g. para. 489).

[34] As well as the Laidler (1989) paper mentioned above, see also e.g. Walters (1970) and Goodhart (1973).

[35] The inconsistency of the Radcliffe Report with Wicksellian analysis was emphasized by Dacey (1960, p. 120).

[36] February 4, 1970, testimony, to Select Committee on Nationalized Industries (1970, p. 219).

[37] Dennis (1981a, p. 141) offers a contrary conclusion, arguing that while U.K. authorities did share the Committee's dismissal of the significance of the money stock, "the operation of policy is indicative of a rejection of the specific details of the Report, particularly with respect to the transmission mechanism of monetary policy… Therefore it is incorrect to overplay the significance of the Report in the design of U.K. monetary policy in the 1960s." To this end, he claims that U.K. authorities did not share the Committee's doubts about the interest elasticity of aggregate demand (1981, p. 139). This claim, however, is incorrect: our quotations from a key Treasury adviser (Balogh) and a principal monetary policy maker (Callaghan) echo the elasticity pessimism expressed by the Committee and by Bank of England officials. Consistent with our evidence, Bell (1970, p. 287), a former Treasury advisor, noted that "the traditional view in both Whitehall and Threadneedle Street is that borrowers are interest-insensitive." (Whitehall and Threadneedle Street are the locations in London of the Treasury and Bank of England, respectively.)

[38] And Goodhart (1973, p. 506) judges that the authorities were "in broad agreement" with the Report's conclusions.

inflation in 1955 and 1957, as well as their judgment that those attempts had turned out to be ineffective. It thus served as a "*coup de grace*"[39] on lingering minority views in officialdom regarding the importance of monetary policy. Harold Wilson, Prime Minister for most of the 1960s,[40] accepted "the devastating analysis of the Radcliffe Report about over-reliance on monetary policy,"[41] and the Treasury under Wilson's administration featured as senior personnel several academics who had shaped the Report's findings, including Alec Cairncross, Nicholas Kaldor, and Robert Neild. The judgments of the Radcliffe Committee underpinned policymakers' renewed emphasis in the 1960s on fiscal policy for aggregate demand management and incomes policy for inflation control.

Lionel Robbins was a prominent advocate of the conventional monetary view of inflation over this period, first as an occasional adviser to the Government in the late 1950s and, from 1959, as a member of the House of Lords and critic of the nonmonetary approach to inflation control taken by successive governments.[42] As early as 1954, Robbins observed that while "the years since the war have witnessed a gigantic experiment, so to speak, in fiscal control… without recourse to the more old-fashioned instruments of monetary policy," he was confident that "any doubts of the capacity of monetary policy to control inflation [would] vanish" if monetary policy was used consistently for that purpose.[43] Robbins, in fact, believed that the event that had entrenched the nonmonetary view as official policy was not the release of the Radcliffe Report, but the resignation in January 1958 of Chancellor Thorneycroft and two other Treasury ministers. Robbins quoted a Keynesian colleague at the London School of Economics as saying of this event: "This is the best news we have heard for many a long day; it is the death of the quantity theory of money."[44]

In retrospect, it is surprising that this episode was seen as a blow to the quantity-theory perspective, because the issue that prompted Thorneycroft and his colleagues' resignation was the failure of Thorneycroft's proposals for cuts in government spending, not monetary policy actions. Indeed, Thorneycroft's post-resignation speech to Parliament questioned the ability of the government to affect aggregate demand via monetary policy instruments.[45]

What the 1958 episode does highlight, however, was the misconception at the time among U.K. policymakers that an automatic, mechanical link existed between government spending or deficits and money creation. By contrast, the standard modern position is that such a link arises only if the monetary policy reaction function creates one. Overstatement of the deficit/money growth link remained prevalent in U.K. policy circles until the 1980s,[46] but was especially severe in these early debates, engendering the confusion that fiscal conservatism and tight monetary policy were synonymous. One of the figures who propagated this confusion was Enoch Powell, who had been among the Treasury ministers resigning in 1958. In later years Powell would encourage the view that he was an early U.K. monetarist. But his policy prescriptions constantly conflated fiscal tightening and monetary

---

[39] As Schwartz (1969, p. 38) puts it.

[40] Wilson served as Prime Minister for the periods October 1964–June 1970 and March 1974–April 1976.

[41] Harold Wilson, *House of Commons Debates*, July 26, 1961, page 445.

[42] See Robbins (1979) for a collection of his speeches.

[43] Robbins (1954, pp. 82–83 and 85).

[44] Lionel Robbins, *House of Lords Debates*, April 10, 1968, page 399.

[45] "I do not believe [the control of inflation] lies in an answer to the question whether we should use Bank Rate or physical controls. To tell the truth, neither of them works very well." Peter Thorneycroft, *House of Commons Debates*, January 23, 1958, page 1296.

[46] See Section 4.

restraint: as late as 1980, Powell was calling on the government to "tax heavily, ruthlessly and comprehensively" as a means of reducing monetary growth.[47] For that matter, some of Powell's emphasis on fiscal policy was based on a cost-push view of inflation: in 1968, he blamed inflation on the channel running from taxes to costs, which was a standard 1960s Conservative Party position but quite inconsistent with viewing inflation as a monetary phenomenon.[48] Nevertheless, Powell came to be identified with the minority in the 1950s and 1960s that emphasized the importance of monetary policy; and, as Robbins suggested, the fact that Powell was widely known not for economics but as an extremely controversial social critic certainly did not help in making the advocacy of monetary policy a respectable pursuit.[49] The situation was the upside down of later U.S. developments: whereas the advocacy of supply-side economics by leading U.S. political figures in the 1980s gave the false impression that supply-side economics was a major school of thought in the economics profession, the emphasis on monetary policy by figures on the U.K. political fringe made it seem that belief in monetary policy had had little basis in economic theory.

3A.2 Developments in the 1960s

The U.K.'s adherence to a fixed exchange rate continued in the 1960s, and some policy tightenings were dictated by exchange-rate considerations, including 1964, as noted, and 1966. Nevertheless, the exchange rate constraint did not prevent a substantial loosening of monetary policy during the 1960s relative to the 1950s, reflecting the consolidation of the nonmonetary outlook to macroeconomic management. This loosening was feasible in part because foreign exchange controls permitted substantial short-run departures of U.K. monetary policy from purely external considerations. Indeed, one empirical study has gone so far as to conclude that in the U.K., "interest rates apparently were fully insulated from U.S. interest rates during both the fixed-rate and floating-rate regimes" (Throop, 1980, p. 14). This finding surely overstates the actual circumstances, but makes it likely that while exchange-rate considerations dictated infrequent adjustments of the intercept term in the U.K. policymakers' interest-rate reaction function, they were not an overriding constraint on that reaction function. In the event, the U.K. reaction function produced an upward trend in money growth and inflation during the 1960s that made continued adherence to a fixed exchange rate infeasible.

Some accounts of developments in policy following the exchange-rate devaluation of 1967 suggest that the U.K. shifted sharply at that time toward greater reliance on monetary policy in controlling aggregate demand. In particular, the U.K.'s commitments to the IMF in 1968 and 1969 included targets for Domestic Credit Expansion (DCE),[50] and this has

---

[47] Andrew Taylor, "Powell Calls for Big Tax Rises," *Daily Express* (London), September 6, 1980, page 4. Similarly, in 1970 Powell had said that deficit spending "can only [produce] one result: the Government will create sufficient extra money to meet its expenditure." Powell, "Balance of Payment and Prices," June 6, 1970 speech, reprinted in Wood (1970, pp. 92–97); quotation from page 96.

[48] See Peter Jay, "Powell's Theory of Inflation: A False Premise," *The Times* (London), May 16, 1968, page 32. The tax-cost-push view of inflation was also endorsed by the Conservative Party's economic spokesman, Iain Macleod (e.g. in his "Iain Macleod" column, *Daily Mail* (London), September 20, 1966, page 6), and shaped both the Conservative Party's platform for the 1970 general election and the early policies of the Heath Government (see Nelson, 2004).

[49] Speech by Lionel Robbins, *House of Lords Debates*, November 23, 1972, page 1073.

[50] Letters of Intent were written to the IMF by Chancellor of the Exchequer Callaghan in November 1967 and Chancellor Jenkins in May 1969 (reprinted in Wadsworth, 1973, pp. 484–490). The Wilson Government's decision to set DCE targets, according to Wilson, was made at the end of 1967 at IMF instigation (Wilson

sometimes been treated as a watershed for the increased importance of monetary policy. Prime Minister Harold Wilson, for example, later wrote that "[a]t the end of 1967... monetary aggregates began to play a more important role in the conduct of monetary policy," and the "role of monetary policy was then further enhanced in 1969."[51] One financial commentator in 1969 even described the government as "bowing to that new god, the money supply."[52]

In retrospect, it is hard to see why this period was regarded as such a watershed. Within a few years, it was clear that "[c]ontrary to early expectations[,] the 1969 commitment to a specific DCE target did not signify a major change in policy,"[53] and Gowland's (1978, p. 5) conclusion that "it was very much the mixture as before, even after the adoption of a DCE target" seems much more on target than the proclamations by commentators at the time. The lack of a genuine policy shift was no doubt in part because the conversion was in rhetoric rather than practice: Keegan (1985, p. 41), for example, claims that the Chancellor of the Exchequer, Roy Jenkins, was privately dismissive of the monetarist critique of old-fashioned Keynesianism.

But even judged on their public declarations, the authorities provided few grounds to expect a major change in emphasis. The DCE targets were part of a package that included strong emphasis on nonmonetary techniques: Jenkins' 1969 Letter of Intent stated that monetary policy's role was as "support to fiscal policy," and the promised policy package also gave prominence to incomes policy for inflation control.[54] And judged by their impact on monetary policy, the commitments to the IMF were not a substantive change, because DCE targeting was compatible with a Radcliffian approach to monetary policy. The Radcliffe Report had emphasized concepts of aggregate credit with a corresponding downgrading of the importance of monetary aggregates. The emphasis on DCE was in keeping with this attitude: the Bank of England said in 1969 that the U.K. authorities had agreed on the DCE target because of their "belief that the rate of growth of the money supply... is an inadequate indicator of monetary conditions."[55] Consistent with this, the Bank of England Governor testified in 1969: "What we are trying to do primarily is to contain the whole corpus of credit..."[56] The interpretation by many commentators, on the other hand, that the government now emphasized money supply, largely reflected the fact that these commentators treated credit control as synonymous with money supply control.[57] But close DCE control need not translate into tight money supply control, and, in the event, did not: the U.K. had external surpluses in 1969-70 that permitted achievement of the DCE target alongside rising base

Committee, 1980, p. 79), which is consistent with the Bank of England's account that "[i]n 1968 and 1969, in agreement with the International Monetary Fund, quantitative limits were set for domestic credit expansion" (in "The Gilt-Edged Market," *Bank of England Quarterly Bulletin* (June, 1979), Vol. 19(2), pp. 137–148; quotation from page 138). However, of the 1967 and 1969 Letters of Intent, only the latter referred to DCE targets; the 1967 letter referred to Callaghan's "expectation" of slower growth in bank credit expansion and the money supply.

[51] Wilson Committee (1980, pp. 79 and 16).

[52] Patrick Sergeant, "Bets on Bank Rate," *Daily Mail* (London), May 14, 1969, page 13.

[53] Kern (1972, p. 37).

[54] From Jenkins' May 22, 1969, Letter of Intent (in Wadsworth, 1973, p. 489).

[55] *Bank of England Quarterly Bulletin Supplement: Domestic Credit Expansion* (September, 1969), page 363.

[56] Governor Leslie O'Brien, May 21, 1969, testimony, in Select Committee on Nationalized Industries (1970, p. 75).

[57] The slippage was evident in a commentary by a U.K. merchant banker who discussed the Chancellor's targets "for the growth of the money supply (or more correctly, domestic credit expansion)..." Geoffrey Bell, "Britain Must Reassess Her Economic Armoury," *The Times* (London), September 29, 1969, "International Scene" section, page III.

money growth and cuts in official short-term interest rates. The rising money growth was welcomed by Chancellor Jenkins, who thought one virtue of the DCE target was that "it enables the money supply to grow faster—and legitimately faster—if we are doing better overseas."[58]

Chancellor Jenkins' conduct of macroeconomic policy over this period won him a reputation as an orthodox or "austere" economic manager; this apparently led to unsuccessful efforts to recruit him in 1979 as the first Chancellor of the Exchequer in the Thatcher Government,[59] as well as the praise from Goodhart (1997, p. 852-853) that "Roy Jenkins injected some sanity in 1968-69." But this reputation for austerity is justified only by the substantial fiscal tightening Jenkins enacted over this period, and not by his approach to monetary policy. Not only did money growth rise under Jenkins, but his short-term interest rate decisions in 1969 opened up a deviation of interest rates from the prescriptions that a Taylor rule now suggests were appropriate—a deviation that Jenkins' successors in the 1970s would continue and magnify. Furthermore, both as Chancellor (1967-70) and as Labour Party economics spokesman (1970-72), Jenkins would take a cost-push view of inflation, leading to his recommendation in 1971 of demand stimulus combined with compulsory price controls (see Nelson, 2004). In 1983, Jenkins would lead the Social Democratic Party on an election platform that again included compulsory price controls. Therefore, while Jenkins has been described as "the grandfather of New Labour" and therefore as an influence upon the policies of the current U.K. government,[60] that description is inappropriate as far as macroeconomic policy is concerned, since Jenkins belonged to the old nonmonetary tradition in economic management.

The Bank of England

In discussing monetary policy over this period, we have focused upon developments in the *executive* branch of the U.K. government. The reason is that the Bank of England was not independent; official statements by the Bank are useful as articulations of government policy, but the Bank itself was not the maker of monetary policy. Well into the 1970s, the Bank of England instead placed primacy on its role as a "sponsor" of the City of London: as a conduit that could communicate the views of the financial community to the government, in much the same way as the Department of Industry informs the government about the concerns of industry (Goodhart, 1972, p. 463). As the Governor of the Bank put it in 1969, the Bank had "a view influenced by the market conditions in which it lives."[61] The importance assigned to this function reflected both the Bank's lack of a policymaking role and the relatively low priority the Bank placed on macroeconomic analysis. For it was in this period that the Bank conformed to what Brunner (1981, p. 23) calls "City Syndrome," whereby expertise in central banking corresponds to a good understanding of the day-to-day psychology of the U.K. financial markets, with macroeconomic knowledge merely an optional extra. As of 1959, the notion that the Bank of England would devote substantial resources to economic analysis was considered sufficiently unlikely that in the James Bond novel *Goldfinger*, after Bond is told

[58] Jenkins (1969, p. 1214).

[59] See Campbell (2003, p. 10) and Therese Raphael, "Blair's Mentor, Thatcher's Maker," *Wall Street Journal Europe*, January 8, 2003, page A11.

[60] Former Labour Cabinet Minister Tony Benn, quoted in Raphael, "Blair's Mentor, Thatcher's Maker."

[61] Governor Leslie O'Brien, April 30, 1969, testimony, in Select Committee on Nationalised Industries (1970, p. 17).

he is going to meet "the head of the Bank's research department," he is informed that this department is "nothing more or less than a spy system" (Fleming, 1959, p. 47).

The Bank did not have a Research Department in reality, though it did have an Economic Intelligence Section. Many economists on the Bank staff in the 1950s and 1960s, however, learned economics during the period of "Neanderthal Keynesian" U.K. academic thought, with their views on monetary policy shaped further in that direction by the Radcliffe Report. Consequently, senior Bank economists during this period tended not to be monetary specialists. It is perhaps significant that when in 1968 the Bank hired an economist with a monetary economics background, the event was considered unusual enough to merit a news item in the London *Times*.[62]

3B The Nonmonetary Approach to Inflation Control (1955-79)

We divide our discussion of the nonmonetary approach to inflation control into the1950s and 1960s (Section 3B.1) and the 1970s (Section 3B.2).

3B.1 1955 to 1969

As we mentioned in Section 3A, cost-push theories of inflation held a prominent place among policy officials in the 1950s. These theories tended to produce advocacy of wage and price controls or other incomes policies as the means of controlling inflation. On the other hand, the import-price-push view of inflation was one of the reasons behind support for fixed exchange rates among economists. For example Hanson (1962, pp. 343, 256) said that a "devaluation of sterling... would be disastrous for Great Britain [i.e., the U.K.]" because "the effect of higher import prices is to raise wages and set the inflationary spiral in motion again." This import price-wage-price spiral view has no more merit than other variants of the cost-push theory of inflation; but unlike the other variants, this particular view served in the 1950s and early 1960s as a restraining force on U.K. monetary policy.

Domestic wage-push views of inflation were also prevalent. In the early 1960s, in line with its diagnosis that "inflation... is a cost-push problem,"[63] the Conservative Government began a series of attempts at a voluntary incomes policy, as did the Wilson Government in 1964-66. The Wilson Government then imposed compulsory wage-price controls in 1966-67, and again attempted thereafter to organize a voluntary policy regarding nominal wage growth. When wage growth and inflation rose in 1969-70, the Government placed the blame on an import price-wage-price spiral in the wake of the 1967 devaluation.[64]

3B.2 1970 to 1979

The period 1970-79 is covered in detail in Nelson (2004) and Nelson and Nikolov (2004), so we provide only a summary here. Under the leadership of Edward Heath, the Conservative Party had criticized the incomes policies of the Wilson Government. For example, Heath had

---

[62] "A Goodhart at the Bank," *The Times* (London), May 20, 1968, page 8. The new Bank employee was Charles Goodhart, who subsequently recalled that he was told upon joining that "the Bank is a bank, and not a study group" (Goodhart, 2004).

[63] Chancellor of the Exchequer Reginald Maudling, *House of Commons Debates*, November 5, 1962, page 621.

[64] For example, in June 1970 Home Secretary Callaghan said that while "the doctrine of economics is left to wiser heads than mine," the government's "principal concern is the level of wages increases." Quoted in "New Wages Freeze on the Way?," *Daily Mail* (London), June 4, 1970, page 1.

said of the 1966 wage-price freeze: "Never before has there been such interference with business and commerce, nor with the normal process of law."[65] However, it was also clear that these objections were focused on the compulsory character of the controls rather than on the underlying cost-push view of inflation. The Heath Government elected in 1970 accordingly took a variety of nonmonetary measures intended to fight inflation: manipulation of prices of government-owned industries (especially in 1970-72), attempts to keep wage growth for government employees down (1970-71), income tax cuts to fight a wage-price spiral (1970), and a sales tax cut (1971). These measures culminated in mandatory wage and price controls during the Heath Government's last fifteen months in office.

The succeeding Wilson Government had a "Social Contract" agreement with unions designed to restrain wage growth, and also attempted to manipulate prices directly by another sales tax cut (1974) and subsidies to key commodity prices (1974-75).[66] The Social Contract agreement also meant that wage restraint was intended to be traded off against fiscal measures to boost disposable income, such as income tax cuts. This partly accounts for the large number of Budgets enacted by the 1974-79 Wilson and Callagan Governments—which various accounts give as anywhere from 12 to 14.[67]

In February 1979, following the collapse of the Social Contract, Prime Minister Callaghan signed a new agreement with the union leadership, entitled the "Concordat," which announced a package to bring inflation down to 5 per cent by 1982. As with many of the nonmonetary measures against inflation during the 1970s, plans to stimulate aggregate demand formed part of this package, highlighted by Callaghan's statement in a television interview that the U.K. would have a "steaming" economy in 1982.[68] In the normal course of events, the design of the Government's April 1979 Budget could be expected to be driven by tax-cut measures to support the Concordat. But on March 28, 1979, the Callaghan Government was defeated in the House of Commons by one vote on a confidence motion, forcing a general election. This meant that Callaghan could remain in office until the election, but could not introduce policy changes before the election; consequently, the government's April 1979 Budget was a "caretaker" package not guided by the Concordat proposals. The victory of the Conservative Party at the May 1979 general election then brought the era of the nonmonetary approach to inflation control to an end.

Post-mortems on the 1970s

A detailed post-mortem on the U.K.'s Great Inflation is given in the 2004 papers cited above. Some flavor of the explanation offered there is given by considering two explanations that do not work—one based on a nonmonetary view of inflation, the other that rests on the monetary view.

---

[65] "Heath Vows: We'll Fight All the Way," *Daily Mail* (London), October 6, 1966, page 1.

[66] Accounts differ on whether the Wilson Government also continued the Heath Government's compulsory price controls. Friedman and Schwartz (1982, p. 119) characterize the compulsory controls as ending with Heath's departure, whereas Brittan and Lilley (1977, p. 18) portray the Wilson Government as "maintaining and intensifying the price controls it had inherited." Nelson and Nikolov's (2004) econometric modeling of inflation over this period suggests that the price controls are best characterized as not continuing beyond Heath's government.

[67] According to *Whitaker's Almanack 1979* (1978, p. 358), the April 1978 Budget was the Labour Government's thirteenth, which would make the 1979 Budget its fourteenth. A separate count at the time of the April 1979 Budget listed that Budget as the twelfth.

Advocates of the cost-push or nonmonetary explanation for inflation not only have the problem of overcoming the logical inconsistencies inherent in that explanation, but also of explaining why the nonmonetary measures taken against inflation did not work. A recent attempt to defend the nonmonetary explanation is Bernstein (2004), who blames the take-off in inflation in the early 1970s mainly on the abandonment of incomes policy and the 1973 oil shock; similarly, he attributes the declines in 1976-78 and after 1980 largely to incomes policy and falling commodity prices, respectively.[69] The failure of the nonmonetary approach to inflation is then principally attributed to individuals' weaknesses, such as: "Heath was so lacking in political savvy that it remains a source of amazement that he could have risen to the top of a major political party" (Bernstein, 2004, p. 232). But the approach to inflation control that Heath undertook was not out of line with those undertaken by his predecessors and successors. Indeed, Harold Wilson later categorized 1973-75 as a single "phase" of macroeconomic policy, thereby conceding the continuity of his own policies with those of Heath.[70] The nonmonetary measures Heath embraced were in line with official advice, to such an extent that *The Economist* later judged that Heath "relied too heavily on civil servants."[71] Nor were these measures taken without Cabinet debate and consent. A senior Cabinet minister in Heath's government has written, "For my part I never found any difficulty in expressing my views, and nor to my knowledge did anyone else. If they were silent it was by choice."[72] Consistent with this account, Margaret Thatcher has admitted that she did not oppose in Cabinet debates the price controls and similar measures introduced by the Heath Government.[73]

In short, the fundamental problem with 1970s macroeconomic policy was not a reflection of the idiosyncrasies of individual policymakers, but was instead the nonmonetary framework that guided successive governments.

Another explanation of the U.K.'s Great Inflation, which was founded on acceptance of the monetary explanation but is nevertheless faulty, is that Chancellor of the Exchequer Nigel Lawson gave in 1984.[74] Lawson claimed that prior to the election of the Thatcher Government, U.K. policymakers used macroeconomic policy to achieve output and employment goals, and microeconomic policy to achieve inflation goals, while the Thatcher Government reversed the assignment of instruments in pursuing those goals.

Lawson's characterization of both employment and inflation-control policy is an oversimplification and factually inaccurate in several important respects. Consider first employment policy. Contrary to Lawson's characterization, policymakers in the 1960s and 1970s did use a concept of productive potential as the reference value for output, with demand management viewed as the means of matching demand levels to that supply goal.[75] The central problem with this approach was not that policymakers believed that potential was subject to manipulation by demand management, but instead that their estimates of potential

---

[68] James Callaghan, interview on *Panorama* television program, February 26, 1979, quoted in Cockerell (1989, p. 245).

[69] Bernstein (2004, pp. 214, 244, 534). Another aspect of Bernstein's nonmonetary explanation of inflation—the 1972 tax cuts—we consider in Section 8.

[70] Wilson Committee (1980, p. 10).

[71] "A Celebrated Failure," *The Economist* (London), July 10, 1993, page 83.

[72] Geoffrey Rippon, "Loyalty and Dissent in the Party," *The Times* (London), October 12, 1981, page 7.

[73] Thatcher (1995, pp. 220, 224).

[74] See (e.g.) Keegan (1985, p. 216).

[75] See Nelson and Nikolov (2003) for a detailed discussion.

were mistaken (biased upward). This error was of the same character as that in the U.S. during the same period—whose importance is highlighted by Orphanides (2003, 2004). In addition, as we have already noted, the importance of monetary policy relative to other demand-management tools was underestimated prior to the 1970s.

It is also problematic to characterize the pre-1979 inflation-control regime as "microeconomic." For one thing, policymakers did realize that output above potential contributed to inflation. Even under the pre-1979 approach, therefore, they were willing to tighten demand if they felt the output gap was positive. This willingness did not do much to keep inflation under control because, as noted above, they too infrequently appreciated that the output gap was positive (and, when they were willing to tighten, underestimated the importance of the need for monetary tightening relative to fiscal tightening).

Another important aspect of pre-1979 macroeconomic policy was that, even when they did not realize the output gap was positive, policymakers *did* use macroeconomic policy to control inflation, but did so in a counterproductive way. For example, tax cuts and interest-rate cuts were advanced as anti-inflation measures, either as cost-reducing devices in their own right or as support for incomes policy packages. In addition, the authorities' nonmonetary framework meant that they saw output below potential as something that worsened inflation, via a unit-cost-push channel, rather than a disinflationary tool. Thus, so long as policymakers thought output was below potential, they were inclined to use macroeconomic policy to push it back to potential.[76] Again, this factor reaffirms the importance of policymakers' errors in overestimating potential output as a significant contribution to policy mistakes.

A more accurate characterization of the pre-1979 policy framework, and thus the U.K.'s Great Inflation, is instead that given by Allan Meltzer in 1976 Congressional testimony:[77]

> For decades influential British economists argued that it was unnecessary to control the rate of monetary expansion. Some argued that the way to end inflation was to stimulate the economy by government policies that create jobs and output. By increasing output they hoped to lower prices or the rate of inflation. Contrary to experience everywhere they sought to end inflation by stimulating the economy. The result was predictable, and both the predictions and the results are part of British history.

4 BROAD MONEY TARGETING

In this section we consider the period of broad money targeting in the U.K. (1976-85), starting with an analysis of the sequence of events that led to that policy (Section 4A), then providing a critical discussion of the official monetary analysis that underlay the pursuit and choice of the targets (Sections 4B and 4C).

---

[76] For example, the Heath Government's policy was described in 1970 as one in which "more growth will give higher productivity to provide further relief on unit wage costs" ("The Economy: A Very Awkward Course," *The Bankers' Magazine* (August, 1970), Vol. 205(1517), pp. 96–98; quotation from page 97). Roy Harrod was one of many U.K. economists supporting this view, contending that "an increase in demand should be a helpful factor in the fight against wage-price spiraling" (Harrod, 1972, p. 62).

[77] Meltzer (1976, p. 179).

4A The Kremlinology of Monetary Targets

Targets for broad money growth in the U.K. were formally announced in July 1976. While their public disclosure reflected pressure from financial markets, monetary targets had been used within the Treasury and the Bank of England since 1973 (Healey, 1990, p. 491), which in turn followed what the Bank of England later called the adoption of an "aim of regulating the growth of the money supply" in 1971.[78]

These developments occurred despite continuing strong attachment among U.K. policy officials to the nonmonetary approach to economic management. For example, Rowan (1973, pp. 36-37) observed that "it is clear that the authorities do not accept that either a restrictive monetary policy or a restrictive fiscal policy would make a useful contribution to reducing cost inflation… [T]he Bank [of England] probably sees fiscal policy as the main means of controlling demand[,] and 'incomes policy'… as offering the best hope of containing inflation." And several appointments during 1973-74 consolidated the position of the hard-liners: Christopher Dow (a major influence on the Radcliffe Report) became Economics Director at the Bank of England in early 1973, and when Harold Wilson returned to office in March 1974, Nicholas Kaldor again became a senior advisor to the Chancellor of the Exchequer, while Thomas Balogh actually became a member of Wilson's ministry. These personnel changes reinforce the puzzle of why U.K. policymakers actually moved away from the traditional nonmonetary approach to demand management and toward monetary targeting during the 1970s.[79]

As observers such as Keegan (1985, p. 100) have noted, there is an element of "Kremlinology" in analyzing U.K. monetary policy over this period, because while policy decisions were undoubtedly the outcome of much internal debate, the details of internal deliberations were not disclosed officially, with a monolithic view being presented publicly. In the present instance, the debate within the government was between the advocates of greater use of monetary policy and the traditional U.K. hard-liners.

One can rationalize the increased role for monetary aggregates in monetary policy from 1971, despite the hard-liners' strength, by continuing the "Kremlinology" analogy. The policy of détente was adopted in the Soviet Union in the 1970s in part because it had elements that appealed to both "reformers" and "hard-liners" within the Kremlin: to the reformers, détente was a means of achieving a genuine thawing of international relations and promoting internal reform; while to the hard-liners, détente offered an opportunity to "lock in," via international agreements, recognition of postwar borders imposed by Soviet military power.

By analogy, the growing interest in monetary aggregates in the 1970s had some appeal to both reformers and hard-liners in U.K. policy circles. To reformers, it was a shift away from the traditional nonmonetary framework. To hard-liners, there was a positive side to each of the steps in 1971, 1973, and 1976, that seemingly attached monetary policy ever more firmly to monetary aggregates.

Regarding the initial 1971 shift, Gowland (1978, p. 40) contends that hard-liners at this time might have increased their interest in money supply series, despite regarding credit and liquidity as the important aggregates for monetary policy. The reason, he speculates, is that

---

[78] "The Gilt-Edged Market," *Bank of England Quarterly Bulletin* (June, 1979), Vol. 19(2), pp. 137–148; quotation from page 138. Similarly, the OECD (1982, p. 78) judged that "[t]he focus of [U.K.] monetary policy shifted during the early 1970s toward control of various monetary aggregates."

[79] Though retaining, as we will see, nonstandard views on how to control monetary aggregates.

the 1971 reforms reduced the regulation of banks, which might have had the effect of making broad money a less distorted proxy for a wider liquidity aggregate than previously. Gowland's speculation was borne out by disclosures by a Bank of England official in 1982 (Fforde, 1983).[80] Fforde noted that policy officials had been able to reach agreement because "the use of a broad money target could be justified by reference to rather different theories about the importance of 'liquidity' and 'credit'" (1983, p. 53)—or, as Fforde's discussant put it, U.K. officials could "justify monetary targeting in nonmonetarist terms" (Davis, 1983, p. 68). Indeed, during 1971 the Bank of England Governor described monetary policy as "control over liquidity,"[81] thereby leaving nebulous whether monetary aggregates were being given importance in their own right. In the event, the issue became moot, as over 1971-73 the overriding interest of the authorities was in stimulating the economy, and so rapid growth in a variety of monetary and credit aggregates was permitted.

The acceptance by the hard-liners of the 1973 shift to an internal monetary target is only slightly more difficult to rationalize.[82] The main departure from the Radcliffian position by the authorities in 1973 was their renewed deployment of direct controls over bank balance sheet growth—which the Radcliffe Report had criticized as ineffective, and which again created the scope for money growth to diverge from the "liquidity" concept. The hard-liners nevertheless probably accepted this departure on pragmatic grounds. For one thing, not all the hard-liners who were prominent in 1973-74 shared the Radcliffe Report's negative view of direct controls; Kaldor, for example, had decided that the 1971 deregulation was a "disastrous reform" and preferred "the well-tried methods" of direct controls.[83] But more fundamentally, the reason the Heath and Wilson Governments favored direct controls to rein in broad money growth was to avoid the need for interest-rate increases. Whatever reservations Dow and others had about the effectiveness of direct controls on banking activity, they would have sympathized with the sentiment that interest-rate increases should be avoided. According to the hard-liners' and the Government's cost-push view of inflation, interest-rate increases were doubly undesirable: to the extent that they reduced aggregate demand, they added to unemployment without fighting inflation, and to the extent that they raised costs, they actually contributed to inflation.

---

[80] Fforde's paper was an official account of policy developments, and therefore can be presumed to have had top-level clearance from both the Bank of England and the Treasury. Nevertheless, there is evidence in the paper that the clearance may have been rushed, resulting in the final product being unusually candid. For example, Fforde gives the wrong date both for the release of the Radcliffe Report (corrected in the *Bank of England Quarterly Bulletin* version of his article) and the first 1974 election (an error that likely would have been corrected if a Treasury minister had read the article in detail). In addition, a footnote in Fforde's paper also downplays monetary expansion as a source of the U.K.'s 1970s inflation, contradicting the Thatcher Government's official position.

[81] Leslie O'Brien, "Key Issues in Monetary and Credit Policy," May 28, 1971, speech, *Bank of England Quarterly Bulletin* (June, 1971), Vol. 11(2), pp. 195–198; quotation from page 197. The labeling of the 1971 reforms as "Credit Control" had raised suspicions from the start that there had been little change by the authorities from the Radcliffian position (Johnson, 1971a).

[82] Paralleling the increased internal interest in monetary targets at this time was growing discussion of the money supply in U.K. policy debate. For discussion of this, see Keegan (1984), Smith (1987), and Parsons (1989, Ch. 6).

[83] Nicholas Kaldor, *House of Lords Debates*, June 11, 1980. pp. 466–467.

The introduction of announced monetary targets (initially for M3, then Sterling M3)[84] in 1976 likewise had its bright side for the traditional critics of monetary policy. The shift to broad money targeting did not end the nonmonetary approach to inflation control; rather, as Allsopp (1991, p. 23) observes, "the emphasis of counter-inflation policy remained on incomes policy throughout this period." Nor did monetary targets even come to dominate short-term interest-rate decisions. On the contrary, the credit counterparts approach to money supply analysis (see Section 4B below) led the authorities to believe that the monetary targets could be achieved largely by fiscal actions. Indeed, very soon after the introduction of monetary targets, the authorities used short-term rates to impose what Goodhart (1984a, p. 18) describes as "almost pegging" of the dollar/sterling exchange rate, a policy that produced sharp cuts in nominal and real interest rates; and when in 1977 *The Economist* referred to "the government's new economic policy," it was to this exchange-rate policy, not to the monetary targets.[85] The hard-liners had considerable reason to be pleased with the state of macroeconomic policy, as it was adhering to a "sixties-style" combination of incomes policy and pegged exchange rates, rather than to an inflation-oriented monetary policy. Thus, despite official monetary targeting from 1976, a real break from the nonmonetary approach to inflation control did not occur until the Thatcher Government's election in 1979.

4B The Credit Counterparts Approach

During the broad money targeting period, the U.K. authorities made use of an identity describing commercial bank asset and liability growth, known as the "credit counterparts" identity, as a guide to the determination of monetary growth. Along with several outside U.K. economists, they argued that the counterparts identity shed light on the link between budget deficits and deposit creation, and also provided a reason for targeting broad money growth instead of a narrower monetary aggregate. But these arguments were flawed: the credit counterparts identity does not, in fact, shed light on the link between budget deficits and deposit creation, nor does it provide a reason for targeting broad money growth instead of a narrower monetary aggregate.

The credit counterparts identity is simple to exposit in generic form. Neglecting the non-earning assets of commercial banks, their total assets may be written as:

Total commercial bank assets=Bank lending to government+Bank lending to private sector

while on the liabilities side

Total commercial bank liabilities = Total deposits + Total nondeposit liabilities.

---

[84] The original broad money targets, and much early 1970s U.K. discussion, referred to M3, but Sterling M3 (which excludes foreign currency deposits at U.K. banks) soon became the targeted aggregate. The change was technically justifiable, but also probably influenced by the fact that Edward Heath had taken to using the argument that since M3 contained foreign deposits, he had been justified in disregarding the growth in that aggregate. Edward Heath, *House of Commons Debates*, March 10, 1976, page 466.

[85] "Gilts: Interest Grows as Interest Falls," *The Economist* (London), August 13, 1977, pp. 87–88; quotation from page 87.

With the "budget deficit" defined as the change in total borrowing by the government, and assuming the central bank does not directly acquire newly issued securities,

Budget deficit=Change in bank lending to government
+Change in nonbank private sector lending to government.

The credit counterparts identity follows as:

Change in total bank deposits=Change in lending to private sector+Budget deficit
-Change in nonbank private sector lending to government
-Change in total nondeposit liabilities.

From this identity, the authorities concluded that there was a one-for-one relationship between absolute changes in the budget deficit and in Sterling M3 (which was, after all, currency plus total bank deposits), unless the budget deficit was financed by selling securities to the nonbank private sector.[86] This conclusion was inappropriate: it amounted to using the identity to make a partial equilibrium rather than a general equilibrium analysis. The identity does not provide a good guide to the economic behavior that determines broad money growth. Various misleading aspects of the policy conclusions that came out of the credit counterparts identity are highlighted in Parkin (1982), Darby and Lothian (1983), Allsopp and Mayes (1985), and Schwartz (1985), and we synthesize and build on these critiques in this section.

There is a longstanding confusion in monetary economics about the implications of commercial bank lending to the government. Friedman and Schwartz (1963, p. 566) document that the Federal Reserve in the 1940s treated commercial bank purchases of government securities as similar to central bank purchases of government debt in that both imply higher money growth. As they note, this conclusion was incorrect. Central bank purchases of government debt (including purchases of securities initially acquired by the private sector), not offset by other transactions, expand the monetary base and, together with the interest-rate reactions associated with the change in the base, create the conditions for an expansion for the total deposits of the commercial banking system. On the other hand, commercial bank purchases of government securities, for given monetary base, must be at the expense of greater lending to the private sector, since the unchanged monetary base means that no conditions for an expansion of overall commercial bank deposits have been created. These behavioral factors mean that, the credit-counterparts identity notwithstanding, the division of the budget deficit between commercial bank and nonbank financing is unimportant for monetary control.

Nonetheless, the belief that commercial bank purchases of government debt stimulated money growth remained prevalent in the U.K., including among U.K. monetarists, such as Walters (1969),[87] and in such inaccurate descriptions such as that of *The Economist* that it corresponded to "printing money through borrowing from the banks."[88] The credit counterparts identity appeared to provide an underpinning for this belief, which probably contributed to the popularity of the counterparts approach in the U.K. Cobham (2002, p. 21)

---

[86] It further led to the misguided policy of "overfunding," discussed in Section 5B.1 below.

[87] "One method of financing the deficit is for the Government to borrow from the banking system… [which] clearly increases the quantity of money." (Walters, 1969, pp. 1181-1182).

[88] Editorial, "Agenda for the Tories," *The Economist* (London), July 2, 1977, pp. 9-10; quotation from page 9.

dates the counterparts approach to articles by U.K. government officials in 1966, but the approach was exposited earlier by Holtrop (1957), the Governor of the Netherlands central bank, who had also testified to the Radcliffe Committee (Holtrop, 1958). Holtrop's original exposition had included the key fallacious policy conclusion that emerges from the counterparts approach: "borrowing by the Treasury from the commercial banking system has, by itself, exactly the same inflationary character as borrowing from the central bank" (Holtrop, 1957, p. 316).

Numerous exponents of the credit counterparts approach have stated that the identity can only be applied to a broad aggregate like Sterling M3 and not a transactions money aggregate like M1 (e.g. Bank of England, 1984, p. 45); and it was this property, according to a Bank of England official, that "turned the decision" in determining the authorities' preference for Sterling M3 over M1 targeting.[89] But the claimed property is incorrect both in principle and as a matter of history. It is incorrect in principle because the counterparts identity *does* hold when M1 deposits constitute the "bank deposits" aggregate; one simply needs to define the non-M1 deposit component of Sterling M3 as "nondeposit liabilities." It is incorrect as a matter of history because the originator of the counterparts approach—Holtrop—used it to analyze the determination of M1, not broad money.[90]

The claim that the counterparts identity applies only to Sterling M3 deposits does, however, throw light on the views of its exponents. It would appear that the U.K. advocates of the counterparts approach were attached to it precisely because they believed the appropriate measure of money was one that moved closely with aggregate credit. This is perhaps most clear from the discussion of Congdon (1982, p. 129), who argued that the counterparts approach was a good way of analyzing money creation in the U.K. but not in the Federal Republic of Germany, because in the latter country variations in banks' equity issues drove a large wedge between broad money and aggregate credit growth. But the insistence that money and credit move together does not provide a good criterion for defining money, for the credit/money distinction is crucial to much of the quantity-theory and monetarist literature, and is central also in modern optimizing models where it is services of money, not credit, that enter the utility function. The appropriate conclusion from Congdon's observation is instead that the counterparts identity should not have been at the center of monetary analysis in the U.K. or any other country, and that it should not have played a part in deciding the issue of which monetary aggregate the authorities should target.

4C The Choice of Broad Money

As the Bank of England Governor acknowledged in 1978, "The view that monetary aggregates matter does not in itself imply a choice of any particular aggregate."[91] But until the

[89] Allen (1982, p. 104).

[90] "[A] shift from time deposits to current deposits, i.e. a creation of money…" (Holtrop, 1958, p. 266). See also the discussion of Holtrop's views in "The Banking Sector and Monetary Policy," *Midland Bank Review* (Winter, 1978), pp. 19–25. Geoffrey Bell, who was one of the figures who introduced credit counterparts analysis to the U.K. in 1966 (Cobham, 2002, p. 21), himself favored a definition of money considerably narrower than the official M3 series (Bell, 1970).

[91] Governor Gordon Richardson, "The Building Societies in a Changing Financial Environment," May 18, 1978, speech, published in *Bank of England Quarterly Bulletin* (June, 1978), Vol. 18(2), pp. 245–249; quotation from page 247.

early 1980s, the issue was settled as far as the authorities were concerned: as Cobham (1991, p. 43) notes, since "they first began to talk in terms of monetary aggregates, the U.K. monetary authorities had shown a preference for broad money as the best measure." Indeed, two striking features of U.K. discussions of monetary targeting are, first, the number of arguments made in favor of broad money measures, such as Sterling M3, over narrow aggregates such as the monetary base (M0) or M1; and second, the poor quality of these arguments. In fact, it seems clear that the authorities would have been better served in both the 1970s and 1980s in focusing on narrower aggregates, particularly the monetary base, as the measure of money in making interest-rate decisions.

Predating even the monetary targeting period, several commentators who believed that an M1-type measure was appropriate for monetary analysis in the U.S. sought to rationalize the interest in broad money in the U.K. The U.S. monetary economist Lauchlin Currie, for example, wrote in 1934 that "[i]n Great Britain [i.e., the U.K.] and Canada[,] competition between banks has led to a relaxation of the prohibition against the drawing of checks against time deposits" (Currie, 1934, p. 19). On the basis of this argument, one might infer that it was appropriate to treat Sterling M3 or other broad aggregates as a measure of transactions money. Even U.K. authorities could not accept this argument—it was clear that time deposits and similar instruments were not equivalent to demand deposits as media of exchange. Thus the U.K. authorities acknowledged in 1970 that the M1 series was "based more firmly on the distinguishing function of money as a medium of exchange."[92] Though the M1 aggregate was abolished in 1989, the authorities continue to acknowledge the distinction between broad money and transactions money, for example by reporting Divisia versions of the M4 series.[93]

It was also claimed by proponents of broad money that narrow measures such as M0 and M1 failed to predict the take-off in U.K. inflation in the 1970s, particularly the peak in 1975, whereas Sterling M3 did so (e.g. Bank of England, 1984, p. 45). Sterling M3 did rise at a greater rate in 1971-73 than either M0 or M1, and more closely matched in its percentage-point increase the subsequent rise in inflation. But this did not reflect aberrational behavior on the part of the narrow aggregates. For M0, one important factor was that the cut in reserve requirements by the authorities in 1971 produced the equivalent of about six percentage points of money base growth, so one would expect deposit money to rise by more than base money over this period (Pepper, 1994, p. 244). In addition, M0 and M1 had larger interest elasticities than Sterling M3, on account of the substantial interest-bearing component of broad money. Under those circumstances, it is to be expected that the rise in inflation to exceed the rise in money growth—given that, in the U.K. from 1972, nominal interest rates too were increasing. Such a money growth/inflation pattern is a fundamental part of the adjustment of prices to a monetary expansion, and qualitatively the same pattern was observed in the M1 growth/inflation relationship during the rise in inflation in the U.S. (Barro, 1982).

Another argument, as we have discussed, was that Sterling M3 was regarded as preferable to M1 because of the direct link between budget deficits and Sterling M3 claimed by advocates of the credit counterparts approach. For example, in 1979, Alan Budd, later an

---

[92] HM Treasury, "A Note on Definitions of the Money Supply," *Economic Trends* (August, 1970), Vol. 202(8), pp. xi–xii; quotation from page xi.

[93] Other early arguments, such as in Newlyn (1962, pp. 7–9), that attempted to justify broad money for the U.K. rather than M1 on grounds of institutional differences between the U.S. and the U.K, proved equally shaky (see Friedman and Schwartz, 1970, pp. 118–121).

adviser to the U.K. government (and much later, one of the original members of the Bank of England's Monetary Policy Committee) claimed: "M3 is the preferable measure amongst those available because of its direct link with the government's fiscal and financial policy" (Budd, 1979, p. 12). The link between deficits and broad money growth suggested by this approach, had already meant that the monetary targets were one factor guiding fiscal policy in the early monetary targeting period (1976-79). The belief in a link was enshrined in the "Medium-Term Financial Strategy" (MTFS) announced alongside the 1980 Budget, setting out multi-year plans for reductions in Sterling M3 growth and the deficit. Fortunately, however, 1980 turned out to be the last budget where the broad money targets were a major consideration in setting fiscal policy.[94] But in any case, the credit counterparts identity was not a valid grounds for preferring Sterling M3 as the measure of money.

It was also claimed, both by Treasury Ministers Howe and Lawson in 1981[95] and by outside commentators such as Congdon (1995, p. 18), that movements in M1 and the monetary base could not meaningfully register excessive or inadequate money creation, because private sector behavior determined the split between deposits and M1 deposits, and between currency and total deposits. To be an argument in favor of Sterling M3 or M4, the argument requires it to be the case that the private sector's portfolio adjustments cannot change the aggregate stock of broad money. This claim is not correct: every monetary aggregate, under modern institutional arrangements, corresponds to the quantity of nominal money demanded by the private sector. The monetarist claim that central banks can create an "excess supply" of money does not amount to a denial of this reality, but instead rests on the fact that open market operations alter the quantity of nominal money demanded. The "excess money supply" concept does not require a lack of intersection between demand and supply curves for money, just as the "output gap" concept does not deny that aggregate demand and supply curves continuously intersect. Both concepts instead highlight that macroeconomic policy can create quantities (of money and output, respectively) that are "excessive" relative to a price-stability baseline, and which therefore trigger price-level responses.

Finally, the fact that Friedman and Schwartz (1963, 1970) used a broad money concept (old M2) in their analysis of the U.S., and justified it by appealing to the "temporary abode of purchasing power" or "asset" function of money, does not provide much support for the emphasis on broad money in the U.K. Friedman and Schwartz (1970) specifically excluded certificates of deposit from their definition of money; whereas in the U.K., not only were CDs included by the authorities in the Sterling M3 definition, but their growth was a large contributor to the divergence between broad and narrow money growth in 1971-73. In fact, within the U.K., the authorities' inclusion of CDs in the M3 definition had been questioned as early as 1970 (Bell, 1970).

---

[94] An individual who served as a junior Treasury minister over this period later claimed that Sterling M3's high growth led to the tightening of fiscal policy by Chancellor Howe in his 1981 Budget (Ridley, 1991, p. 182). But Howe (1994, p. 205) says that broad money behavior played a "very modest role" in he formation of the 1981 Budget, which seems more plausible, especially as Margaret Thatcher's newly appointed economic advisor (Alan Walters) preferred the narrow measures of money. It is also consistent with Howe's statement in his Budget speech that "underlying financial conditions have, as the Government intended, been tight" (*House of Commons Debates*, March 10, 1981, page 762).

[95] For a statement to this effect by Howe, see *House of Commons Debates*, March 10, 1981, page 762; while one by Lawson is quoted in Keegan (1989, p. 78). The same argument figured in the Callaghan Government's preference for Sterling M3 (Allsopp, 1991, p. 30).

The arguments in favor of broad money appear weak, but can more positive arguments be made in favor of the narrow definitions? It was Friedman and Schwartz (1970, p. 145) who also provided a practical argument for regarding the narrowest measures of money as more reliable indicators than broad money. They argued: "In many a country... the meaning of different categories of bank deposits has altered as banks have reacted to government regulations and interventions"—in the U.K. case, principally quantitative controls on banks' balance sheets—so that it could be "preferable to return to earlier definitions of 'money' as currency (or high-powered money) solely and to omit all deposits." Their general argument applies best to currency, but applies also to the U.K.'s monetary base (M0) series, which is largely currency and for which the required-reserve component is not typically a large contributor to the annual growth rate.[96] A dissertation by one of Friedman's students pursued Friedman and Schwartz's argument. In the published version of the dissertation, the author remarked that the "United Kingdom currently provides an instructive example" of their point (Lothian, 1976, p. 67).

Lothian was referring to the U.K.'s marginal reserve requirement, labeled the "Supplementary Special Deposit" or "corset" scheme, introduced in late 1973 with the explicit aim of lowering M3 (or Sterling M3) growth without altering interest rates. The corset scheme was specifically designed to curb broad money growth by inducing slower growth in certificates of deposit. Since these instruments were, as noted above, among the most questionable elements of the broad money definition, it is doubtful whether the corset scheme would have had a restrictive effect on aggregate demand even if had reduced CD growth and not promoted any kind of bank evasion. But, of course, the corset *did* lead to efforts by the banks to evade the new control; and with interest rates low and reserve growth high during much of the corset period, the evasion took the form of the creation of deposit substitutes. The outcome was that in the period during which the corset was imposed (or in danger of being reimposed), 1973 to 1980, Sterling M3 growth was a far less reliable measure of money growth than was monetary base growth.

With the corset's abolition in mid-1980, annual Sterling M3 growth rose to rates of around 20 per cent. Various auxiliary explanations have been offered for rapid broad money growth over this period; for example, Meltzer (1981, p. 25) suggests that income tax cuts led to a shift to time deposits, Allen (1982, p. 99) and Keegan (1985, p. 146) mention "distress borrowing" by corporations, and Walters (1986) stresses the effect of sterling appreciation on household wealth. These explanations, however, by themselves only explain why certain classes of deposits or loans should grow in relative terms, not why aggregate broad money growth rose. Ultimately, there is no getting away from the explanation that "[e]vidently banks' (and their customers') ingenuity and determination to avoid corset penalties had been underestimated" (Bootle, 1985, p. 327), and that consequently broad money growth in 1980 gave a misleading picture of monetary conditions—a fact the authorities quickly acknowledged.

---

[96] Since 1981, required reserves have not been a component of the official M0 series. Over 1955–2004, changes in reserve requirements have had direct implications for the reserves component of the M0 series only in 1971 and 1981; the required reserves (Special Deposits) that resulted from operation of a variable reserve requirement over 1961–1981 are not part of the M0 series (Capie and Webber, 1985, p. 12).

Money base growth, on the other hand, reached low single-digit levels in the early 1980s, accurately reflecting the restrictive monetary policy in force.[97] It was this situation that led Karl Brunner, when talking to Margaret Thatcher in 1980, to emphasize the monetary base, using much the same argument as Friedman and Schwartz (1970). "From the start we told her it was in part a data problem," Brunner recalled shortly afterwards. "M1 is too narrow and M3 is much too broad… So long as there is this data problem, the central bank should focus on the monetary base."[98] Thatcher heeded this advice, indicating in a 1981 television interview that while she was "not relying on M1" and that rapid M3 growth had been due to the fact that "we took off that thing known as the Bank of England corset," she felt that the "monetary base happens to be an extremely important [aggregate]… We do look at monetary base."[99] Thus the weight given to the monetary base increased, although the Government rejected the option of monetary base control and continued to use the short-term interest rate as a policy instrument.

Ongoing institutional changes in the 1980s continued to make Sterling M3 and M4 less reliable than base money as an indicator for monetary policy. Cobham (2002, p. 42) argues that since the standard deviation of the broad money velocity growth rate was not higher in the 1980s than previously, the broad money/nominal income relationship was not "more variable and more uncertain" in the 1980s. But a second-moment statistic like the standard deviation of the growth rate understates the uncertainty about velocity when, as in the U.K., policymakers' beliefs referred to the *level* of the series. The U.K. authorities had in 1980 given their estimate of a trend in Sterling M3 velocity of about +1.25% per year (HM Treasury, 1980). By 1986, the deviation of actual Sterling M3 velocity from this trend stood at 15% or more, while M4 velocity stood at a level at least 10 percent below what might have been suggested by its pre-1979 trend.[100]

While inflation targeting has reduced the attention given to monetary aggregates in U.K. policymaking, both the monetary base and broad money are discussed as indicators, and so the issue of which series is more reliable remains important. The same considerations that led to policymakers' disillusionment with broad money in the 1980s should also lead today's policymakers to prefer the monetary base as the measure of money.

5 Flaws in Monetary Policy Execution (1955-85)

The execution of monetary policy had a number of flaws both during the period of nonmonetary approach to demand management and during the monetary targeting period. Some of these flaws were shared with other countries; some were specific to the U.K.; and some (such as lack of transparency about its interest-rate decisions, and over-reliance on

---

[97] Bernanke, Laubach, Mishkin, and Posen (1999, p. 149) report U.K. base money growth as falling from 12% to minus 2% over 1980–82. Part of this decline, however, reflects regulatory changes in 1981 which reduced required reserves and shifted the remaining required reserves out of the monetary base definition. Our own series that adjusts for this change still shows a major decline over 1980–82, from 12% to below 1%.

[98] Karl Brunner, quoted in Lindley H. Clark Jr., "Battle of the Bank of England," *Wall Street Journal*, April 7, 1981, page 35.

[99] Margaret Thatcher, interview with Brian Walden, *Weekend World*, London Weekend Television, February 1, 1981, Margaret Thatcher Complete Public Statements Archive, Thatcher Foundation website.

[100] And unlike the later break in trend of M0 velocity, which followed the adoption of inflation targeting, the trend-breaks in broad money velocity did not all have an obvious economic interpretation.

reserve requirements as a policy instrument) the U.K. shook off earlier than other countries. We divide our discussion of the conduct of monetary policy into short-term interest-rate policy (Section 5A) and other policy instruments (Section 5B).

5A Short-Term Interest-Rate Policy

After giving some background to the conduct of interest-rate policy in the U.K. (Section 5A.1), we look at two problems with interest-rate policy formulation: neglect of the real rate/nominal rate distinction (particularly important before 1970) and inadequate nominal-rate responses to inflation (especially important during the 1970s).

5A.1 Interest Rates and U.K. Policy

In the U.S., the formal acknowledgment by the Federal Reserve Board in 1994 that it used the Federal funds rate as its instrument, and the prompt disclosure of its chosen values for that instrument, were regarded as a watershed. In the U.K., however, there was no corresponding watershed, because the authorities' use of a short-term interest-rate instrument, and its chosen instrument value, were public knowledge throughout the 1950s, 1960s and into the 1970s. When Jonson (1976, p. 996) wrote in the *Journal of Political Economy* that "U.K. monetary policy is conducted by setting some important nominal interest rates," it amounted to a simple statement of fact, whereas, at the time, a corresponding statement applied to the U.S. would have been controversial (though accurate). There was also no episode in the U.K. corresponding to the U.S. experience of 1979-82, during which use of an interest-rate instrument was dropped in favor of a nonborrowed reserves operating target. In these respects, there has been a degree of continuity in the conduct of monetary policy in the U.K. not present in the U.S.

The continuity is reflected in the similarity of coverage of monetary policy decisions in the 1950s and 2000s:

"[The] Bank of England boosted to 3½% from 3% the cost of money it will lend through the discount markets… [T]o businessmen and the man in the street it's the key to all interest rates. Changes in its level govern bank charges and personal loans, interest on bank deposits, mortgage rates and others." (*Wall Street Journal*, January 28, 1955)[101]

"The Bank of England yesterday moved to head off a recession by dramatically slashing interest rates to their lowest level since Winston Churchill was Prime Minister… Following the announcement, a flurry of lenders were quick to pass on the latest cut to customers, while others said they were reviewing their rates." (*The Sun*, November 9, 2001)[102]

Despite this continuity, much discussion prior to the 1990s of the U.K. authorities' conduct of monetary policy was clouded by misconceptions. The abolition of interest-rate pegging by central banks in the early 1950s coincided with the abolition of price controls in many countries, including the U.K. This probably encouraged a belief that central banks' influence over interest rates rested on a suppression of market forces analogous to that associated with price controls. The false analogy between price control and interest-rate control in turn encouraged the view that, as financial markets became progressively more

---

[101] "Bank of England Raises Discount Rate in Mild Move on Inflation," *Wall Street Journal*, January 28, 1955, page 11.

[102] Ian King, "4% Mortgage Delight as Rates Hit 46-Year Low," *The Sun* (London), November 9, 2001, page 8.

sophisticated and deregulated, the U.K. authorities' ability to manipulate interest rates would wear off. Complementing this view was the influence of the Gurley-Shaw (1960) and Radcliffe Committee positions that financial innovation was creating conditions where private intermediaries would be able to expand their balance sheets independently of the actions of the monetary authorities, with the result that the determination of interest rates would become outside the influence of central banks.

Along these lines, both academic and financial-market commentators on the U.K. scene in the 1960s and 1970s made claims that the era of an official interest-rate instrument was ending. For example, a 1964 discussion of monetary policy in Western Europe stated: "Bank [R]ate, as a policy instrument, has lost some of its former importance… and is apt to be a follower rather than an initiator of policy" (Beckhart, 1964, p. 96). And in October 1969, the financial column of the London *Daily Mail* stated: "Time was when all London interest rates were geared to Bank Rate. But that is long since past… Bank Rate, in fact, is meaningless."[103] In January 1972, the same column stated: "Nowadays the Bank influences rates through open market operations, and Bank Rate follows interest rates rather than leads them."[104] Nearly five years later, in November 1976, a column entitled "What Happened to Bank Rate" began: "The Bank of England has pulled its Minimum Lending Rate, successor to Bank Rate, out of the firing line and into reserve. MLR's meaning has changed, its importance has diminished. The Bank has other forces at its command, and now will use them more freely."[105] Thus in 1964, 1969, 1972, and 1976, the obituary was written for interest rates as a meaningful policy instrument in the U.K.—yet in 2004 the monetary authorities employed an interest rate as an instrument just as they did in 1955.[106]

In fact, the conditions under which central bank actions cease to be a strong influence on short-term interest rates never arrived in the U.K. In a Gurley-Shaw (1960) type world, financial innovations do result in the elimination of a demand for base money, and so the fading away of central-bank influence over interest rates, broader monetary aggregates, and aggregate demand. But in actual practice, banks and other intermediaries have continued to find it convenient to use balances at the central bank as a means of settling interbank debt; combined with the demand for currency by private households, this ensures a positive demand for the monetary base. At a minimum, this ensured a long-run central-bank influence on nominal interest rates by being able to influence the expected-inflation component of nominal rates. But when there is some degree of price stickiness, open market operations that alter the nominal monetary base will alter the real monetary base in the same direction, and thus imply that central bank operations have a powerful short-run influence over both nominal and real short-term interest rates. There are grounds for expecting these qualitative conditions to continue to prevail, both in the U.K. and elsewhere (Woodford, 2001). And since these conditions have prevailed throughout 1955-2004, it follows that the repeated

---

[103] Patrick Sergeant, "Bank Rate: The Fiction," *Daily Mail* (London), October 30, 1969, page 15.

[104] Patrick Sergeant, "Will It Matter If Bank Rate Goes Down?", *Daily Mail* (London), January 20, 1972, page 21. Also in 1972 a book on the U.K. economy by a financial journalist claimed, "Bank Rate is much less important nowadays than it was, say twenty years ago… [I]nterest rates generally do not follow Bank Rate" (Davis, 1972, p. 24).

[105] Christopher Fildes, "What Happened to Bank Rate," *Daily Mail* (London), November 8, 1976.

[106] The policy rule guiding instrument choices, of course, changed substantially from 1955 to 2004, as we discuss below (Section 5A.3).

statements in U.K. debate that loss of central bank influence on interest rates was at hand were misguided.

What, then, was behind the periodic commentary about monetary policy was losing control of rates? The quotation given above from 1964 probably reflects the incorrect "price control" analogy, while that from 1969 was probably driven by a misinterpretation of the implications of financial liberalization and global financial integration. The 1972 declaration that Bank Rate now follows market rates, on the other hand, likely reflects initial confusion about the implications of the financial deregulation measures (Competition and Credit Control) introduced in 1971. These reforms were designed to encourage greater competition among commercial banks, particularly with regard to the interest rates offered by those banks. Such reforms may have been interpreted as implying a permanent loss of official influence on market rates, whereas, in fact, they are better regarded as causing a one-time permanent shift in the spread between rates offered to customers by commercial banks and official interest rates.

Another factor, discussed by Goodhart (1992, p. 324), is that the monetary authorities in the 1970s and 1980s themselves encouraged the view that interest rates were market-determined, as this served as a "smokescreen." For the U.S., John Taylor observed in 1982 that if the perception that the central bank was no longer setting interest rates had made it "easier politically" to carry out a disinflation, since the change in perception was "reducing political pressures on the Fed to lower interest rates."[107] A successful smokescreen, in other words, could reduce the assignment of blame to central banks for "high" nominal interest rates.[108] As one U.K. financial columnist put it in 1984, there were "frequent official claims when interest rates are rising that they are 'being pushed up by the market' and that it would be misguided, difficult or even impossible to resist the pressures."[109]

Gowland (1978, p. 51) and Goodhart (2004) mention specifically the replacement of Bank Rate with Minimum Lending Rate in October 1972 as one reform motivated by "smokescreen" considerations—as Gowland put it, creating a "cloak [over] policy changes." Some contemporary observers did take the 1972 reforms at face value, and so erroneously regarded the authorities as having abandoned an interest-rate instrument.[110] For the most part, however, most financial market and academic observers quickly realized after each reform that the authorities had not abandoned interest rates as their control variable. Tew (1979, p. 253), for example, noted that in the 1970s "the Bank [had] as effective a control over rates…

---

[107] John B. Taylor, August 31, 1982 letter to Senator Roger W. Jepsen, published in Joint Economic Committee (1982), pp. 156–159; quotations from page 157.

[108] See Mishkin (2001) for a recent application of the "smokescreen" argument to Federal Reserve policy over 1979–82; in particular, Mishkin (2001, p. 2) argues that "the 1979 policy shift... was a smokescreen to obscure the need of the Fed to raise interest rates to very high levels to reduce inflation." A very early exponent of this position was Anna Schwartz in a 1984 *Wall Street Journal* interview, which gave her judgment as that in 1979–82 "the Fed embraced monetarist principles as a smokescreen for raising interest rates and reducing inflation." See Lindley H. Clark Jr. and Laurie McGinley, "Money's Role: Monetarists Succeed in Pushing Basic Ideas But Not Their Policies," *Wall Street Journal*, December 10, 1984, pages 1 and 16. Some doubts about the applicability of the "smokescreen" interpretation to 1979–82 are expressed by Bindseil (2004).

[109] Samuel Brittan, "A New Look at 'Monetary Base,'" *Financial Times* (London), June 4, 1984, page 15.

[110] For example, Derek Porter, "Bank Rate Is Up 1pc," *Evening News* (London), June 8, 1978, stated that "Bank Rate… returned to the City after a six-year absence last week." This was also the interpretation of Beenstock (1980, p. 28). In fairness to these authors, Milton Friedman has himself admitted to having made similar misinterpretations of U.S. developments, conceding that he was among those who "have repeatedly licked our wounds when we mistakenly interpreted earlier Fed statements as portending a change in operating procedures." Milton Friedman, "Has the Fed Changed Course?," *Newsweek*, October 22, 1979, page 35.

as it had enjoyed in the 1960s." The 1976 newspaper column quoted above also establishes that the 1972 reform had not succeeded in "fooling" the market about the importance of policymakers' influence. The attempt described in that column to downplay the role of Minimum Lending Rate (MLR) was, in turn, quickly abandoned: during 1977, the government, as noted above, attempted to restore fixed exchange rates, and so no longer had any interest in hiding its control of interest rates. In this environment, *The Economist* noted that "the Bank effectively tells the discount market what rate it wants,"[111] while a London financial broker was quoted as accurately observing: "The authorities are trying to hold the pound steady and… interest rates are the variable."[112]

Even after the authorities resumed a free float late in 1977, financial commentators recognized that private commercial interest rates were, as before, governed by the authorities' actions on the official interest rate.[113] An academic study in 1979 stated simply that rates on "short-term securities in the United Kingdom… have been administered by Bank Rate policy and, more recently, through alterations in the Minimum Lending Rate" (Foster, 1979, p. 152). Consistent with this, the Bank of England Governor acknowledged in 1978 that "[t]he execution of monetary policy relies importantly on the control and movement of short-term rates of interest,"[114] while the following year Margaret Thatcher publicly explained her government's increases in the MLR in reaction-function terms.[115] This directness continued in 1980, with Chancellor of the Exchequer Geoffrey Howe stating: "The level of interest rates is determined by the requirements of domestic monetary policy."[116]

Both Smith (1987, p. 96) and Goodhart (2004) nominate the Bank of England's abolition of the Minimum Lending Rate in 1981 as another reform motivated by "smokescreen" considerations—which a Bank of England official effectively admitted at the time when he said that MLR had been abolished because "[d]eclared changes in MLR tended to be political events of considerable significance for the government" (Allen, 1982, p. 109). This reform, however, was even less successful than the 1970s attempts to cloak the authorities' manipulation of short rates. Soon after the early 1980s reforms, Allan Meltzer accurately judged that they were a change "in name but not in fact; [the U.K.] continues to aim at interest-rate [operating] targets,"[117] while Congdon (1982, p. 80) stated: "The Bank [of England] can keep rates within its 'unpublished' target band. The contention that short-term interest rates are market-determined in Britain is a serious misunderstanding."[118] And official statements by policymakers in the 1980s acknowledged the authorities' continued use of short rates as an instrument: for example, Chancellor Lawson's 1983 Mansion House speech

---

[111] "Goodbye to the Duke of York," *The Economist*, January 15, 1977, pp. 72–73; quotation from page 72.

[112] Nigel Althaus, senior partner of the Pember and Boyle brokerage company, quoted in Patrick Sergeant, "Home Loans Should Follow MLR Down," *Daily Mail* (London), April 26, 1977.

[113] E.g. Patrick Sergeant, "Is Money Really All That Matters?," *Daily Mail* (London), November 26, 1977.

[114] Governor Gordon Richardson, "The Building Societies in a Changing Financial Environment," May 18, 1978, speech, published in *Bank of England Quarterly Bulletin* (June, 1978), Vol. 18(2), pp. 245–249; quotation from page 247.

[115] For example, in a November 17, 1979 speech to Conservative Trade Unionists, Thatcher gave the "background to the increase... in the MLR which we announced." Margaret Thatcher Complete Public Statements Archive, Thatcher Foundation website.

[116] Geoffrey Howe, July 28, 1980, testimony, in Treasury and Civil Service Committee (1981, p. 201).

[117] From page 13 of his October 6, 1981, Congressional testimony, in Joint Economic Committee (1981).

[118] Similarly, Nicholas Kaldor observed in February 1982 that "*de facto*[,] the Bank of England exercises the same control over money market rates as before" (Kaldor, 1982, p. 112).

described the factor's underlying his "short-term interest-rate decisions" (quoted in Smith, 1987, p. 117).

Thus, despite their short-lived efforts to suggest otherwise, the U.K. monetary authorities have consistently used a short-term interest rate as their policy instrument. In fact, even the changes in the particular rate used as the instrument—e.g. from Bank Rate to Minimum Lending Rate, and in recent years, repo rate—have been of little macroeconomic significance, because all series have been closely related to the Treasury bill rate. Thus, it is the bill rate we focus upon when we come to characterize the monetary policy reaction functions of the authorities during 1955-2004 (Section 5A.3).

5A.2 Real vs. Nominal Interest Rates

That policymakers controlled short-term interest rates was well enough understood in the U.K. from the 1950s onward. That "high" nominal interest rates did not necessarily imply tight monetary policy was far less well understood. In particular, discussions prior to the late 1960s show a striking lack of interest in the real/nominal interest rate distinction. This problem went to the very top level of policymaking, with former Prime Minister Anthony Eden displaying his own confusion on the subject in a 1957 letter to his successor, Harold Macmillan, where Eden asked, "How can one talk of a property-owning democracy and a seven per cent Bank Rate?"[119]

But postwar U.K. monetary economists also rarely focused on the subject until the monetarist critique brought it to the fore in the late 1960s. For example, the 600-page, approximately 264,000-word *Readings in British Monetary Economics* (1972) contained only *four sentences* that mentioned the real/nominal interest-rate distinction—and all four sentences were from articles published in 1970-71, the very end of the period covered by the *Readings*.[120]

The Radcliffe Report, it is true, as well as some of the financial press, discussed the issue of whether index-linked bonds were desirable.[121] But such discussions put the focus on the *supply-side* consequences of low real interest rates—i.e., the implications for the purchasing power of saving and for capital accumulation—and even this channel was discounted, since the Radcliffe Report, like the authorities, judged that saving was quite interest-inelastic.[122]

The *demand* implications of the Fisher relation were neglected: little attention was given to the fact that reductions in real rates were a stimulus to aggregate real spending, and, therefore, in the face of rising inflation, a given level of policy tightness required higher nominal rates. That aspect of the Fisher relationship was clouded by the constant references during the 1960s to the prevailing 7 or 8 percent Bank Rate as a "crisis" rate. As noted above, a revival of interest in the Fisher relation did finally occur in the late 1960s. An early discussion in the press that perceived the importance of the Fisher relation for aggregate demand was that in *The Observer* in 1969: "Eight per cent sounds horribly high; it is nothing

---

[119] Quoted in Thorpe (2003, p. 574).
[120] Johnson *et al* (1972).
[121] E.g. Patrick Sergeant, "Savings Chief Studies Cost-of-Living Bonds," *Daily Mail* (London), May 3, 1966, page 13; and Radcliffe Committee (1959, paras. 572–573).
[122] Radcliffee Committee (1959, para. 554).

of the kind… If prices are rising at the rate of 5 per cent, as they did last year, then Bank Rate at 8 per cent is a mere bagatelle—a true rate of no more than 3 per cent."[123]

In policy, financial, and academic circles, discussion of the real rate/nominal rate distinction exploded in the early 1970s. Thus it appears appropriate to conclude that lack of understanding of the Fisher relationship was an impediment to good policy formulation in the U.K. up to the late 1960s, but not thereafter. The problem in the 1970s was predominantly policymakers' continuing belief that expected inflation could be manipulated by nonmonetary devices, not their failure to appreciate the importance of the expected-inflation component of nominal interest rates.

5A.3 Interest-Rate Reaction Functions

Studies of U.K. monetary policy since the 1960s have estimated interest-rate reaction functions, although most early studies (e.g. Goodhart, 1973) do not present estimates comparable to those in recent papers, mainly because they have the price level on the right-hand side instead of the inflation rate. To give some simple characterizations of U.K. monetary policy over the last half-century, we present in this section simple interest-rate reaction functions estimated on annual data.

Following Taylor (1999), our estimated specification has the nominal short rate (in our case, the Treasury bill rate) as the dependent variable, with the right-hand-side variables the contemporaneous values of annual consumer price inflation and the deviation of log real GDP from a broken linear trend (the breaks in the trend, in our case, taking place in 1974 and 1981). We use annual-average data. The data refer to recent revised vintages, despite the quantitative importance of real-time output gap mismeasurement for the U.K. Estimates in Nelson and Nikolov (2004) suggest that gap revisions do not have the powerful effect on policy-rule estimates for the U.K. that Orphanides (2004) found for the U.S.

We consider several sample periods: 1955-1978; the subsample 1970-1978 taking in the last years of the nonmonetary approach to inflation control;[124] and the period of inflation-oriented monetary policy 1981-2003. We start the sample period for the inflation-oriented monetary policy in 1981 rather than 1979 because 1979 average data include some behavior from the Callaghan Government's incumbency, while the inflation data for both 1979 and 1980 are affected by the Thatcher Government's 1979 increase in Value Added Tax.[125]

The table shows that the policy-rule response to inflation was *very* weak before 1979. The 1955-78 estimated inflation response is not much higher than that for 1970-78; evidently, the 1955 and 1957 tightenings in response to rising inflation do not make a great impression on the estimates.[126] The period of an inflation-oriented monetary policy (1981- 2003) is

---

[123] Anthony Barbridge, "Last Laugh for the Bankers," *The Observer* (London), March 2, 1969, page 10. See also Margot Naylor, "Your Real Mortgage Rate Hasn't Changed," *Daily Mail* (London), October 27, 1969, page 11.

[124] The floating of the exchange rate in June 1972 did not represent a major break from the monetary policy regime in force since 1970, because in 1970 and 1971 "the external situation ceased to be the dominant consideration in the application of domestic policies" ("Annual Monetary Survey—1971: A Sound External Situation," *Midland Bank Review* (May, 1971), reprinted in Wadsworth, 1973, pp. 412–432; quotation from p. 412); and, as noted earlier, even the late 1960s tightening measures consisted more of fiscal than monetary restriction.

[125] In quarterly policy-rule estimates, Kara and Nelson (2004) control for this tax increase and show that once this is done, rule estimates for the whole post-1979 period is similar to those for the inflation targeting regime.

[126] A much larger inflation response (2.397) is reported for the period 1958–76 by Budd and Burns (1981, p. 139). Their specification, however, includes the current account balance and exchange-rate change as additional explanatory variables, making the estimated response to inflation difficult to interpret.

associated with a response to inflation above unity, paralleling Taylor's (1999) estimates of this specification for the U.S. over 1987-97. Within the 1981-2003 era, the inflation targeting period (1993-2003 in annual data) appears to exhibit a larger response to inflation and a smaller one to output deviations, though the low variability in the data (itself, of course, a symptom of successful stabilization policy) and the small number of observations produce low *t*-statistics for our estimates. The point estimate of 1.4 on inflation is close to Chancellor Gordon Brown's characterization of current U.K. arrangements: "For a 1 per cent rise in British inflation, the British interest rate would, other things being equal, tend to rise by 1.5 per cent."[127]

Table 1. Interest-rate reaction functions for the U.K.: Annual data

Sample period	Inflation response	Detrended output response	R^2
1955-1978	0.330 (t = 7.45)	0.318 (t = 1.83)	0.731
1970-1978	0.279 (t = 3.97)	0.875 (t = 2.96)	0.778
1981-2003	1.050 (t = 8.04)	0.445 (t = 3.05)	0.786
1993-2003	1.397 (t = 0.91)	0.187 (t = 0.48)	0.103

Note: Dependent variable is the nominal Treasury bill rate (annual average).

5B Inappropriate Monetary Control Devices (1955-85)

A focus on the shortcomings of interest-rate policy, while identifying important problems with past U.K. monetary policy, does not adequately address some key flaws in the policy record. In particular, we look now at various other monetary control devices used in the U.K. from 1955 to 1985—long-term debt operations, lending controls, cash reserve requirements, and secondary reserve requirements—and argue that all were inappropriate. A unifying principle in our criticism should be mentioned at the outset. It could well be, and we believe is indeed the case, that there are important channels in the transmission mechanism of monetary policy not captured by the effect of policy on the path of the nominal short-term interest rate. But it does not follow that one should expect monetary policy to have effects on aggregate demand by employing devices that leave the nominal short rate unchanged. We will argue that, on the contrary, such an expectation is fallacious, and that embrace of this fallacy accounts for the repeated use of the devices that we now describe.

5B.1 Long-Term Debt Operations

If the U.K. authorities' attempts to portray the short-term interest rate as market-determined were an attempt to deceive the public, their attitude to the determination of the long-term interest rate was instead a case of self-deception. Denying the expectations theory of the term structure—as well as plausible generalizations of that theory—the authorities in the 1960s and 1970s both talked and acted as though the long-term government bond rate was

[127] Gordon Brown, *House of Commons Debates*, June 9, 2003, page 410.

a policy instrument, which could be manipulated independently of the short-term rate. For example, the *Bank of England Quarterly Bulletin*'s description of developments in the long-term securities market in early 1969 was that "[d]uring the period the authorities generally *allowed* yields to rise,"[128] and similarly, later in the year "[t]he authorities allowed yields to rise very sharply…"[129] The authorities left no doubt of their view that they could manipulate long rates independently of the short rate with their March 1969 account: "a rise in U.K. interest rates other than the very shortest was seen as an appropriate accompaniment to the measures which had been taken to restrain domestic demand; and the authorities reverted to a policy of allowing any weakness to be fully reflected in [long-term bond] prices."[130]

Before discussing *how* the authorities thought monetary policy could manipulate long-term interest rates, let us first consider *why* the authorities regarded management of the long-term rate as a desirable policy. Here their justification changed over time. An early rationale, inherited from the "cheap money" period of 1939-51 during which both short and long rates were pegged, was the central bank's traditional debt-management role. The Radcliffe Committee had concluded, "In our view debt management has become the fundamental domestic task of the central bank."[131] In line with this, the Bank of England described its long-term operations as guided by the aim of "maximization of demand for British government debt,"[132] while Walters (1970, p. 44) contended that this constituted the principal aim of U.K. monetary policy for the entire postwar period. Schwartz (1985) argues that from this aim the authorities took it as an "article of faith" that "debt management requires administered changes in interest rates," leading to official attempts to administer the long rate.

A second rationalization for the authorities' interest in administering long rates, of increasing prominence from the late 1950s, was manipulation of the long rate for aggregate demand control. The long-term rate had been one of the few observed interest rates that the Radcliffe Report had expressed some constructive remarks regarding its relevance for aggregate demand, though it had discounted the importance of even this rate.[133] Similarly, the Bank of England Governor in 1978 recounted that "one strand" of official thinking in the 1950s and 1960s was that the long-term rate had a role in stabilization policy beside its function in "merely financing the Government,"[134] while the Bank of England publicly emphasized this role in 1966, stating that its purpose in long-term bond transactions was "to assist economic policy by promoting or sustaining the most appropriate pattern of interest rates" and specifically "seeking to influence the behavior of prices and yields"[135] of long-term securities. The demand-management rationale is also evident in the March 1969 Bank of

---

[128] *Bank of England Quarterly Bulletin* (June, 1969), Vol. 9(2), page 138 of "Commentary" (pp. 129–144). Emphasis added.

[129] *Bank of England Quarterly Bulletin* (September, 1969), Vol. 9(3), page 287 of "Commentary" (pp. 275–291).

[130] *Bank of England Quarterly Bulletin* (March, 1969), Vol. 9(1), page 16 of "Commentary" (pp. 3–20).

[131] Radcliffe Committee (1959, para. 982).

[132] "Official Transactions in the Gilt-Edged Market," *Bank of England Quarterly Bulletin* (June, 1966), Vol. 6(2), pp. 141–148; quotation from page 148.

[133] The Radcliffe Committee said that the authorities should be "taking a view on long rates rather than short," on the grounds that the latter had "some impact" on total demand (1959, paras. 499–500). From this, Hawtrey (1959, p. 253) judges that the Committee's prescription was to "influence the long-term rate… to regulate demand." This interpretation, however, misses the pessimism the Committee felt about monetary policy; and in Artis' (1961, p. 360) assessment, the Report's pessimism encompassed doubt about the elasticity of aggregate demand with respect to both short and long rates.

[134] Gordon Richardson, "Reflections on the Conduct of Monetary Policy," February 9, 1978 speech, *Bank of England Quarterly Bulletin* (March, 1978), Vol. 18(1), pp. 31–37; quotation from page 32.

England statement quoted above, while Goodhart (1972, p. 460) went so far as to say that "an understanding of the Bank's view of [the long-term bond] market is an absolute precondition to comprehension of recent monetary policy in the U.K."

How do these rationalizations for the manipulation of the long rate stand up today? There seems little merit in the debt-management justification for controlling the long rate. Rather, it has become standard practice for central banks, to the extent they have a "banker to the government" function, *not* to interpret their role as an obligation to attempt to determine the prices at which the debt will be sold in the long-term market. As for the demand-management rationale, macroeconomic analysis today does lend support to the notion that long-term rates matter more than short rates for aggregate demand—subject to important qualifications that we will discuss at the close of this section. But the 1960s position of the authorities is still hard to defend, because even if (real) long rates are important for total demand, the U.K. official thinking on how monetary policy could affect (real and nominal) long rates seems, in retrospect, unsatisfactory.

How *did* the authorities see their influence over the long rate working? A U.S. observer, Kareken (1968, p. 101), interpreted the authorities' references to their influence on the long rate as amounting to the claim that their short-rate policy affects "expectations about tomorrow's interest rates and thereby today's long-term rates"—that is, via a standard expectations channel. This interpretation, however, is too generous to the authorities, while also underestimating their ambitions. It is too generous because it presumes that the authorities' view of how they could affect long rates fell within a defensible economic theory. It underestimates their ambitions because the authorities in the 1960s felt that their ability to manipulate long rates went well beyond their influence on expectations of future short rates.

In fact, the authorities' estimation of their ability to affect long rates expanded during the 1960s and became quite unorthodox. These changes were clearly influenced by the Radcliffe Report. In some respects, the Radcliffe Committee's sketch of how monetary policy could affect long rates was quite standard and modern: for example, at one point it stated that a change in Bank Rate—i.e., in the official short-term interest rate—could be expected to induce a larger movement in the long rate (in the same direction) if the Bank Rate movement was expected to be long-lasting.[136] But the Report also suggested that the authorities could go further in moving the long rate if they followed a less "passive" attitude in the long-term bond market, and that they "must have and must consciously exercise a positive policy about interest rates, long as well as short, and about the relationship between them."[137] Influential "City" economists also claimed that such a policy was feasible; for example, Dacey (1960, p. 123) dismissed the importance of Bank Rate but argued that long-term debt sales can "always" produce a desired increase in the long rate; while *The Banker* editorialized that "more positive tactics in the gilt-edged [i.e., long-term securities] market" would give the authorities an instrument distinct from Bank Rate "for the purpose of bringing about... changes in longer rates" (1960, p. 226). In light of this kind of analysis, the authorities' belief in their ability to affect the long rate via long-term debt operations was hardened. Indeed, by 1969, their confidence in affecting the long rate via direct intervention contrasted with their

[135] "Official Transactions...," pp. 146 and 141.

[136] "It is generally agreed that the more temporary a rise in short rates is expected to be, the less it will cause long rates to rise; correspondingly, the more temporary a drop s expected to be, the less will long rates fall." (Radcliffe Committee, 1959, para. 447).

[137] Radcliffe Committee (1959, paras. 552 and 982).

pessimism about the expectations channel, which they felt was frustrated by "often volatile" attitudes on the part of private market participants.[138]

The Bank of England did state in 1961 that "it was not the practice of the authorities to support [bond prices] in the sense of pegging,"[139] and similarly Goodhart (1984b, p. 92) notes of the 1960s as a whole that "[n]o attempt was made to peg long rates," but the very fact that management of the long rate short of a peg was seen as a feasible policy is jarring from a modern perspective. And to a remarkable degree, private-sector observers accepted the premise that the authorities were manipulating the long rate independently of the short rate. For example, the Midland Bank (a commercial bank), in its commentary on the "emergence of a gap between short and long rates from early 1970," offered the explanation that the authorities had reduced short-term interest rates and intervened in the long-term market to prevent the decrease from being transmitted to long rates.[140] By contrast, a more standard interpretation would see the long-rate response as purely a market-driven Fisher effect in the wake of a monetary policy easing. Similarly, *The Bankers' Magazine* said in 1969 that the Bank of England had "allowed prices to fall and yields to rise" in the long-term market, instead of interpreting such behavior as a Fisher effect.[141]

The authorities clearly encouraged the idea that bond market intervention can permit management of the long rate. What are the merits of this idea? Obviously such intervention—for a given path of the short rate—does not provide a feasible means for affecting long-term rates if the strict expectations theory of the term structure is valid. Interestingly, the type of actions favored in the U.K. would also be ineffective in influencing the long rate in an extended version of term-structure theory such as that in the Brunner-Meltzer (1973) type of monetarist model.[142] In this more general model of monetary transmission, it continues to be the case that the central bank cannot set the long rate independently of the short rate; rather, operations on base money affect both rates. The difference from the standard model is instead that the response of the long rate (and other asset prices) to actions on base money goes beyond that the response of the path of the short rate. The U.K. authorities' view, on the other hand, clearly suggested that the authorities could set the two rates independently, manipulating the long rate for a given path of short rates, and for a given path of the monetary base. Their position was therefore inconsistent with both standard and extended theories of the term structure—and was, in fact, an untenable position.

The fact that the Bank of England's debt operations did not, in fact, give it scope to manage the long rate, gradually forced itself on the authorities and outside observers during the 1970s, as the Fisher effect became the overwhelming factor driving long-rate movements. The Bank's description of the bond market in 1979 acknowledged inflationary expectations as

---

138 *Bank of England Quarterly Bulletin Supplement: Domestic Credit Expansion* (September, 1969), page 365.

139 *Bank of England Quarterly Bulletin* (September, 1961), Vol. 1(3), page 12, quoted in Tew (1979, p. 233).

140 "The Gilt-Edged Market and Credit Control," *Midland Bank Review* (August, 1971), reprinted in Wadsworth (1973, pp. 65–75); quotation from page 71. Also, McRae (1969, p. 1174) claimed that official debt sales had "stopped the fall in short-term interest rates from being transmitted to the longer end" in 1958, a period the Radcliffe Report approvingly described as one where long-rate behavior was "near to being decided by official action" (1959, para. 553).

141 "Money and Banking," *The Bankers' Magazine* (April, 1969), pp. 258–260; quotation from page 260. In addition, Walters (1965, p. 8) claimed that, for given Bank Rate policy, the authorities' long-term operations had "a direct effect on the [bond] yield," while Crockett (1973, p. 195) interpreted the rise in long-term rates in the decade to 1960 as evidence of a tightening of U.K. monetary policy.

142 In addition to the discussion that follows, see Andrés, López-Salido, and Nelson (2004) and Bernanke and Reinhart (2004) for detailed analysis of these issues.

the dominant factor, phrasing the problem as that "investors may lack confidence in the outlook, for example in respect of wage demands and industrial disturbance and their implications for future inflation, and in the economic and financial policies being pursued."[143] Incidentally, the fact that monetary policy was listed as the third item driving inflationary expectations (or fourth, if monetary policy is classified under "financial policies" rather than "economic policies") behind labor and industrial factors, reaffirms the grip that nonmonetary explanation of inflation had on official thought in the late 1970s.

Over 1975-79, the authorities continued to take actions to influence the long rate but did so via sharp increases in the short rate.[144] They thus reverted to reliance on the expectations channel as the means for influencing the long rate.

Despite the adoption of a more standard attitude to long-rate determination, central bank operations in long-term markets *continued* to be assigned an importance by U.K. policymakers from the mid-1970s that they did not merit. The Bank of England Governor said in 1978 that "the importance attached to operations in the gilt-edged market" now lay in their significance "in terms of the monetary aggregates."[145]

The belief that long-term debt sales were important for the government's Sterling M3 target had its origin in the credit counterparts approach to monetary control, already discussed. A Bank official expressed the philosophy simply (Coleby, 1983, p. 61): "The sale of any form of public sector debt to the nonbank public will, in principle, help to restrain M3 [growth], because the public sector will have a correspondingly reduced need to borrow from the banking system." This philosophy led the authorities to regard it as important to finance the budget deficit by sales of long-term debt to the nonbank private sector (in preference to the main alternative of selling short-term securities to the commercial banks). In addition, it led to the policy of "overfunding"—the sale of *more* long-term debt to the nonbank sector than necessary to finance the budget deficit.

Strong claims have been made about the effects of the overfunding policy and of its abandonment in 1985.[146] Congdon (1992, p. 227) asserts that overfunding was "immensely useful as a means of curbing the growth of the monetary aggregates," while Pepper and Oliver (2001, p. 47) claim that the abandonment of overfunding did "harm to the U.K. economy" by pushing up broad money growth and thereby producing an "inflationary boom." And even discussions that question the significance of overfunding—for example, Dow and Saville (1988) and Cobham (2002)—take for granted that overfunding had a negative effect on Sterling M3 growth.[147]

By contrast, an alternative approach, more consistent with standard economic theory, is that overfunding had *no* overall effect on broad money growth (and by extension, neither did the attempts in 1976-81 to restrain money growth by shifting the financing of the budget

[143] "The Gilt-Edged Market," *Bank of England Quarterly Bulletin* (June, 1979), Vol. 19, No. 2, pp. 137–148; quotation from page 139.

[144] See Artis and Lewis (1981, p. 76) and Dennis (1981b, pp. 262–269).

[145] Gordon Richardson, "Reflections on the Conduct of Monetary Policy," February 9, 1978 speech, *Bank of England Quarterly Bulletin* (March, 1978), Vol. 18(1), pp. 31–37; quotation from page 32.

[146] Goodhart (1992, p. 326) gives 1981–85 as the period of overfunding policy. In addition to these years, the official figures suggest overfunding also took place in the financial year 1977/78 (Temperton, 1986, p. 51).

[147] For example, Cobham (2002, p. 25) frames the doubts about overfunding as: "it became increasingly unclear whether the overall effect on monetary growth was real or cosmetic." That way of framing the issue accepts the premise that banks' deposit and asset growth were reduced by overfunding, but suggests that nonbank credit creation compensated for slower balance sheet growth by banks. The discussion that follows will instead dispute that there was any effect of overfunding on money growth at all.

deficit from purchases of debt by banks to purchases by the nonbank sector).[148] It follows that the abandonment of overfunding did not contribute to the late 1980s expansion of aggregate demand. To see why overfunding should not be expected to be effective in restraining deposit growth, let us consider two cases: one where the long-term interest rate does not enter the money demand function, the other where it does.

If short-term interest rates are the only opportunity cost variable in the broad money demand function, then central bank operations in the long-term market—which were regarded as a separate policy instrument precisely because they left short rates unchanged—should not be expected to affect the quantity of money demanded. Then attempts to control deposit growth by changing the quantity of debt sold to commercial banks are subject to the same critique as the whole credit counterparts approach to controlling money growth. That is, with the reserve position of the commercial banking system unchanged by the operation, and with the quantity of money demanded by the public the same as before, commercial banks will offset the effect on their total asset growth of fewer purchases of government debt by expanding their loans to the private sector. Broad money growth will be unaffected by overfunding.

In the case where long rates do enter the money demand function, there is scope for overfunding operations to affect money growth, *provided* the operations affect the long rate. During the early years of Sterling M3 targeting, almost all discussion treated long-term debt sales to households as having an automatic negative effect on deposit growth, implied by the credit counterparts identity, and did not portray the effect as contingent on the operations being able to affect long-term rates. In other words, the justified doubts that the authorities had acquired regarding their ability to influence the long rate via these sales did not cause them to doubt the effectiveness of these sales in restraining broad money growth. But, as we have discussed, the claimed restraining effect on broad money growth *did*, in fact, require that the sales affected the long rate. This fact was noted late in the monetary targeting period by a U.S. observer (Davis, 1982a, p. 56):

> [T]here are some in the United Kingdom who believe that… [short-term] interest rates are not an effective tool for controlling [Sterling M3]. Rather the best tool that is available to the Bank of England is to try to directly influence the movement of this aggregate by debt management operations that, in effect, shift the yield curve.

Within the U.K., discussions of the overfunding policy from the mid-1980s did increasingly discuss its effects in terms of any influence on long rates.[149] These discussions

---

148 Articulations of this no-effect view were rare in the U.K. during the monetary targeting period. As far as the authorities were concerned, Chrystal (1999, p. 198) argues that they believed "that debt sales to banks involved printing money" until 1993. An articulation of the opposing view from an academic economist was Allsopp (1981, paras. 134–135), who stated specifically that (for the reasons discussed here) overfunding's effect on bank asset growth would be offset by growth in other commercial bank assets. Macroeconomic models of the U.K. economy that embedded the expectations theory of the term structure (e.g. Minford, 1980) also implicitly amounted to a rejection of the official position on overfunding.

149 See e.g. Bain (1983, p. 6), Temperton (1986, p. 53), Miles and Wilcox (1991, p. 242), and Robertson (1992, p. 184), as well as "Casting Government Bread on the Water," *The Times* (London) ("Finance and Industry" section), June 5, 1984, page 14, and Samuel Brittan, "A Fresh Look at the U.K. Economy," *Financial Times* (London), August 2, 1984, page 16. As late as 1992, however, the effect of debt management operations on broad money was described by one financial columnist as "an arithmetic certainty" that could be relied upon regardless of whether those operations moved long-term rates (Anthony Harris, "A New Twist to Ease the Slump," *Financial Times* (London), July 20, 1992, page 17).

did at least grasp what overfunding had to do to have an effect on aggregate broad money growth.

There are, however, no grounds for expecting overfunding to have had an effect on long-term interest rates, because the overfunding operations had the same feature as the Bank of England's 1960s operations in long-term markets—that is, their effect on the monetary base was sterilized. With the path of short-term interest rates and the path of monetary base unchanged by overfunding operations, there is no justification either from the expectations theory of the term structure or from a monetarist perspective to expect overfunding to affect long-term interest rates. Therefore, the conclusion remains that the U.K. authorities' long-term operations had no effect on money growth. Consistent with this conclusion, reduced-form empirical evidence for the U.K. does not support a link between overfunding and either long-term rates or broad money growth (Miles and Wilcox, 1991; Chrystal, 1999).

We conclude that the U.K. authorities' actions in the long-term markets did not provide it with a separate instrument for influencing either money or interest rates distinct from its open market operations. Indeed, to the extent that such operations as overfunding convinced the authorities they needed to do less with their short-term interest rate to achieve monetary restraint, these operations made policy easier than intended in the 1960s, 1970s, and 1980s, not tighter. The reassignment in 1998 of debt-management functions from the Bank of England to the Debt Management Office therefore did not sacrifice room to move for monetary policy, but instead signified a realistic recognition on the part of the authorities that "debt management is not a major tool of monetary policy."[150]

Curiously enough, alongside the fallacious ideas that guided the U.K. authorities' operations in long-term markets were some observations that were worth pursuing and which identified what proved to be resilient stylized facts. The Bank of England in 1966 had observed that among the regular purchasers of long-term debt were "institutions [which] fall into fairly homogeneous groups with broadly similar investment preferences."[151] Along the same lines *The Economist* noted in 1965 that pension and life insurance funds were not "interested in stock with less than five years to maturity;"[152] the shorter-term securities being demanded by commercial banks.[153] This stylized fact continues today, with Chrystal (1999, p. 194) observing: "most of the long-term [U.K.] government debt outstanding is held by pension funds and insurance companies. Banks prefer short-term debt holdings because they have short-term liabilities, and they need to hold some safe liquid assets."

These stylized facts have important implications for the transmission of monetary policy. Andrés, López-Salido, and Nelson (ALSN) (2004) show that the existence of agents who subscribe exclusively to long-term debt is a crucial condition for making the long rate appear in the aggregate IS function in an optimizing macroeconomic model. Otherwise—for all the stress in the literature on long rates—one obtains the standard IS equation, where what matters for aggregate demand is the integral of the path of short rates. In the standard model, therefore, deviations of the long rate from the expected path of short rates are irrelevant for aggregate demand; on the other hand, in ALSN's framework, these deviations are relevant because the long rate appears directly in the IS equation. ALSN further modify the standard

---

150 *Debt Management Review*, July 1995, quoted in Goodhart (1999, p. 63).

151 "Official Transactions in the Gilt-Edged Market," page 144.

152 "The Gilt-Edged Market," *The Economist* (London), March 20, 1965, page 1338.

153 Similarly, the OECD (1982, p. 76) observed that "commercial banks rarely purchase" long-term U.K. government debt. See also Radcliffe Report (1959, para. 547).

model to accommodate the monetarist or Tobinesque assumption that long-term securities are not perfect substitutes for other assets. In particular, reflecting the stylized fact noted above, ALSN's modification makes those agents who hold both short-term and long-term assets prefer, other things equal, to hold the former. This creates an extra transmission channel in the model, whereby monetary policy affects the long rate both via the expectations channel and the risk premium. But this channel requires that the monetary policy actions affect the monetary base, and so does not provide a justification for the U.K. authorities' operations in the long-term market over 1958-85, which by design left the monetary base unchanged.

5B.2 Credit Controls

Credit controls were official requirements (labeled "directives" or "requests") that the commercial banks to keep their increase in loans to the private sector to a specified limit (or "ceiling"). These controls applied to the "clearing banks" up to 1961, and were extended thereafter to other commercial banks. They were used so vigorously during the 1960s that they have been described as the "main instrument" of monetary policy prior to their abolition in 1971, and by former Prime Minister Wilson himself as his "principal technique of monetary control" in the 1960s.[154]

Direct controls on lending appealed to policymakers because they believed credit was an economically significant variable, while the controls appeared to avoid the need to use interest rates to restrict credit or aggregate demand. Prime Minister Harold Macmillan saw this as one attractive feature of controls,[155] and Wilson admitted that this had been his "main reason for applying direct controls."[156]

Interest-cost-push views of inflation were also a factor leading to support for controls. For example, in 1965 a London financial columnist wrote: "The aim must be to cut the internal cost of money by reducing interest rates but at the same time to exercise control over the amount of credit. In other words—cheaper money, but less of it."[157] He was evidently voicing an opinion that was shared by key policy advisors such as Nicholas Kaldor. Kaldor praised controls as "the way in which credit expansion has been controlled ever since the war,"[158] while criticizing interest-rate increases because "interest costs are passed on in higher prices in much the same way as wage costs."[159] Kaldor's fellow advisor Thomas Balogh was attracted to credit controls on the additional grounds that the demand for loans was insensitive to interest-rate changes (Balogh, 1958).

As might be expected, the controls became ineffective as a means of restricting aggregate credit in the economy, due to more credit being intermediated through the unregulated portion of the financial system. The considerable scope for evasion is shown by the fact that at the time of their abolition in 1971, controls applied to 200 commercial banks, but only 20 of 1500 finance houses, none of 300 investment trusts, none of 150 unit trusts, and none of 500 building societies.[160]

It would be a mistake, however, to rest the judgment that credit controls were an ineffective monetary policy instrument solely on the existence of a large uncontrolled

[154] Brown (1981, p. 2); Wilson Committee (1980, p. 178).
[155] See Dell (1996, p. 232).
[156] Wilson Committee (1980, p. 178).
[157] Gerald Colverd, "Fighting a Battle That Has Already Been Won," *Daily Mail* (London), April 30, 1965, page 17.
[158] Nicholas Kaldor, *House of Lords Debates*, June 11, 1980, page 467.
[159] Kaldor (1982, p. 62).

component of lending. In a standard macroeconomic model, as we noted earlier, it is money balances rather than the stock of credit that pins down the price level. Suppose the lending by the unregulated sector created corresponding liabilities that do not substitute closely for bank deposits. Then the disintermediation induced by credit controls might still have a meaningful contractionary effect on aggregate demand by slowing growth of money relative to growth in credit (Lewis, 1980).

Unfortunately, this argument does not apply to the practical experience of the U.K., and therefore cannot salvage the case for credit controls. First consider the case where a narrow aggregate such as M1 or the monetary base is the appropriate definition of money. It is likely, as we discuss in the next subsection, that nonbank financial institutions did not produce deposits in the 1960s and 1970s that substituted closely for M1 transactions balances. But credit controls were nevertheless ineffective, because in the 1960s they were directed at all banks, including those that created primarily non-M1 deposits. Thus, insofar as credit controls indirectly restricted deposit growth, they did so in restricting M3 growth, with no necessary implications for growth in M1.

Consider now the case where a broad money concept is the appropriate definition of money. Further make the generous assumption that the credit controls, which really applied only to lending to the *private* sector, had a restrictive effect on total balance sheet growth of commercial banks—i.e., that their slower lending to the private sector was not offset completely by greater acquisition of government securities. Even making this assumption, the conclusion is that credit controls failed to produce a meaningful monetary restriction. Disintermediation encouraged not only growth in nonbank lending but, on the liabilities side, growth in instruments that were close substitutes for banks' time deposits, especially building society deposits. Broad money growth, correctly defined, was not restricted by the credit controls.

The authorities could, if they wished, have inhibited the extent to which credit controls promoted the creation of deposit substitutes. A tight interest-rate policy and accompanying slower growth in base money would have stifled the private sector's ability to create deposit-like instruments. But credit controls were intended precisely as a device which reduced the recourse to a tight interest-rate policy. The bottom line is that the critique of credit controls today is precisely the same as that made fifty years ago: "control of the cash base will secure the Chancellor's objective *without* directives[,] whereas the most perfect implementation of the directives, without any contraction of the cash base, will make no contribution whatever."[161]

A postscript on the U.K.'s experience with credit controls came in 1980, when two figures who had both featured prominently in U.K. policy debates offered their assessment of controls. While Harold Wilson had used controls frequently during his 1964-70 incumbency, his conclusion in 1980 was that they "inhibited competition among banks and between them and other financial institutions, thus protecting market shares and discouraging innovation. [They] also became less effective with the passage of time."[162] Milton Friedman, submitting evidence to the House of Commons Treasury and Civil Service Committee, delivered a briefer verdict: "There is, in my opinion, no case whatsoever for direct controls on credit."[163]

[160] Figures from Bank of England official's handwritten notes on Hodgman (1971), late 1971.
[161] Newlyn (1955, p. 289).
[162] Wilson Committee (1980, p. 178).
[163] Friedman (1980, p. 61).

5B.3 Cash Reserve Requirements

Until 1981 the U.K. authorities imposed two types of cash reserve requirement: a cash reserve ratio of 8% on "clearing banks," cut to 1.5% in 1971; and a variable reserve requirement known as calls for "Special Deposits," initially (1961) imposed on the "clearing banks" but imposed on all commercial banks from 1971. The variable reserve requirement was set at zero in 1980 and was discontinued thereafter, while mandatory reserve requirements were substantially altered in 1981 and, as we will see, ceased to be part of the conduct of monetary policy. As a result, over the last 25 years the U.K. has had an environment where reserve requirements are at low levels and are not seen as essential to monetary policy. This outcome represented a victory for the arguments against reserve-requirement changes as a monetary policy instrument.

The traditional critique of variations in cash ratio requirements as a monetary control device is that they do nothing that cannot alternatively be achieved by open market operations (Friedman, 1960, pp. 47-48; Johnson, 1971b, p. 143), since both actions can be thought of as working on a requirement-adjusted monetary base series. In the U.K. in the 1960s, a second prominent criticism—analogous to the criticism of credit controls—was that binding reserve requirements encouraged the growth of depository institutions that were not subject to the requirement, with the eventual prospect of reserve-requirement changes losing their equivalence to open market operations and becoming ineffective (e.g. Johnson, 1971b, p. 144). U.K. policy actions in the 1960s and early 1970s were perhaps less subject to the second criticism than was thought at the time. For while official regulation did promote disintermediation and the creation of deposit substitutes, these activities was strongest in creating alternatives to time deposits. Building societies and similar nonbank institutions were less adept, especially before the 1980s, at creating close substitutes for demand deposits.[164] As reserve requirements until 1971 fell predominantly on the "clearing banks" and so the main creators of transaction deposits, they probably did have a restraining effect on the M1 aggregate and therefore transactions money. Certainly the sharp rise in the M1 multiplier following the cut in the cash reserve ratio in 1971 is evidence that the cash ratio had a restraining effect on M1 creation.[165]

But cash reserve requirements were subject to the first criticism in the preceding paragraph, as well as to a third criticism, less commonly made at the time, which reinforces the first criticism. This is that a reserve-requirement increase, in conditions of an unchanged choice for the short-term interest rate, simply leads to the extra reserves being provided to the commercial banks. The monetary base rises to compensate for the increase in reserve requirements, and wider monetary aggregates and market interest rates are unaffected.[166] Not only are variations in reserve requirements ineffective, but their presence as a policy instrument may encourage the authorities to regard other, effective policy actions—especially an increase in the policy rate—as unnecessary.

---

[164] For example, Morrell (1987, p. 28) characterizes the situation during the 1960s as one where "[b]uilding society transactions… would ultimately be reflected in movements in bank balances," while Thompson (1986, p. 27) characterizes the 1980s as the period where building societies "progressively turn[ed] themselves into conventional banks with checking account facilities."

[165] Howard and Johnson (1982, p. 160) claim that the 1971 cut in reserve requirements did not alter the M1 multiplier. This claim seems to be a product of problems with the M1 series they use. Capie and Webber's (1985, p. 109) series on the M1 multiplier clearly exhibits a marked increase in late 1971.

[166] See Meltzer (2001), and for specific applications of the argument to the U.K.'s system, Gibson (1964), Crouch (1967, pp. 4.13 and 4.22), and Norton (1969, p. 192).

This danger became a reality in 1970 when the Heath Government increased Special Deposits as a monetary tightening measure, in preference to increasing Bank Rate.[167] This ineffective attempt at tightening, together with the conscious easing of monetary policy from April 1971, contributed to the very expansionary monetary policy of the early 1970s and subsequent rise in inflation.

Variations in reserve requirements continued to be used as a policy instrument during the 1970s. Since 1980, however, the authorities have taken a much more enlightened view of the role of reserve requirements. The authorities' *Monetary Control* document in 1980 emphasized that some balances at the Bank of England were required for the authorities' "point of control over short-term interest rates,"[168] but in 1981 the 1.5% cash ratio was abolished, allowing the demand for reserve balances to emerge voluntarily.[169] Special Deposits were also effectively abolished, ending variations in reserve requirements as a policy instrument. For the purposes of financing the Bank of England, a new mandatory cash ratio (initially at 0.5%) was introduced, imposed on banks and a variety of other financial institutions. These funds were impounded by the authorities and thus could not serve to carry out transactions between the Bank of England and the commercial banks.[170] The fact that the new reserve requirement was not a monetary policy instrument was emphasized by the fact that the resulting funds were excluded from the official definition of the monetary base,[171] although for some analytical purposes it would be legitimate to include them.[172]

The very low levels of reserves that emerged from this system did attract some criticism: for example, Karl Brunner said in December 1981 said that the fact that banks were "able to run on virtually no reserves... is really a subsidy to the City."[173] But such criticisms have not stood the test of time, and it has been much more common to regard the low level of reserves as a sign of efficiency: as a low tax on banking, rather than a subsidy to banking. At the same time the framework where open market operations work off voluntarily-held balances, with (almost) no reserve requirement on financial institutions, has come to be seen as sufficient for central bank control of aggregate demand while simultaneously lowering welfare costs (e.g. Dotsey, 1991; Woodford, 2001).

---

[167] The Government's view of variations in Special Deposits as a substitute for interest-rate actions could also be found among outside commentators. For example, financial columnist Patrick Sergeant wrote in early 1971: "I think Mr. Barber [the Chancellor of the Exchequer] will have to cut Bank Rate soon, though this will not mean relaxing the squeeze—he could keep money scarce by Special Deposits and a variety of other measures." "Stampede for Gilts," *Daily Mail* (London), January 16, 1971, page 14.

[168] HM Treasury and Bank of England (1980, Annex A, para. 7).

[169] In July 2004 the Bank of England announced reforms that would continue to make the holding of reserves voluntary, but are designed to increase the predictability of the levels of reserve balances held with the Bank. The reforms encourage financial institutions to notify the Bank of their chosen average reserve level over the month ahead. In the words of the Bank's July 22, 2004 press release, the reserves are "voluntary" in the sense that the institutions choose the target levels, but "required" in the sense that adherence to these chosen levels is a binding undertaking by the institutions. In return, the reserves bear interest at a rate equal to the Monetary Policy Committee's (MPC's) chosen policy rate. The Bank's principal motivation for this reform was to reduce the fluctuations of overnight market interest rates around the MPC's policy rate (Bank of England, *Reform of the Bank of England's Operations in the Sterling Money Market*, May 2004, para. 13).

[170] Woodford's (2001, p. 320) position that the U.K. has "completely eliminated reserve requirements" is thus a slight overstatement, though accurate as far as operational balances are concerned.

[171] See Temperton (1986, p. 76).

[172] For example, they should be included in the monetary base series is used to compute the own rate on money, as in Friedman and Schwartz (1982, p. 260).

[173] Quoted in Newton (1983, p. 206).

Very soon after the onset of present arrangements, a U.S. observer accurately saw the U.K. system as a benchmark for other systems, such as the U.S., that then relied more heavily on required reserves: "it is clear that the central bank could exert relatively large immediate interest-rate effects with only rather small-sized variations in its own portfolio—much like the situation apparently facing the Bank of England, whose money market operations focus on the quite small clearing balances at the Bank" (Davis, 1982b, p. 30). Thus, while the U.K. authorities made mistakes in its use of reserve requirements for monetary policy that mirrored those in other countries, they were among the world leaders in dismantling the reserve-requirement system.

5B.4 Secondary Reserve Requirements

A secondary reserve requirement is a reserve requirement imposed on commercial banks that requires banks' holding of Treasury bills, or of cash reserves plus bills, be equal to some minimum ratio to total deposits. In the U.K., the authorities until 1981 imposed a virtual secondary reserve requirement on banks—initially in the form of the Liquidity Ratio (which was 28% at the time of its abolition in 1971) on clearing banks, then from 1971 the 12.5% reserve assets ratio[174] on all banks. In principle these ratios could be satisfied by holding base money (and, to a limited extent, other assets) rather than Treasury bills, but the fact that desired cash ratios[175] were low and Treasury bills bore interest meant that banks has an incentive to satisfy the liquidity ratios principally by holding short-term government securities.

While the liquidity ratio was introduced in the 1940s as a prudential measure, rather than for monetary policy purposes,[176] it came to be regarded as significant for monetary analysis. Both the Bank of England[177] and influential observers such as Dacey (1960) and Sayers (1957), as well as the Radcliffe Report (paras. 376, 583), attached behavioral significance to the ratio of banks' liquid assets to their total balance sheets—on the grounds that a fall in the ratio below desired levels would force banks to contract their business. The 1960s critics of the official view argued, correctly, that the flaw in this approach was that commercial banks could restore their liquidity ratio by bidding away existing government securities from nonbank holders, without any contraction in aggregate bank assets or liabilities (e.g. Crouch, 1964, p. 926).

This criticism certainly identified a flaw in official monetary analysis of the time, but it is doubtful whether it also found a major source of *policy mistakes*. Such a finding would require that the liquidity ratio was actually regarded by the authorities as an instrument of monetary policy. Thomas Wilson (1957, p. 241) claimed that they did do so, stating: "Credit policy in Britain has been operated by means of the liquidity ratio… [using] the liquidity ratio

---

[174] The reserve assets ratio was cut to 10% shortly before its 1981 abolition (Tew, 1981, p. 13).

[175] Or desired excess cash reserve ratios, for those banks subject to cash reserve requirements.

[176] See Crockett (1973, p. 182) and HM Treasury and Bank of England (1980, para. 3.4).

[177] See e.g. the quotations in Crouch (1964, pp. 926–927) of the Bank of England's submissions to the Radcliffe Committee. In addition, Goodhart (1999, p. 54) states that "the key role of the liquid assets ratio was endorsed by both the Bank of England and the Treasury, and accepted by most other economists who considered the issue." This included Lionel Robbins who, while challenging the low weight assigned by Sayers and the Radcliffe Committee to the role of monetary policy in controlling aggregate demand, accepted their liquid-assets view of money creation (Robbins, 1961).

in order to check the growth of deposits."[178] But it is very unlikely that the liquidity ratio was deployed much for this purpose, because, as discussed in Section 3A, restraining money growth was not a major concern of the authorities, especially after 1957. The liquidity ratio thus did underpin a flawed view by U.K. authorities of money supply determination, but correcting that flaw need not in itself have led to a different monetary policy, since official analysis gave little importance to the money stock.

It also appears that, contrary to the perception of contemporary observers such as Thomas Wilson, the liquidity ratio was hardly used at all by the authorities as a monetary policy instrument. When a critique of U.K. monetary policy appeared in the *Journal of Money, Credit and Banking* in 1971 (Hodgman, 1971), a Bank of England official wrote in the margin of the Bank's subscription copy of the article, "*At last an academic who realizes that we have used Liquidity Ratio as a control* [*device*] *for* <u>*only a few months*</u> *during the last 25 years*! *But just as we have abandoned the system*!"

This suggests that the authorities did not regard the liquidity ratio as a central policy instrument, and treated it less prominently than other quantitative devices and Bank Rate. Its principal attraction to the authorities was not for implementing monetary policy but, as discussed below, to subsidize the financing of government debt. The official's comment quoted above is unfair to academic economists in one important respect: the Bank of England Governor had given credence in 1969 to viewing the liquidity ratio as a control device.[179] But perhaps it was during 1969 that the "few months" of the use of the liquidity ratio actually took place.[180]

The "abandonment" of the liquidity ratio referred to in the preceding quotation referred to the introduction of a new set of regulations on the banking system with the 1971 Competion and Credit Control reforms. Though abolishing the liquidity ratio, these new arrangements introduced a new type of secondary reserve requirement, applying to all commercial banks (rather than the clearing banks alone, as the liquidity ratio had). The new "reserve assets ratio" required that an amount equal 12.5% of bank liabilities be held in the form of specified assets, which included Treasury bills, soon-to-mature long-term securities, and (up to a low maximum) certain commercial bills.

The creation of the new secondary reserve requirement set off a fresh guessing game among commentators on U.K. monetary policy on its role. The predictable first reaction was to regard it as a new device, again based on the "liquid assets" theory of money creation, for controlling the aggregate balance sheets of the banking system. Alternative accounts of U.K. monetary policy differ on the reserve assets ratio actually served as part of the authorities' monetary control apparatus; indeed, there is not always agreement between different accounts by the same author. Thus Congdon (1992, p. 216) criticizes Friedman's (1980) attack on the reserve assets ratio as reflecting Friedman's "imperceptiveness" about U.K. institutional arrangements, but Congdon (1978, pp. 47-48) criticized the reserve assets ratio using an

---

178 Similarly, Johnson (1956, p. 6) claimed that the liquidity ratio "can without exaggerating be said [to be] ... the significant ratio through which monetary policy operates." He renounced this view in Johnson (1971b, p. 144).

179 "[C]ontrary to a lot of popular belief, the cash ratio is not the fulcrum for credit policy; it is the liquidity ratio... The liquidity ratio, however, is the traditional fulcrum on which monetary policy is based." Governor Leslie O'Brien, May 14, 1969, testimony, in Select Committee on Nationalized Industries (1970, p. 52).

180 Consistent with this conjecture, Tew (1981, p. 12) says that the "liquid asset ratio did not bite seriously in any year except 1969." Crockett (1973, p. 182) also suggests that the liquidity ratio may have been used for monetary control in 1951, during the transition from the "cheap money" policy.

argument *identical* to that Friedman made. This argument, in turn, corresponds to that raised by Laidler (1981, p. 177), who said, "I have, from their very inception, been critical of that provision of the Competition and Credit Control rules that makes Treasury Bills (not to mention certain private sector Bills) a component of the reserve base."

The criticism of Congdon, Friedman, and Laidler of the reserve assets ratio was presumably based on the following argument. The ratio might encourage commercial banks to regard Treasury bills as the equivalent of bank reserves, in the same way that they did during the postwar "cheap money" period when the price of securities was pegged in money terms (Friedman and Schwartz, 1963, p. 563). Under those circumstances, open market operations (switches between base and short-term securities) no longer produce predictable effects on deposit creation, because they no do not affect the base-plus-securities aggregate that matters for banks' expansion.

This criticism, however, was not actually valid in practice. The analogy between the cheap money period and the period of the reserve assets ratio (1971-81) breaks down because in the latter period, rates on U.K. Treasury bills and other short-term securities varied widely over time; although short-term rates were a policy instrument, their rate was not pegged. Thus, however much the ratio's presence tended to create equivalence between base money and bills, the variations in the return on bills broke that equivalence. Commercial banks did not have grounds, in making decisions affecting monthly or quarterly movements in their balance sheets, for treating securities and base money as equivalent.[181]

The reserve assets ratio not only did not make commercial banks treat Treasury bills as equivalent to base money; it was not in fact used as a policy device for controlling the money stock (or total bank credit). As the OECD put it (1982, p. 78): "The reserve asset requirement… was never intended and has never been used as a vehicle for direct control of the credit pyramid."

What then was the function of the reserve assets ratio? Congdon (1992, p. 216) suggests the ratio's role was as a prudential regulation, but the authorities in their *Monetary Control* document (1980) explicitly said that the "reserve ratio was not intended as a prudential control."[182] Artis and Lewis (1981, p. 63) suggest that it may have come to be perceived as a prudential ratio over time, but Llewellyn (1981, p. 96) notes that it was not a meaningful prudential ratio by the late 1970s. Artis and Lewis (1981, p. 63) also suggest that the reserve assets ratio was intended as a "'second leg' of interest-rate policy." In their 1980 document the authorities similarly claimed that the reserve assets ratio had been intended as "an element in the control of short-term interest rates," but in the same document they acknowledged that demand for base money was sufficient to achieve that control (1980, paras. 3.6, 3.8).

The actual function of the reserve assets ratio seems instead to have been unrelated to either the monetary policy or prudential concerns of the authorities. Instead, it was simply a means of subsidizing official sales of government debt. By forcing commercial banks to demand government securities, a secondary reserve requirement tends to lower yields on those securities relative to a situation where the government and the private sector fully compete for funds. This effect underlay Brunner and Crouch's (1967, p. 109) judgment that "the liquid assets ratio is, to call a spade a spade, purely a device to reap 'monopsonistic

---

[181] Dean (1975, p. 69) is a discussion of secondary reserve requirements that recognized this point.
[182] HM Treasury and Bank of England (1980, Annex A, fn. 4).

profits' for the Exchequer."[183] Apparently the subsidization of government debt was also a motivation for imposing the reserve assets ratio in 1971 (Brown, 1981, p. 4). The reserve assets ratio was thus a straightforward successor to the liquidity ratio in being a tax on banks, though with the tax extended to the entire banking system instead of clearing banks alone. The abolition of the reserve assets ratio in 1981 brought this tax to an end.

6 Monetary Policy Developments in the 1980s

Our discussion of 1980s developments covers first the early 1980s disinflation (Section 6A) then the subsequent upsurge in inflation (Section 6B).

6A The Disinflation of the early 1980s

In this subsection we focus on the period from 1979 to 1983, considering first the events that were the background to policy decisions (Section 6A.1), then the behavior of inflation and real variables during the disinflation (Section 6A.2).

6A.1 Background to the Disinflation

The economic policies of the Thatcher Government elected in May 1979 were outlined in the speech opening Parliament, written by the government but by tradition read out by the Queen. A key passage of the Queen's speech was: "My Government will give priority in economic policy to controlling inflation through the pursuit of firm monetary and fiscal policies."[184] The reference in this passage to "firm monetary and fiscal policies" rather than monetary targeting (let alone to any specific definition of the money supply) brings out the most fundamental break from the past in 1979: the assignment of inflation control to monetary policy rather than incomes policy. This break in policy behavior has outlasted both the Thatcher government and monetary targeting, and has persisted to the present day. It was a more fundamental policy shift than the introduction of the inflation targeting framework introduced by Chancellor of the Exchequer Norman Lamont in 1992; and, indeed, acceptance of the validity of the 1979 shift made inflation targeting possible.[185]

Why did this policy shift prove lasting? It was certainly not because of a wide consensus in favor of the new government's reassignment of instruments. Opposition by U.K. economists to the Thatcher Government's policies was particularly strong during the disinflation and recession that took place during its first term. Public critics of the government included not only former officials who continued to adhere to the Radcliffian tradition, such as Nicholas Kaldor and Robert Neild, but also the noted general equilibrium theorist Frank Hahn. Hahn laid out his critique in a series of lectures in 1981, published as Hahn (1983), in which he questioned the link between expansionary monetary policy and inflation, and recommended that the government's tight monetary policy be abandoned in favor of

---

183 "The Exchequer" is a term that stands in for any revenue-collecting branches of the U.K. government.

184 May 15, 1979 Queen's speech, quoted in *Whitaker's Almanack 1980* (1979, p. 361).

185 Advocates of monetary targeting during the 1970s emphasized the implied shift in the role assigned to monetary policy. For example, Friedman (1977, p. 13) observed that the "essence" of his argument "was to suggest that monetary policy is an appropriate and proper tool directed at achieving price stability or a desired rate of price change."

expanding demand. Hahn expressed legitimate concerns about the complexity of defining the natural rate of unemployment for an economy as complex as the U.K., yet his policy prescription was to have demand management guided by a full-employment target rate of unemployment—*a.k.a.* the natural rate of unemployment. The tension between these positions was not lost on the late Herschel Grossman, who suggested that "the weakest aspects of these lectures are Hahn's attempts to evaluate and prescribe monetary policy," which, as Grossman noted, were out of date in light of "the realization by economists and persons of affairs, including Mr. Callaghan and Mrs. Thatcher, that his simplistic approach... provides no operational bounds on either monetary expansion or inflation."[186] A review by Goodhart (1983) reached a similar judgment—"I found some of the assertions about more practical matters dubious and/or unhelpful." Nevertheless, critiques such as Hahn's conferred legitimacy on the older nonmonetary approach to inflation, and likely contributed to the fact that at the 1983 election the three principal opposition parties all advocated a return to compulsory price controls. At the election, these parties received over 53% of the popular vote. It was the fact that the Government faced a divided opposition that prevented a reversion in 1983 to pre-1979 policies.

But developments in 1983 do not explain why the Government was able to maintain a tight monetary policy over its first term and thus achieve the early 1980s disinflation. In terms of pressure for a policy reversal in its first term, what really mattered was not the presence of outside critics but the strength of Thatcher's *internal* opposition—in her Cabinet and parliamentary party. In fact, Thatcher's first Cabinet was nevertheless dominated by senior figures from the Heath Government, many of whom remained sympathetic with the traditional nonmonetary approach to fighting inflation. The disillusionment with traditional policy had in fact been deeper among some of the Callaghan Government's team than among many of Thatcher's senior personnel; reflecting this, Thatcher actually appointed a former member of Callaghan's Cabinet as a junior minister in her government, while she has also stated that she would have liked to appoint Callaghan's son-in-law to her Cabinet because of his "understanding of monetary economics."[187]

Nor was it just Heath's former subordinates who criticized the shift in economic policy. As Lamont later observed with understatement, "Mrs. Thatcher had her problems with Ted Heath."[188] Since losing the Conservative Party leadership to Thatcher in 1975 the former Prime Minister had criticized her rejection of incomes policy in favor of monetary policy, and kicked off a fresh campaign in late 1980 in the form of a radio debate with Milton Friedman and criticism of the Thatcher Government's economic policy in a House of Commons debate.[189] Government figures occasionally attempted to suggest that Heath was now too marginalized for his criticisms to be damaging,[190] but this is belied by Harris' (1988, p. 36) observation that when Heath spoke out, "every time he did so received wide publicity" and such criticism was privately "welcomed" by several members of Thatcher's Cabinet. Indeed, Nigel Lawson, Chancellor of the Exchequer from 1983, judged that Heath's criticisms of

---

[186] Grossman (1984, p. 339).

[187] Thatcher (1995, p. 368). The individual in question was Peter Jay, Callaghan's then son-in-law, a former Economics Editor of *The Times*, and since 2003 a Director of the Bank of England.

[188] Norman Lamont, quoted in Benedict Brogan, "Tories 'Could Be Out of Power for a Generation'", *Daily Telegraph* (London), August 24, 2001, pages 1 and 4.

[189] See Campbell (1993, pp. 722–725).

[190] See e.g. Ridley (1991, p. 173).

monetary policy did political damage to Lawson as late as 1988,[191] while Thatcher herself has acknowledged that the "highly publicized attacks from Ted Heath" played a part in the sequence of events in 1989-90 that led to her removal.[192]

Why then did the internal opposition to Thatcher's policies not lead to a policy reversal during the crucial years of the disinflation: 1979 to 1981? Several accounts have speculated that Thatcher was close to being forced by Cabinet into a policy change during 1980 and 1981. Most of these accounts, however, mix together reversals in fiscal policy and monetary policy. It was the absence of a change of direction of monetary policy that was really crucial for securing the fall in inflation in the early 1980s.[193] Postwar economic policy arrangements traditionally gave the Cabinet considerable authority over fiscal policy but not monetary policy. Monetary policy decisions tended to be decided away from Cabinet by the Prime Minister and the Chancellor of the Exchequer, and this remained the case in the early 1980s. There were few precedents for other ministers to intervene in major monetary policy decisions, and those precedents suggested that only very senior non-economics ministers, such as the Foreign Secretary, could do so, as had occurred in the early 1950s when Anthony Eden was Foreign Secretary.[194]

The lack of a monetary policy reversal by the Thatcher Government therefore seems best explained by the fact that the *most senior* Cabinet members did not promote a change. Chancellor Howe and the other Treasury ministers were committed to disinflation, while Lord Carrington, Foreign Secretary over 1979-82, apparently did not challenge the Government's economic policy in Cabinet discussions, despite being privately skeptical.[195] If—as had been mooted before Thatcher's first Cabinet was appointed—Thatcher had instead made Roy Jenkins Chancellor of the Exchequer and Heath Foreign Secretary, it is much more likely that these two longtime advocates of incomes policy would have forced a reversal in monetary policy in 1980 or 1981, and consequently terminated the disinflation effort.

6A.2 Character of the Disinflation

Some accounts claim that the early 1980s disinflation was more drastic than intended. For example, Gilbody (1988, p. 252) claims that nominal GDP growth from 1980 "was declining… at a considerably faster rate than the gradual slowdown" planned by the Government. These accounts are, however, contradicted by two facts: first, inflation and nominal GDP growth if anything overshot their planned values in 1980; and second, in 1982/83 nominal GDP growth was close to that envisaged by the Government in 1979-80 (Bean and Symons, 1989, p. 16). So the decline in nominal GDP growth from 1979 to 1983 as a whole was as intended by policymakers, while the path to the desired rate featured overshoots, not undershoots.

---

[191] See Lawson (1992, pp. 847–848).

[192] Thatcher (1993, pp. 749–750).

[193] Some accounts (such as William Keegan, "Mrs. Thatcher, Myth Snatcher," *The Observer* (London), May 9, 2004, "Business" section, page 8) claim that the Thatcher Government shifted to a much easier monetary policy in early 1981. But these accounts confuse nominal and real interest rates. While short-term nominal interest rates were reduced from their 1979–80 peak (which is the basis for Minford's (1993, p. 412) statement that in 1981 the "decision was taken to loosen monetary policy"), real interest rates *increased* after 1980, and the lack of a policy reversal is also reflected in the fact that money base growth continued to be low in the five years after 1981.

[194] See Thorpe (2003, pp. 372–373).

[195] On Carrington's skepticism, see Ridley (1991, p. 173), and his refraining from debating economic policy, Keegan (1985, p. 201).

The unanticipated aspect of the disinflation instead took the form of surprises about the initial breakdown among the components of demand. First, as Bean and Symons (1989, p. 16) note, the split of nominal GDP growth between real growth and inflation was very unfavorable in 1980, with nominal GDP growth rising yet the level of real GDP contracting. Real GDP performance continued to be poor in 1981: while technically the recession ended that year, uninterrupted growth did not begin in 1982.

The early 1980s contraction was also manifested in a sharp rise in unemployment, from about 5.3% in mid-1979 to over 11% by the end of 1982. In judging the likely implications of the contraction for inflation, the authorities tended to place less weight on unemployment than on monetary and spending indicators in judging the likely impact of the slowdown for inflation. For example, Charles Goodhart testified in July 1980: "we do not know what level of employment or unemployment is consistent with a desired rate of inflation... you cannot go back to the old policy of trying to aim for a particular level of employment."[196] In the same week, Prime Minister Thatcher cited reductions in overstaffing by firms as one source of the rise in unemployment.[197]

In one sense, the behavior of unemployment during the recession itself does not seem too puzzling, in the sense that the behavior of unemployment was not too puzzling: the rise in unemployment was roughly three times as large as that in the only previous recession, 1973-75, but so too was the fall in GDP.[198] But this is not strong evidence that the rise in unemployment purely reflected the fall in aggregate demand, because both 1975 and 1979-81 saw major withdrawals of subsidies to government-owned industries, and so both periods probably brought some hidden structural unemployment out into the open.[199]

The suspicion that the natural rate of unemployment was undergoing change was borne out in the economic recovery beginning in 1981, during which unemployment continued to rise until 1986. Beside change in the labor market, another factor making for a break in the GDP/unemployment relationship during the 1980s was a faster rate of productivity growth and potential output, which reversed some of the post-1973 slowdown.[200] This development was just the opposite of that predicted by some observers during the early 1980s recession. Hahn (1983, p. 96) argued that the Thatcher Government's disinflation would have permanent negative effects on potential GDP, due to the contraction in investment and therefore the physical capital stock during the early 1980s recession.[201] Estimates of potential output by Backhouse (1983, p. 212) seemed to support this conjecture: deriving estimates of potential based on annual estimates of the U.K. capital stock, Backhouse found that growth in potential output had been below 2% over 1974-80 and had then fallen further in 1981. Estimates based

---

196 Charles Goodhart, July 7, 1980, testimony, in Treasury and Civil Service Committee (1981, pp. 67–68).

197 Robert A. Erlandson, "Mrs. Thatcher Hangs Tough on the Economy," *Detroit Free Press*, July 10, 1980, page 16A.

198 The 1973–75 recession is the only pre-1979 postwar GDP contraction in Birchenhall, Osborn, and Sensier's (2000) chronology for the U.K. (The 1960s contractions studied by Friedman and Schwartz, 1982, are growth recessions.)

199 See Section 9.

200 Some observers suggested that the measured improvement in productivity was spurious, being simply the mirror image of the contraction in employment (e.g. Keegan, 1985, p. 203). Microeconomic data and subsequent macroeconomic developments did not support this hypothesis (see Bean and Symons, 1989, p. 41).

201 The authorities had earlier endorsed the view that actual investment developments have an effect on growth in potential GDP. For example, the Bank of England's "Economic Commentary" in 1976 had stated: "the persistent weakness of manufacturing investment is probably now inhibiting the underlying growth of productive potential" (*Bank of England Quarterly Bulletin* (March, 1976), Vol. 16(1), pages 3–17; quotation from page 6.)

on current data, on the other hand, continue to support the finding of weak growth in potential in 1974-80, but suggest that from around 1981 potential output underwent a shift to a *higher* average growth rate. Real GDP growth over 1981-2003 (a long enough period to be indicative of the behavior of potential growth) was 2.6%, compared to 1.7% over 1974-79 and 0.9% over 1974-80.

One important factor to be considered is whether slower growth in the capital stock during the early 1980s recession should have been taken as implying slower growth in potential, even in principle.[202] In any event, the rapid investment during the 1973 boom was followed by a slowdown in U.K. productivity, while contraction in investment in 1980 was followed by a reversal of much of the post-1973 productivity slowdown. Evidently, on both occasions any effect on future potential growth from slower capital accumulation was swamped by structural changes that worked in the opposite direction.

6B The Late 1980s Increase in Inflation

Measured by RPI inflation, there was a marked deterioration in U.K. inflation performance from the late 1980s, with the four-quarter inflation rate peaking at 10.4% in 1990 Q3. If the RPIX series (which excludes mortgage interest payments) is instead used, and if the distorting effect on price indices of the introduction of the poll tax in 1990 is also excluded, four-quarter inflation instead peaked at 7.2% in 1990 Q4. This rate still represented a major deterioration—an increase in the four-quarter rate of 3.5 percentage points since the first quarter of 1988.

Given that by the 1980s U.K. policymakers had accepted the important role for monetary policy in controlling inflation, how did the upsurge of inflation come about? For his part, the Chancellor of the Exchequer, Nigel Lawson, stated shortly after his resignation in 1989 that while the inflation problem did reflect excessive growth in aggregate demand, his policies were not to blame because, he claimed, "I didn't boost demand at all." Instead, he argued, the source of the expansion of demand was the "increase in personal borrowing… far greater than anything I expected."[203] Lawson reaffirmed his diagnosis in 2003, claiming: "The people who really caused a lot of problems in the 1980s were the lenders."[204]

This interpretation of events is not plausible because the rise in inflation can be readily accounted for by prior developments in money base growth. The four-quarter growth of M0 rose 3.9 percentage points from 1986 Q1 to 1988 Q4, which, with a two-year lag between movements in the monetary base and movements in inflation, matches quite closely the 3.5 percentage-point rise in inflation over 1988-90. If anything, the increase in RPIX inflation is low relative to the increase in money base growth; there is certainly no major excess of inflation over base growth requiring explanation. Accounts such as Lawson's that assign special importance to the behavior of banking or lending institutions therefore do not stand up.

---

202 Neiss and Nelson (2003) argue that the actual capital stock should not be used in computing potential GDP, which instead should be generated by estimates of how the capital stock and other productive inputs would behave in a flexible-price equilibrium.

203 Lawson, November 5, 1989, television interview, *The Walden Interview* program, quoted in Watkins (1992, p. 112).

204 Quoted in Ed Crooks, "Lord Lawson: 'There and Booms and Busts: People Don't Like It,'" *Financial Times* (London), February 7, 2003, page 15.

The take-off in money base growth over 1986-88 did reflect a change in monetary policy priorities. In the period 1981-86, money base behavior was given weight by policymakers in making their interest-rate decisions, whereas it was not thereafter. As we have seen, Margaret Thatcher publicly endorsed the monetary base as a significant monetary policy indicator in early 1981, while Minford (1993, p. 413) claims that the key outcome out of internal deliberations in 1981 was that "M0 [is] the key indicator to guide interest-rate changes." This principle was eventually ratified by the prominence given M0 in Chancellor Lawson's 1983 "Mansion House" speech and the government's projections for base money growth from the 1984 Budget onward; and Artis and Lewis (1991, p. 171) judge that movements in base money "were an argument in the interest rate reaction function—a leading one..." While Goodhart (1992, p. 319) reported, "I cannot identify any monetary decision since 1985 in which the growth rate of M0 has played a significant part," this actually dovetails well with the observation that the take-off in money base growth began from early 1986, since that period was distinct from the 1981-85 period where money base developments were given considerable attention by policymakers.

Lawson (1992, pp. 805, 938) argues that money base growth could not have guided him to tighter policy during 1986-87 on the grounds that its growth rate reached only high levels in the first half of 1988. This claim is supported by the judgment of Bernanke, Laubauch, Mishkin, and Posen (1999, p. 151), who note the moderate calendar-year growth of base money in 1987. These assessments do not do justice to the quality of base money growth during this period because, as noted in Walters (1990, p. 102) and above, the take-off in base money growth began during 1986; the weak calendar 1987 growth reflects a low growth rate in the final quarter of 1987, interrupting a rising trend.

Apart from reduced attention to money base growth, what were the distinguishing features of the more inflationary monetary policy after 1981-85? There is general agreement that a major difference was the increased interest by policymakers, specifically Chancellor Lawson, in fixing the exchange rate. In 1980, Charles Goodhart, testifying to a parliamentary committee and therefore acting in the role of a spokesman for official policy, stated: "The level of the exchange rate is not an element of the Government's policy objectives."[205] Similarly Chancellor Howe observed in 1980, "We have said very often that it is our policy to leave the exchange rate to be determined primarily by market forces."[206] These statements were clearly obsolete over 1987-90, when interest-rate movements in the U.K. intentionally mimicked those of the Bundesbank in an attempt to create conditions similar to membership of the Exchange Rate Mechanism. The rising money base growth pattern in 1987-88 indicates that the early stages of this managed exchange rate policy amounted to an easing of monetary policy.

Nicholas Ridley, a member of the Cabinet over this period and a Treasury minister in the early 1980s, argued that policymakers in the late 1980s and early 1990s embraced cost-push views, in contrast to the early Thatcher Government period.[207] As evidence for this claim, Ridley offered a passage from the U.K. Treasury's 1990 *Financial Statement and Budget Report* which stated that the exchange rate "can also play a direct part in raising inflation; a lower pound tends to lead to higher import prices in sterling terms."[208] This passage does not,

---

[205] Charles Goodhart, July 7, 1980 testimony, in Treasury and Civil Service Committee (1981, p. 65).
[206] Geoffrey Howe, July 28, 1980, testimony, in Treasury and Civil Service Committee (1981, p. 199).
[207] Ridley (1991, pp. 193–194).
[208] Quoted in Ridley (1991, p. 194).

in fact, amount to a break from the Treasury's early 1980s position: in a February 1981 parliamentary submission, the Treasury had said that exchange-rate movements had "a direct impact on domestic prices—both by reducing the cost of imports and by putting pressure on producers of domestic substitutes to price competitively."[209] And belief in a strong exchange-rate channel of the type described is consistent with belief in a monetary view of inflation, since the former can be regarded (together with the output-gap channel) as the conduit by which monetary policy affects inflation. Indeed, contrary to Ridley's interpretation, the Treasury explicitly said in 1990: "Inflation is a monetary problem and so monetary policy has to be in the forefront of the battle to conquer it."[210]

Nevertheless, it is likely that the U.K. authorities had too much confidence in the *quantitative* significance of the exchange-rate channel, producing misjudgments about the extent to which exchange-rate stability itself created conditions for low inflation.[211] Symmetrically, they may have underestimated the relative importance of the output-gap channel in the determination of inflation. Such an error was compounded by the fact that U.K. policymakers again severely underestimated the size of the output gap over this period (see Nelson and Nikolov, 2003, for estimates of the errors).

The element of validity in Lawson's claim that he did not stimulate demand is that his monetary policy actions never brought real interest rates down to the negative levels of the 1970s. In fact, real interest rates during the period of monetary expansion, 1986-88, were higher than the levels observed during the low-inflation period of the 1990s. The rise in aggregate demand and inflation in the late 1980s suggests that, high as real interest rates were, they should have been raised to still higher levels.

7 Monetary Policy Developments from 1990 to 2004

The 15 years 1990 to 2004 divide evenly into the period preceding Bank of England independence (Section 7A); and the first seven-and-a-half years of the operation of monetary policy being the responsibility of the Monetary Policy Committee (Section 7B).

7A 1990 to 1997

From the vantage point of the beginning of 1993, the two most significant events in U.K. monetary policy in the early 1990s probably seemed to be entry into the Exchange Rate Mechanism in October 1990 and its forced exit (with a large exchange-rate depreciation) in September 1992. In retrospect, however, the two most important monetary policy events of the early 1990s were first, the monetary union opt-out provision negotiated for the U.K. by the Major Government with the European Union countries at the end of 1991, and the introduction in October 1992 of inflation targeting in the U.K. The switch to inflation targeting in 1992 commenced a regime that continues to the present day. The long-lasting

[209] Quoted in Hall (1983, p. 98).
[210] HM Treasury, *Financial Statement and Budget Report 1990/91*, page 11.
[211] The exchange-rate channel in practice appears weak. In this light, Kara and Nelson (2003) argue for treating the exchange-rate channel in the U.K. as part of the output-gap channel rather than an extra channel by which monetary policy affects CPI inflation.

nature of U.K. inflation targeting in turn reflects the U.K. government's use (in both 1997 and 2003) of the opt-out provision, in the absence of which the U.K. would be part of the euro area.

As noted above, the U.K. was a member of the ERM over 1990-92, a period which overlaps closely with the U.K.'s last recession to date. The principal criticism of ERM membership is that it made the recession worse by forcing on the U.K. tighter monetary policy than desirable. The Chancellor of the Exchequer for most of the ERM period, Norman Lamont, has endorsed this criticism.[212] But the era's Prime Minister, John Major, has argued that the criticism does not apply to 1991 or early 1992, and that it was "only in the final few months of our membership that the tensions between domestic monetary policy and exchange-rate management became acute."[213] In support of this claim, he notes that the U.K. authorities were able to cut interest rates throughout 1991 while belonging to the ERM.[214] This observation does not, however, preclude the possibility that the cuts in U.K. interest rates during ERM membership were less than could have been achieved under floating rates. The experience of Australia, which had floating exchange rates over this period, supports the notion that the ERM was a serious constraint. Lamont (1999, p. 90) acknowledges that the "British situation was similar to Australia" over this period, in the sense that both countries had overheated economies in the late 1980s and underwent a permanent shift to low inflation in the early 1990s. But short-term nominal interest rates over 1989 Q4-1992 Q3 were cut by 12 percentage points in Australia compared to only 5 percentage points in the U.K., while real interest rates fell by less than 2 percentage points in the U.K. and by more than 6 percentage points in Australia. This suggests that fixed exchange rates were indeed a serious constraint on U.K. monetary policy over the whole of 1990-92.

Major (1999, p. 340) claims that ERM "membership turned Britain into a low inflation economy" and that "the ERM gave credibility that our policy would otherwise have lacked." The evidence is not strong, however, that the ERM conferred on the U.K. extra benefits in inflation control distinct from those inherent in keeping monetary policy tight. Much of the fall in inflation occurred in 1991 and 1992, which (with the lag in the effect of monetary policy actions) is most plausibly attributed to the tightening of monetary policy that preceded formal ERM membership. ERM membership clearly did not produce a costless disinflation, so that it cannot be said to have satisfied that definition of "credibility"; indeed Major's own description of ERM membership is that it "hurt, but it worked" (Major, 1999, p. 341).

The concept of "credibility" that Major evidently has in mind is the shift of agents' expectations to an environment of permanently low inflation. His own evidence that the ERM achieved this is that nominal wage growth never fell below 7.5% during the 1980s, even when price inflation was low, but did settle at lower levels during ERM membership and thereafter.[215] But U.K. productivity growth was higher in the 1980s too, so nominal wage growth is not directly comparable across the two decades. And with forward-looking price-setting, low inflation in the face of rapid current wage growth can be a sign of high, not low, policy credibility.

A better indication of a permanent shift in agents' expectations about the regime is the behavior of the demand for the monetary base. In the U.K. in the 1970s and 1980s, the

---

[212] See Lamont (1999).
[213] Major (1999, p. 663).
[214] Major (1999, p. 662)
[215] Major (1999, p. 340).

velocity of base money seemed to have an inherent upward trend, distinct from the standard determinants of money demand. This suggests that agents felt it worthwhile to intensify their use of cash-saving devices, year in and year out. But in the 1990s this trend came to an end, which suggests that expectations of a regime of price stability had made it no longer worthwhile to deploy further cash-saving devices.[216] The crucial fact is that the velocity trend-break took place in 1993, *after* the U.K. had abandoned ERM membership. So the adoption of inflation targeting seems to have had a more decisive effect on credibility than did ERM membership.

The shift to inflation targeting in October 1992 has a good claim to be regarded as the pivotal monetary policy change of the 1990s. At the time, however, it was easy to discount the importance of this change, and to regard it as an attempt by the Major Government to reduce the political damage from its departure from the ERM. Alan Budd, Chief Economic Adviser to the Major Government, later recalled that ERM exit "was seen at the time, to put it mildly, as something of a failure in economic policy and a certain amount of criticism (some of it violent) was directed at the Government in general and the Treasury in particular."[217] Indeed, as of late 1992, it appeared likely that both Prime Minister Major and Chancellor Lamont would soon be removed from office.[218] As we have seen, the Callaghan Government had to resign in 1979 before it could take any steps to implement its new anti-inflationary policy, and in 1992 it seemed that the Major Government, though offering a more coherent inflation-control package than Callaghan's, might follow the same fate. In the event, while Chancellor Lamont was dismissed in May 1993, Major remained in office, though in a weak parliamentary position.

Growing private sector confidence in inflation targeting, reflected in the 1993 shift in behavior noted above, nevertheless emerged. Undoubtedly some of this came from a factor the authorities did not expect—the failure of the 1992 exchange-rate depreciation to produce an upsurge of inflation, even temporarily. Lingering belief by policymakers in the strength of the exchange-rate channel led them to expect inflation to pick up after the ERM exit, an expectation implicit in Chancellor Lamont's indication in 1992 that "prospective, not current, inflation will be our guide.... [A] low inflation rate today is not in itself a reliable cue for a relaxation of policy."[219] But the exchange-rate depreciation led to shifts in relative prices rather than aggregate CPI inflation. Evidently, low CPI inflation in 1993 was evidently locked in by the preceding years of tight monetary policy.

Confidence in inflation targeting was further consolidated by actions of the authorities to formalize policy arrangements. The first Bank of England *Inflation Report* was published in 1993. In 1994, Chancellor Kenneth Clarke proposed regular publication of a record of the advice he received from the Bank of England Governor on interest-rate decisions. While admitting he was "dubious" about this move because he did not want it to lead to central bank independence, Major approved the proposal, and, as he has written, "[a]s a result of these

[216] See Walters (1995, p. 33) for an early discussion of the break in M0 velocity that offered this judgment. Friedman (1956, point 11) emphasized that an economy's payments practices should be regarded ultimately as a function of the monetary regime, rather than as a technical datum.

[217] Budd (1999, p. 36).

[218] According to Morgan (2001, pp. 447, 514), following the ERM exit Prime Minister Major became the most unpopular Prime Minister since Neville Chamberlain (beating Margaret Thatcher's record).

[219] Lamont (1992, p. 49).

innovations the Bank and the Governor moved a little more beyond the City and into the wider public gaze."[220]

By 2002, however, former Chancellor Clarke felt he had to claim: "I opened up policymaking. Gordon [Brown] taking credit for some dramatic change in policy is a load of old tosh."[221] The reason for these protests is that the changes that Clarke made during his period in office (1993-97) no longer seem significant compared to either the introduction of inflation targeting in 1992 by Chancellor Lamont, or the introduction of Bank of England independence by Chancellor Gordon Brown in 1997.

Bank of England Independence

The literature on central bank independence is vast and we do not touch on it here, instead focusing on key aspects of the U.K. experience.

In testimony given to the Wilson Committee in the late 1970s, the Governor of the Bank of England, Gordon Richardson, used the "independence within government" to describe the Bank of England's role—a phrase identical to that used historically to describe the Federal Reserve's position. His elaboration on this description in his testimony revealed, however, that the analogy with the Fed was inappropriate, as Richardson described the Bank's role as "independence within government, freely—and forcibly on occasions—to express its views to the government."[222]

The description Richardson gave could be applied to any senior civil servant; in no sense did it mean that the Bank of England was independent, either in making or publicly commenting upon monetary policy. Speeches and publications by the Bank typically needed to be cleared in advance by the U.K. Treasury. U.K. governments nevertheless occasionally benefited from the misconception that the Bank of England was able to speak publicly against government policy. For example, a 1980 newspaper report on testimony to a parliamentary committee given by Charles Goodhart and other Bank staff was entitled "Bank's Experts Support Thatcher,"[223] when, in fact, their positions did not entitle them to be anything other than spokesmen for government policy when appearing as Bank representatives at the committee. And in 1976 Harold Wilson had quoted favorable commentary on his government's anti-inflation policy from the *Bank of England Quarterly Bulletin*, asserting that the Bank "is never fearful of expressing its own assessment and judgment," and failing to mention that the contents of the *Quarterly Government* were government-approved.[224]

Turning to authority over policy decisions, Wilson observed in 1980 that there were "some who argue that the conduct of monetary policy the Bank of England should be made more independent of central government constitutionally, and given explicit statutory policy objectives of its own."[225] The reference to "explicit statutory policy objectives" in this statement indicates that, from the outset, the debate over independence of the Bank of England in the 1980s and 1990s focused on whether the Bank should receive "instrument independence" in the terminology of Debelle and Fischer (1994), better known as "operational independence" in U.K. discussions.

---

220 Major (1999, p. 684).

221 Quoted in David Turner, "Five Years of Bank Independence: 'He Hasn't Done as Well as I Did,' Says Clarke," *Financial Times* (London), May 7, 2002, page 3.

222 Governor Gordon Richardon, quoted in Wilson Committee (1980, p. 337).

223 *Daily Telegraph* (London), July 8, 1980.

224 Harold Wilson, *House of Commons Debates*, March 11, 1976, page 641.

The Wilson Committee recommended against Bank of England independence on several grounds, including the constitutional one that independence "would be contrary to the British system and tradition of government."[226] This skeptical attitude toward central bank independence was found in two of Wilson's successors, Margaret Thatcher and John Major. Major relied on appeal to constitutional arguments similar to Wilson's, recounting that he "dismissed the idea [of independence] because I believed the person responsible for monetary policy should be answerable for it in the House of Commons."[227] This specific criticism of independence seems weak, not least because several of those responsible for other areas of policy in Major's government were not members of the House of Commons.

Thatcher argued against central bank independence for the more practical reason that "the control of inflation is ultimately a political problem."[228] Even accepting this position, however, central bank independence can be defended as a system for *maintaining low inflation*, even while broader inflation-control decisions remain with the political leadership. Under the arrangements in force since 1997, a decision for a conscious step down or up in the inflation rate remains the responsibility of the legislative and executive branches of government via the creation of laws that specify the objectives for the Bank of England. The assignment of responsibility for interest-rate decisions to the Bank of England reflects the notion that once an inflation target has been reached, maintenance of inflation at the targeted level requires technical judgments which specialists on monetary policy are best suited to make.[229] Thatcher's case against independence, like Wilson's and Major's, is thus weak when applied to operational independence.

Just as fundamentally, it is unlikely that the Bank of England's independence actually means that the government in power would escape responsibility for serious misses of the inflation target. The return of high inflation would surely be a major electoral liability for the incumbent government, just as high inflation was a major election issue in the 1970s. But such an assignment of responsibility would be appropriate, given that government legislation sets the *framework* for monetary policy, even though the executive branch is uninvolved in specific interest-rate decisions. And symmetrically, just as the Government would not escape responsibility if inflation targets were missed, it has neither denied nor been denied credit for the stable macroeconomic conditions and low interest rate/inflation combinations of recent years. For example, Prime Minister Tony Blair said in the House of Commons on January 26, 2005 that "we are running an economy with low inflation, low mortgage rates and low unemployment."[230]

The attention given by Thatcher and Major to the issue of central bank independence reflects the momentum that the proposal gained over the 1980s and 1990s. In the 1980s it was mainly discussed as a second-best solution. Chancellor of the Exchequer Nigel Lawson, for example, proposed in 1988 to Thatcher that the Bank of England be made independent with a price-stability objective. But he offered this proposal only *after* Thatcher had ruled out his

---

[225] Wilson Committee (1980, p. 339).
[226] Wilson Committee (1980, p. 339).
[227] Major (1999, p. 153).
[228] Thatcher (1993, p. 707).
[229] This is how the system has worked in practice as well as principle, with Christopher Allsopp, a member of the Bank's Monetary Policy Committee over 2000–2003, observing: "The Government has been very good in thinking of the Committee as technical." Quoted in David Smith, "An Appliance of Science for Interest Rates," *Sunday Times* (London), June 23, 2002, "Business" section, page 10.
[230] Tony Blair, *House of Commons Debates*, January 26, 2005, page 302.

preferred option of joining the ERM, and Lawson (1992, p. 868) continued to maintain that an independent Bank of England with a price-stability goal was less desirable than ERM membership by the U.K. This preference was also reflected in Lawson's support for Michael Heseltine's campaign for the Conservative Party leadership in 1990, since Heseltine's platform included a proposal to make the Bank of England independent but to *retain* ERM membership.

In the 1990s, by contrast, the U.K. Treasury began to support as first-best policy the combination of central bank independence plus inflation targeting, and this policy was advocated within the Government by Chancellors Lamont and Brown. Prime Minister Major, however, ruled out the proposal, using the constitutional arguments noted above.[231]

As Lamont noted of his efforts to persuade Major, "My proposals meant that Parliament and Ministers would still have the key role of establishing the objective for the Bank."[232] Major's opposition ensured that independence was not introduced before his defeat in May 1997, but neither Major nor other opponents of Bank of England independence succeeded in forming a truly compelling argument that applied to operational independence. Appropriately, when the newly elected Blair Government announced that the Bank would be made independent, it was the operational-independence character of the proposals that led former Prime Minister Callaghan to announce his support. "The Chancellor of the Exchequer, Mr. Brown, said that to transfer the monetary function to the Bank of England was a bold step. He is right; it is a bold step," Callaghan said in May 1997. "It is made more acceptable because the Government intend to set the targets and will appoint four additional members of the Bank Monetary [Policy] Committee. The system has been shown to work in other countries… It is a step worth trying in this country."[233]

7B 1997 to 2004

"The broad features of the reaction function in place in the United Kingdom increasingly seem to be publicly understood and built into expectations," one of the members of the Monetary Policy Committee, Christopher Allsopp, remarked after some of the dust had settled on the 1997 changes. Thanks to "innumerable speeches, presentations and discussions by members of the MPC," it was "well understood that, should inflationary pressure arise, whether from demand-side or for supply-side reasons, monetary tightening would ensue," including the understanding that "should fiscal policy change, there would be compensating interest-rate reactions to maintain consistency with the inflation target."[234] Another individual who had served on the MPC, Alan Budd, claimed that the new system was "possibly the best system in the world for setting monetary policy."[235]

In discussing the new system, MPC members understandably emphasized the degree of information about monetary policy now released to the public, including the quarterly *Inflation Report* and the release of minutes of the monthly MPC meetings after a two-week

[231] See Major (1999, pp. 153, 684).
[232] Lamont (1999, p. 323).
[233] James Callaghan, *House of Lords Debates*, May 20, 1997, page 313.
[234] Christopher Allsopp, "Macroeconomic Policy Rules in Theory and Practice," *Bank of England Quarterly Bulletin* (Winter, 2002), Vol. 42(4), pp. 485–504; quotations from page 489.
[235] Quoted in Marc Champion and Michael R. Sesit, "Labour Can Thank Bank of England for Its Big Lead: Blair Gained by Giving Up Power over Interest Rates," *Wall Street Journal Europe*, June 1, 2001, page 1.

delay. In another sense, a sign of success of the new system was the less intense discussion within the U.K. of monetary and macroeconomic developments compared to the 1970s, 1980s and early 1990s.[236] The Queen's speech opening the U.K. Parliament on November 23, 2004 began with: "My Government will continue to pursue policies which entrench economic stability and promote growth and prosperity," then immediately moved on to non-economic matters, which subsequent press coverage focused upon. Whereas before the 1970s monetary policy received less attention than it deserved in public debate given its importance for price stability, in recent years the lack of public interest mainly reflects the absence of output or inflation volatility during the inflation-targeting regime.

The most significant change to monetary policy since 1997 came in December 2003 when the inflation target was changed from 2.5% annual growth in the RPIX series to a 2% rate for the new CPI series. As the CPI is designed to correspond to the definition of prices used in the euro area, the switch in target series would smooth a possible transition to euro area membership. That the change in target does not *imply* that U.K. adoption of the euro will necessarily occur is perhaps best shown by remembering Walters' (1986, p. 144) observation that the Bank of England made various changes to its conduct of monetary policy in 1981 that were "desirable in their own right, and which would facilitate a move toward MBC [monetary base control] if that seemed to be the appropriate policy." In the event, a regime change to MBC never took place. Under current U.K. policy, the major steps that would need to occur prior to U.K. adoption of the euro are the U.K. Government's approval of euro area membership after a cost/benefit study, and the passing of euro membership proposals in a national referendum.

7C A Summing Up of the Inflation Record

In Table 2 we summarize the inflation record of successive postwar U.K. administrations. In evaluating the implications of each government's monetary policy decisions for inflation, it is important to allow for a delay between monetary policy actions and the response of inflation. To that end, we report not only the average inflation rate during the life of each government and the average of inflation for the two years.[237] Some skepticism was voiced in the 1970s and 1980s about the existence of a two-year lag between U.K. monetary policy actions and inflation: for example, Allen (1982, p. 104) claims that the belief in a two-year lag emerged from a close match between Sterling M3 growth and subsequent inflation in the early 1970s that did not occur elsewhere in the data. But as we have documented elsewhere (Batini and Nelson, 2001), the evidence for a lag of a year or more before the peak effect of monetary actions on inflation is prevalent across subsamples of the U.K. data. It is present if

---

[236] The current Bank of England Governor, Mervyn King, has cited this state of affairs as a criterion for success, reflected in his oft-quoted position that U.K. monetary policy should be made "boring." See e.g. Scheherazade Daneshkhu and Ed Crooks, "Bank Is Set for Big Changes When King Takes Rein from Sir Edward," *Financial Times* (London), November 29, 2002, page 3.

[237] Our treatment of the 1974–79 Government as a single administration despite the change in Prime Minister from Harold Wilson to James Callaghan in 1976 reflects two factors. First, a single Chancellor of the Exchequer (Denis Healey) served continuously over 1974–79. Second, on his return to office in 1974 Wilson delegated much of the government and party leadership to Callaghan (see Morgan, 1997, pp. 408–409)—to such an extent that Thatcher (2002, p. 371) refers to decisions in 1974–75 as those of "James Callaghan's Labour Government," and Kissinger (1999, p. 913) refers to Callaghan as being Prime Minister in the first quarter of 1976, even though Callaghan did not become Prime Minister until the second quarter of 1976.

narrow money or interest-rate measures are considered instead of broad monetary aggregates, and is pervasive across different monetary policy regimes. Indeed, a 1 to 2 year lag between movements in currency and prices was noted in the U.K. during the nineteenth century, and is detectable if the nineteenth century U.K. data are studied in isolation. Acceptance of a lag of about two years between monetary policy actions and inflation has underpinned the U.K.'s inflation-targeting framework, with Norman Lamont noting in 1992 that "[m]onetary adjustments take time to have effect"[238] and with current policy makers taking a similar view.[239]

Table 2. Inflation records of successive governments

Government	Period in office	Average inflation:		Period used for 2-year-lag calculation	Change in inflation, period in office:	
		While in office	With 2-year lag		With no lag	With 2-year lag
Eden	Apr 55-Jan 57	5.5%	3.5%	Apr 57-Jan 59	+1.1	-0.8
Macmillan	Jan 57-Oct 63	2.5%	3.0%	Feb 59-Oct 65	-2.2	+2.7
Douglas-Home	Oct 63-Oct 64	4.0%	3.9%	Nov 65-Oct 66	+2.5	-1.1
Wilson	Oct 64-Jun 70	4.6%	6.1%	Nov 66-Jun 72	+1.7	+2.4
Heath	Jun 70-Mar 74	10.0%	17.9%	Jul 72-Feb 76	+7.8	+15.4
Wilson/Callaghan	Mar 74-May 79	15.9%	13.7%	Mar 76-Apr 81	-4.4	-9.1
Thatcher	May 79-Nov 90	7.8%	5.7%	May 81-Nov 92	0.0	-8.8
Major	Nov 90-May 97	3.4%	2.8%	Dec 92-Apr 99	-6.7	-0.8
Blair/MPC	May 97-	2.5%[a]	2.3%	May 99-Nov 04	-0.3	-0.2

a. To November 2004.

Allowing for a two-year lag has a material effect on the record of successive governments. In particular, the average inflation rate under the Heath Government goes up from 10% to 17.9% because the peak in inflation in 1975 is now attributed to the monetary expansion in the years to 1973; while the average inflation rate under the Thatcher Government falls because high inflation in 1980 is reassigned to the 1974-79 Labour Government, while the disinflation under the Major Government is now attributed to Thatcher Government policy. The fall in average inflation under the Thatcher Government is, however, the same—just over 8 percentage points—irrespective of whether lags are taken into account. With a two-year lag allowed for, the average inflation rate under the Major and Blair Governments is lower than under any other postwar governments.

An alternative method of assessing the record is to disregard average performance and simply look at whether annual inflation rose or fell. That information too is given in the table. Annual RPIX inflation was the same rate (9.2%) in both May 1979 and November 1990, which is the basis for the criticism that literally no improvement in inflation took place under

---

[238] Lamont (1992, p. 49).

[239] The official description of the MPC's decision-making process states: "the MPC looks at a range of domestic and international economic and monetary factors, which will have a bearing on inflation over the future—usually about two years, this being the time it takes for the full effects of interest rates to work through the economy and impact on inflation." From "Monetary Policy Committee (MPC)," Bank of England website.

the Thatcher Government.[240] But once a two-year lag is allowed for, the improvement in inflation performance under the Thatcher Government is again around 8 percentage points. The inflation fall under the 1974-79 Government is also greater once lags are allowed for.

8 Fiscal Policy

The evolution of fiscal policy in the United Kingdom has been the flipside of the greater importance accorded to monetary policy: fiscal policy received center stage as a demand-management tool prior to 1970, and specific fiscal actions were also thought important in controlling wage inflation, but in recent decades, the emphasis has instead been on the longer-term role. Fiscal policy increasingly has come to be seen as affecting the division of aggregate demand between private and public demand, rather than as exerting a decisive influence on either aggregate demand or inflation. We break up our discussion chronologically, beginning with the pre-1970 period.

8A 1955 to 1969

As we have seen, Lionel Robbins described U.K. macroeconomic policy over 1945-54 as "a gigantic experiment" in activist fiscal policy for demand-management purposes, and this experiment continued over 1955-69. Until the mid-1960s, however, the ratios of government spending and taxes to GDP are instead dominated by downward trends (Figures 3 and 4).[241] An important source of decline in the government spending/GDP ratio is the reduced share of defense spending to GDP, reflecting both the absence of U.K. war engagements in the 1957-81 period and reduced military commitments to former U.K. colonies.

The 1951-64 Conservative Government presided over a sharp cut in the ratio of taxes to GDP. This decline reflects not only the Government's preference for tax cuts as a means of stimulating aggregate demand, but also its subscription to cost-push views of inflation. For example, Alec Douglas-Home, Prime Minister in 1963-64, believed that income tax increases were "inflationary."[242]

Harold Wilson summarized the standard critique of demand management over this period as: "Policy oscillated between expansionary measures designed to reduce the high levels of unemployment and contractionary measures made necessary by subsequent balance of payments deficits. The whole period from the early 1950s to the mid-1960s was aptly labeled 'stop-go.'"[243] Though economic fluctuations over this period would look mild by comparison with later developments, proponents of fiscal policy at the time were clearly disappointed by U.K. performance under fiscal activism. The perceived failure of stabilization policy initially did little to reduce confidence in fiscal policy for demand management. Instead, hard-line

---

[240] See e.g. William Keegan, "Margaret Thatcher, Myth Snatcher," *The Observer* (London), May 9, 2004, "Business" section, page 8.

[241] The ratios plotted are the November 2004 vintage of OECD estimates, available from 1970, with pre-1970 ratios calculated from national sources, spliced in at 1970. The implied Figure 4 closely resembles the tax/GDP series plotted by Beenstock (1979), who also compiled his data from national sources.

[242] Alec Douglas-Home, "They Might Not Save the Pound Again," *Daily Mail* (London), December 1, 1964, page 6.

[243] Wilson Committee (1980, p. 6).

Keynesians such as Dow (1964) cited technical obstacles to the implementation of an effective fiscal policy, such as the low ratio of public investment to GDP, or the impediments to a sufficiently rapid reaction of fiscal policy to economic developments.[244] In crude Keynesian terms, these explanations postulated that the multiplier for autonomous state spending was large, but that the base for the multiplier had been set at too low a value and had not been varied with sufficient speed. Events did not initially produce a rethinking of the relative importance of fiscal and monetary policy; Dow (1964), in particular, reaffirmed his extreme pessimism about the scope for monetary actions to affect aggregate demand.

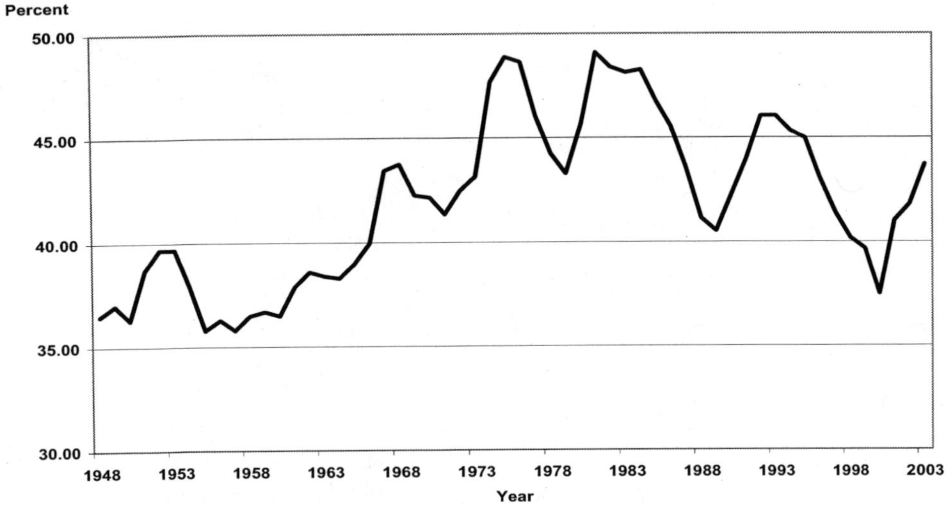

Figure 3: U.K government expenditures (% of GDP)

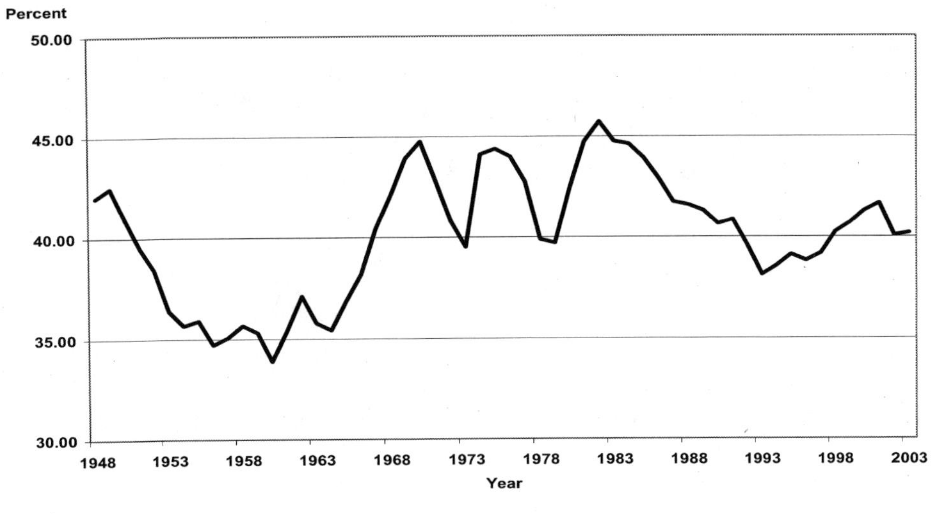

Figure 4: U.K. tax revenues (% of GDP)

244 A detailed discussion of contemporaneous critiques of 1950s and 1960s fiscal policy, such as those of Dow (1964) and Prest (1968), is given in HM Treasury, *Fiscal Stabilisation and EMU* (June, 2003), pp. 34-36.

8B The 1970s and 1980s

Taxation

A striking feature of fiscal developments in the early 1970s is the deep decline in taxes as a share of GDP—a fall of 5.25 percentage points from 1970 to 1973. This fall has been the subject of a flawed interpretation by several observers, who have exaggerated the contribution of fiscal policy to the 1970s inflation. Harold Wilson, for example, cited "large tax cuts in the 1972 Budget" as a major stimulus to aggregate demand,[245] while Bernstein (2004, p. 214) similarly cites the "enormous tax cut in 1972" and "the government's policy of lowering taxes" as the source of the fall to the tax-to-GDP ratio.

These claims are erroneous in two respects: in overstating the contribution of fiscal policy to the expansion of aggregate demand, and in identifying the source of the fall in the tax/GDP ratio. On the first of these errors, it is implausible that the opening up of the budget deficit was central to the take-off of inflation during the 1970s. The behavior of monetary policy was instead decisive for that: it is feasible for monetary policy to be tight in the presence of fiscal expansion. In the event, monetary policy was expansionary in its own right, well beyond any accommodation of fiscal deficits—as shown by the behavior of real interest rates, which fell sharply from 1970, whereas a monetary expansion triggered by fiscal expansion should see real rates constant or rising.

But even the view that the 1970-73 decline in the tax-to-GDP ratio reflects tax cuts is not supportable, once one considers the background in detail. It is true that the Heath Government *intended* to cut this ratio by tax cuts. Keegan (1985, pp. 27-28) instead suggests that the Heath Government did not come into office planning to cut overall taxes relative to GDP, but rather planned tax reform that left the share unchanged. As evidence, he gives a quotation from the Conservative Party's economics spokesman, Iain Macleod, in 1969 that "taxation must be cut. But let us be quite clear what that does and does not mean. It does not mean that by international standards the proportion of income taken in taxation in the United Kingdom tax taken in the U.K. is above average. On the contrary, it is below average: it does mean that we tax the wrong things in the wrong way."[246] But the origin of this quotation, Macleod (1969), indicates that Macleod's statements about tax revenue were inferred from data provided in answers to parliamentary questions in late 1968 and early 1969. It was only later that data on the rise in taxation to GDP under the 1960s Wilson Government became widely available. When they did, Macleod stated: "Total taxation now is 40 per cent of GNP—it was 32 per cent in 1964" and indicated his intention "to bring back the level of taxation to where it was at the beginning of the Labour Party's period of office."[247] Similarly, Heath wrote in early 1970 that he was "determined to reduce direct taxation" on both labor and investment income, and then "reduce taxes still further,"[248] and after his election victory stated: "We repeat our undertakings to reduce the burden of taxation in this country."[249] It is thus clear that the Heath Government did come into office planning to reduce the tax share of GDP.

---

[245] Wilson Committee (1980, p. 7).

[246] The quotation we use here is taken from Macleod (1969, p. 307); the quotation given in Keegan (1985) is clearly based on this source, but slightly paraphrased.

[247] Iain Macleod, *House of Commons Debates*, November 3, 1969, page 666.

[248] Edward Heath, "Less Tax and More Savings," *Daily Mail* (London), February 25, 1970, page 13.

[249] Edward Heath, *House of Commons Debates*, July 2, 1970, quoted in Frank Johnson, "Tax Cuts in Mini-Budget This Autumn, Heath Hints," *The Sun* (London), July 3, 1970, page 2.

As we have discussed, a principal motivation for the Conservatives' interest in reducing taxes in the 1960s and 1970s was a belief in a tax-wage-push view of inflation. An additional important motivation was a belief in the importance of incentive effects of tax cuts. Emphasis on these incentive effects continued under the later Thatcher Government, but members of that Government, such as Howe (1994, p. 128) have emphasized that they "never succumbed" to Laffer-curve views regarding the revenue effects of tax cuts, and so compensated for cuts in income tax rates by other measures to increase revenue (such as the increase in VAT in 1979) or by reductions in spending programs.[250] Indeed, a spokesman for the Thatcher Government wrote in 1979: "Professor Laffer seems to be arguing that taxes should be cut regardless of whether expenditure is cut… No responsible official could advocate this."[251]

The Heath Government, on the other hand, did enter office explicitly basing policy on what was later known as the Laffer curve. The Conservative Party's 1970 election manifesto stated: "We will concentrate on making progressive and substantial reductions in income tax and surtax. These reductions will be possible because we will cut out unnecessary Government spending and because we will encourage savings. And as our national income rises we will get a larger revenue with lower tax rates."[252] Taken in combination with the Government's pledge to reduce the ratio of taxes to GDP, it appears that it had in mind that the tax cuts would generate an increase in real tax revenue, but proportionally less than the increase in real GDP from the tax cuts and other measures, so that the ratio of taxes to GDP would fall substantially.

Therefore, the Heath Government did plan to reduce the tax-to-GDP ratio; and commentators have interpreted the actual fall as reflecting tax-cutting zeal. But in fact the fall reflects factors almost completely different from the tax cuts. While recorded income tax rates were cut—for example, the top-bracket rate was cut from 89% to 75%,[253]—wage and price inflation were so high in the early 1970s that the tax cuts only approximately compensated for the effects of bracket creep, so that household income tax burden did not fall substantially. Nor was the corporate tax burden genuinely reduced: King's (1977, p. 78) estimate of the corporate tax rate is essentially static at 40% over 1970-72, then rises sharply to 49% in 1973.

Rather, the fall in the tax-to-GDP ratio over 1970-73 is a *by-product of the Heath Government's nonmonetary approach to inflation control.* A prominent component of this approach, as noted earlier, was the policy of holding down nationalized-industry prices. A Treasury official testified in 1980 that this policy led to "a considerable acceleration in the public sector borrowing requirement" as "prices got out of line with costs" and the Government injected funds to cover the difference.[254] A similar process took place in the private sector: government pressure for firms not to pass on higher costs into higher prices

---

[250] Bean and Symons (1989, p. 14) similarly observe that the Thatcher Government's attitude to tax cuts was that "there was to be no dabbling in the black arts of the Laffer curve." Some U.S. enthusiasts for supply-side economics did claim that the Thatcher Government's tax cuts were motivated by Laffer-curve considerations. See e.g. John Chamberlain, "Jack Kemp's Tax Ideas Work: Thatcher Has Similar Policy in England," *Fort Lauderdale News*, July 2, 1979, page 18A. But Laffer himself denounced the Government at an early stage for offsetting its income tax cuts with indirect tax increases. See Arthur Laffer, "Margaret Thatcher's Tax Increase," *Wall Street Journal*, August 20, 1979, page 12.

[251] W.S. Ryrie, "Taxation in Britain," *Wall Street Journal*, September 7, 1979, page 18. Ryrie was a U.K. government official designated to explain U.K. economic policy to United States audiences.

[252] Conservative Party Manifesto "A Better Tomorrow," May 1970, quoted in Iain Macleod, *House of Commons Debates*, July 7 1970, pp. 512–513.

[253] Anthony Lewis, "Heath Program Faces Harsh Economic Test," *New York Times*, April 26, 1971, pages 1 and 4.

[254] Peter Middleton, July 4, 1980 testimony, in Treasury and Civil Service Committee (1981, p. 120).

reduced corporate profitability,[255] and this in turn triggered government financial assistance to firms, including outright government takeover of some companies (such as Rolls Royce in 1971). The increased subsidies to the private and public sectors over this period generally counted as "negative taxes," and so reduce the measured ratio of taxes to GDP.

The sharp rise in the tax-to-GDP ratio from 1974 reflects the increase in the effective tax burden from non-indexation of tax scales to rising inflation; cancellation in 1975 of much of the existing system of subsidies;[256] and some explicit tax increases, such as the increase in the top marginal tax rate to 83% in 1974.[257] The last of these measures remained in force for the remainder of the Labour Government's term, leading Pechman (1980, pp. 207-209) to observe:

> The individual income tax starts at a lower income level and has higher initial starting rates in the United Kingdom than in most other countries... The 1978-79 top-bracket rate of 83 percent on earned income was close to the highest in the world; the top rate of 98 percent on investment income was surpassed only in Algeria... The personal exemptions did not keep pace with inflation from 1973-74 to 1976-77, and tax rates were raised significantly in 1974-75 and 1975-76... As a result, between 1973-74 and 1978-79 effective tax rates rose in real terms for practically all taxpayers.

Thatcher (1995, p. 573) states that "low marginal tax rates were the goals in the 1980s; and they were achieved." The Thatcher Government however had an ambiguous record in reducing taxation. Thatcher's economics spokesman, Geoffrey Howe, had said in 1975 that a top income tax rate of 50 per cent was a desirable goal.[258] When it came to office in 1979, however, the top marginal tax rate (on both labor and investment income) was reduced to 60% rather than 50%.[259] Moreover, it was accompanied by a large increase in indirect tax which, together with subsequent tax increases, meant that estimates of the tax on labor are actually higher in 1980-87 than in 1973-79—51% compared to 45% (Nickell, 2003, Table 2). As Figure 3 shows, the share of taxes in GDP also rose over this period. Further cuts in the top marginal income tax rate did not occur until 1988, when it was reduced to its present 40%.

Government Spending

As noted above, the Heath Government entered office pledging to "cut out unnecessary Government spending," but after a slight fall in 1970 and 1971, the share of government spending in GDP rose from by over 6 percentage points in 1971-74 (Figure 3). The peak occurred at 48.9% in 1975. Thereafter, a series of efforts were made to tighten the fiscal stance. Thatcher (1995, p. 569) acknowledges that the reductions in real government expenditure undertaken by the Callaghan Government in 1976 "were significant steps toward

---

[255] According to the *Midland Bank Review* (Winter, 1977), "successive phases of prices and incomes policy restricting profits and dividends reinforced the longer-run effects of the declining profitability of capital" ("The Paradox of Personal Saving," pp. 12–18; quotation from page 14).

[256] Geoffrey Howe (in July 28, 1980, testimony in Treasury and Civil Service Committee 1981, p. 185) described the Labour Government's actions in 1975 as canceling the Heath Government's policy of "hold[ing] nationalized industry prices down by means of subsidies." In addition, the Government withdrew a number of subsidies to food prices it had introduced in 1974.

[257] "Five Years' Hard Healey," *The Economist* (London), April 7, 1979, pp. 76-77.

[258] "Briton Laments 'Fame Drain,'" *Kansas City Times*, Tuesday, September 16, 1975, page 2.

[259] The top rate on investment income was initially cut to 75%.

the kind of approach in which I believed." Indeed, it is fair to say that the Thatcher Government's record on government expenditure did not consist of lower spending but instead, amounted to sustaining the reduction in the ratio of government spending to GDP achieved by the previous administration. The Callaghan Government reduced government spending from 48.7% of GDP in 1976 to 43.3% in 1979; the Thatcher Government did not achieve a lower ratio than this until 1988, and in 1990, Thatcher's last year in office, it rose to 42.2%.

As Figure 3 shows, the government spending/GDP ratio actually rose for much of Thatcher's first term. While Thatcher (1995, p. 571) notes that "the deep recession of 1980/81 pushed [government spending] up," the fastest rate of growth of government expenditure in her first term was actually defense spending.[260] Policy decisions made prior to the Thatcher Government's election almost guaranteed that defense spending would rise in relation to GDP. In May 1978, Callaghan committed the U.K. to 3% per year real growth in defense expenditures into the early 1980s as part of the NATO response to the Soviet military buildup.[261] The Falklands War led to further defense expenditures in financial year 1982/83 as well as reconsideration of planned cutbacks within the defense budget. After Thatcher's first term, defense spending did fall as a fraction of GDP. Despite this source of decline, government purchases of goods and services were actually a slightly higher fraction of GDP in 1987 than in 1979 (Bean and Symons (1989, p. 14).

Deficit Reduction and Privatization

Slower growth in government outlays in the late 1980s, together with rising receipts from the recovery in employment that began in 1986, helped rein in the deficit completely in 1988-89. The precise magnitude of the fiscal improvement, however, was overstated in the U.K. authorities' presentation of fiscal aggregates. In the 1986 Budget, for example, Chancellor Lawson projected a decline in the budget deficit from 10 to 7 billion pounds, but 2.5 billion pounds of the recorded reduction was expected to come from sales of government assets.[262] This tactic had been earlier deployed by the Callaghan Government in 1976 when it announced sales of shares in the government corporation British Petroleum. During the Thatcher Government's privatization program, concentrated in its second and third terms, asset sales became a major source of recorded reductions in budget deficits.

One macroeconomic justification for these sales cited by U.K. policymakers in the 1970s and 1980s was precisely that they contributed to deficit reduction. But this particular justification is highly questionable, reflected in the refusal by outside commentators such as Bean and Symons (1989, p. 17) and Kay and Thompson (1986, p. 27), to regard privatization proceeds as cutting the budget deficit. For one thing, the once-and-for-all nature of privatization revenue distinguishes them from ongoing taxation, and it was on this basis that former Prime Ministers Macmillan and Heath spoke out in November 1985 against the Thatcher Government's treatment of asset sales.[263] But against this criticism the Government

[260] Campbell (2003, p. 170).

[261] James Callaghan, *House of Commons Debates*, June 6, 1978, pages 29-30.

[262] Nigel Lawson, *House of Commons Debates*, March 18, 1986, pp. 170-171.

[263] See Campbell (1993, p. 741; 2003, p. 240). This treatment had earlier been noted as a drawback of the government's reliance on British Petroleum asset sales during the late 1970s, with the *Midland Bank Review* observing: "[To] the extent that the reduction in the Public Sector's Borrowing Requirement is effected by the sale of some public sector assets, such as BP shares... it will only be temporary, unless there is an indefinite

could argue that privatization proceeds were analogous to windfall taxes or temporary taxation; and while temporary tax measures have different effects on private behavior than permanent measures, it remains legitimate to count revenue from temporary taxes as reducing the budget deficit.

A more fundamental criticism, however, underlay economists' critique of the official treatment of privatization proceeds, and was voiced by Milton Friedman when the British Petroleum sales were announced in 1976: "items such as the sale of the British Petroleum assets really do not do anything about releasing more resources for the private sector."[264] A key motivation for deficit reduction in the 1970s and 1980s was the belief that doing so released extra funds in the securities market for existing private-sector projects.[265] But a deficit reduction accomplished by privatization sales does not release extra funds, because the reduced need for the government to issue securities is exactly offset by the creation of a new asset (the share in the privatized enterprise) in need of a private purchaser. From this perspective, asset sales should be regarded as equity finance of a budget deficit: a substitute for bond finance of the deficit, but not a form of tax revenue.

In fact, the illegitimate treatment of asset sales in 1980s fiscal policy went beyond counting them as revenue. The government spending-to-GDP figures published by the U.K. government during the privatization period also need to be treated with suspicion, as they counted privatization proceeds as "negative spending" (Bean and Symons, 1989, pp. 16-17; Keegan, 1989, p. 192). Consequently, official estimates of government spending were artificially deflated over this period. In her memoirs Thatcher (1995, p. 572) used estimates of the U.K. government spending/GDP ratio excluding privatization proceeds, apparently conceding that her government's accounting practice had been inappropriate.

8C The 1990s and 2000s

The early 1990s witnessed a return to budget deficits: over 7 percent of GDP in 1993. Official estimates by the U.K. Treasury of the cyclically-adjusted budget balance suggest that about 3 percentage points of this deficit was due to the automatic reaction to the early 1990s recession.[266]

The striking development in the subsequent recovery is less the reduction in the deficit that occurred, but the generally lower levels of government spending and taxation to GDP in the 1990s compared to prior decades. Government spending falls continuously as a share of GDP during the 1990s recovery, and in the late 1990s falls below 40% of GDP, something it

---

supply of saleable public sector assets. One would presumably stop short of the Crown Jewels." "Economic Outlook," *Midland Bank Review* (Summer, 1979), pp. 1–4; quotation from pp. 1–2.

264 Milton Friedman, quoted in William Lowther, "Healey's Budget Won't Work, Says Friedman," *Daily Mail* (London), December 17, 1976.

265 In a Ricardian world, such a release occurs only with government spending reduction, not with a substitute of (lump-sum) taxes for bond financing. But as we will see, privatization revenue should not be regarded as a substitute either for tax revenue or government spending reduction; it should therefore be rejected as a deficit-reducing measure in both Ricardian and non-Ricardian environments.

266 HM Treasury, *Public Finances Databank* (August, 2004).

never did in the thirty years 1968-97. Taxation falls below 40% of GDP in the early 1990s, and stays below that level until at least 1998.[267]

Over this period, the authorities reaffirmed that fiscal policy would no longer be employed as an important demand-management weapon. For example, shortly after leaving the post of Chancellor of the Exchequer, Kenneth Clarke, remarked: "The control of demand and activity is largely a function of monetary policy, and one sets interest rates to hit inflation targets… The aim of fiscal policy is to produce healthy public finances. Over the cycle, one aims to ensure that there is not excessive borrowing. Fiscal policy is all about tax and is linked to public spending and borrowing."[268] Various reforms to the reporting of public finances by the Blair Government, formalizing the longer-term perspective for fiscal policy, are described in Balls and O'Donnell (2001).

Official Treasury estimates give the share of government spending in GDP in 2003-04 at 40.6%, a rise of 3.5 percentage points above its 1999-2000 trough, but the same share prevailing in the final financial year of the Major Government, 1996-97. By contrast, OECD estimates give the share as 43.7% in 2003, a full 6.3 percentage points above its 2000 trough and 2.4 points above its 1997 level. Besides differences in methodology and data vintage, the discrepancy may be due to the sharp increase in the relative price of government output. The Bank of England's *Inflation Report* in May 2004 reported: "Since 1997 Q1, nominal government consumption… has risen by 62%. Over the same period the [official] measure of real spending has risen by just 14%, with the implied price deflator rising by 42%. By contrast, the CPI has risen by 10% over that period."[269] Consequently, indices of the government-spending-to-GDP share tell different stories depending on whether the spending series used in calculating the share are nominal or real.

The *Inflation Report* suggested that some of the rise in the price of government output reflects improvements in quality and unmeasured increases in quantity.[270] If so, future data revisions may reallocate some of the rise in nominal government spending between prices and output. But on the basis of what is already known, it appears clear that the fall in the government spending to GDP below 40% in the late 1990s has proved transitory and that the government's share of total resources has increased, though not to the levels observed in several years of the 1970s and 1980s.

There are, in addition, several general grounds for preferring expenditure-share ratios based on nominal rather than real spending data (see Whelan, 2000). For the U.K., these arguments have been reinforced by the observation (noted by several U.K. policymakers) that U.K. nominal expenditure series are revised less drastically than the split of nominal spending between real and price components.[271] In light of these arguments, the OECD estimates of the

---

[267] The U.K. Treasury's *Public Finances Databank* gives a sharper rebound in the tax/GDP ratio in the early years of the post-1992 economic recovery than do OECD sources. Both sources agree that the ratio was well below 1990s levels.

[268] Kenneth Clarke, *House of Commons Debates*, July 3, 1997, page 448.

[269] Bank of England, "Measuring the Impact of Government Spending on Inflationary Pressure," *Inflation Report* (May, 2004), page 24.

[270] A report on the issue, *Atkinson Review, Final Report: Measurement of Government Output and Productivity for the National Accounts*, commissioned by the National Statistician in late 2003, was released on January 31, 2005.

[271] See Mervyn King, "The Governor's Speech at the East Midlands Development Agency," *Bank of England Quarterly Bulletin* (Winter, 2003), Vol. 43(4), pp. 476–478; Marian Bell, "Monetary Policy, Data Uncertainty and the Supply Side: Living with the Statistical Fog," *Bank of England Quarterly Bulletin*, (Winter, 2004), Vol 44(4), pp. 510–521. See Mahadeva and Muscatelli (2005) for an analysis of these revisions.

government spending to GDP ratio, using nominal data, are more reliable. Taken at face value, the behavior of this ratio suggests that the role of government has been increased from 2000 to 2003 even more drastically than under the Heath Government from 1970 to 1974, since the former suggest (as noted earlier) a 6.3 percentage point increase in the government/GDP share, vs. a 5.5 point increase over 1970-74. Such a conclusion, however, would not be appropriate. As discussed above, much of the increase in government spending under Heath took the form of increased subsidies, and so was reported as a cut in taxes rather than higher government spending. And the voluntary and compulsory wage and price controls under Heath amounted to a major increase in government command over resources that was not recorded in the government spending/GDP share.

9 Productivity and Economic Growth

Judgments on the U.K.'s economic growth performance in the first quarter-century of the postwar period have tended to become less negative over time. For example, Prime Minister Edward Heath was reported in November 1970 as describing his aim as to shift from the "weakness of the past 25 years toward a coherent and far more effective national performance."[272] By November 1980, Heath's position had changed, as he said he was "not one who apologizes for that period during the post-war years to the middle of 1975."[273] Similarly, a former minister in Heath's Government, Geoffrey Howe, has said: "The quarter of a century between 1945 and 1971 now looks like some kind of economic golden age."[274]

The reason for the changed perspective is the sharp slowdown in GDP and productivity growth in 1974-79 compared to the prior U.K. record. Judged in light of these low growth rates, pre-1974 U.K. growth looks impressive. It also looked favorable compared to prewar historical U.K. performance, as was occasionally noted by observers: Paul Samuelson, for example, said in 1968 that the U.K. "whom we all pity, has averaged faster growth in the postwar era than ever she did in Victoria's glorious days…"[275]

The reason for the frequently negative contemporaneous judgments about postwar U.K. growth performance is that it was less favorable than that of European competitors. While some defenders of the U.K. record attribute the higher European growth purely to recovery of wartime output losses (e.g. Thatcher, 2002, pp. 363-364), this explanation is inadequate since, as has been frequently pointed out, the *levels* of output per person in France and the Federal Republic of Germany moved above the U.K.'s during the postwar decades.[276]

On the other hand, the 1980s and 1990s did not see much further deterioration in the U.K.'s relative position. For example, Prescott (2004, Table 1) reports that the U.K.'s output per person was 67% of the U.S. level in 1970-74 and 68% in 1993-96. The end of the period of severe deterioration reflects both productivity and employment developments. Bean and

---

[272] Quoted in Associated Press, "Heath Outlines Goals", *Kansas City Times*, November 26, 1970, page 9D.

[273] Edward Heath, *House of Commons Debates*, November 27, 1980, page 603. More recently, Heath has partially returned to his 1970 position, describing the pre-1973 period as one of "economic and political decline" which was reversed, although with a lag of "ten or more years," by his bringing the U.K. into the European Union (then the EEC). See Edward Heath, "The Fanatics in the Conservative Party Risk Everything We Have Gained," *The Independent on Sunday* (London), December 29, 2002, page 18.

[274] Howe (1994, p. 162).

[275] Paul Samuelson, "The French Galbraith," *Newsweek*, July 22, 1968, page 73.

[276] See e.g. Caves (1980, p. 136) and Prescott (2004, Table 1).

Symons (1989, p. 15) report a productivity growth rate of 2.2% per annum for the Thatcher government's first nine years in office. The revised data that we use to compute productivity continue to give 2.2% as the annual U.K. productivity growth rate for the Thatcher Government's first nine years in office. If we start the sample in 1981 Q1, representing the point at which the 1980s economic recovery began, and also update the sample, productivity growth continues to record some reversal of the post-1973 slowdown: 2% average annual productivity growth for 1981-2002 compared to 1.4% for 1974-79. Within this average, productivity growth is above 2% in the 1980s and somewhat below 2% in the recovery that began in 1992.[277] The failure of productivity to exhibit a pickup in the 1990s compared to the 1980s has led to initiatives by the U.K. authorities to encourage further innovation by U.K. firms, and in particular to efforts to emulate the revival of productivity growth observed in the U.S.

Actual GDP growth in the U.K. has averaged a higher level in the present recovery than in the post-1981 period as a whole, because faster growth in employment has compensated for the slower growth in productivity. U.K. unemployment rates in the 2000s are close to mid-1970s levels. Estimates of the natural rate of unemployment roughly track the movements in actual U.K. unemployment, including its sharp rise during the 1970s and first half of the 1980s, and sharp fall since 1993. It would be inappropriate, however, to interpret recent declines in the natural rate as simply winding back the supply-side deterioration that caused the rise in the natural rate in the 1970s and 1980s. To see this, it is useful to consider the interpretation offered by Allan Meltzer in 1981: "For many years people were unemployed, but no one knew it. They were hidden away in British Leyland, British Steel, British Airways. These firms were subsidized in part to hide unemployment, to keep workers in the labor force. Mrs. Thatcher took away some of the subsidies, so the workers are now counted as unemployed."[278]

Removals of subsidies took place not only in the early 1980s but in 1975, and were followed by the major privatization programs of the mid-1980s. If Meltzer's interpretation is valid, then examination of natural-rate estimates understates the effects of supply-side improvements on unemployment. Let the *status quo* in 1975 be a natural rate of unemployment of u_a, which is artificially low because of unemployment being hidden by subsidies. Removal of subsidies then raised the natural rate to $u_b > u_a$, while supply-side deterioration raised it further to $u_c > u_b$ by the mid-1980s. The past two decades then saw the natural rate fall back to u_a, but without recourse to subsidies. Because it has emerged without resort to artificial measures to keep unemployment low, current rates of unemployment reflect a stronger supply-side situation than did the same unemployment rates in the 1970s.

The present emphasis on productivity growth as the main source for further supply-side improvement is nevertheless understandable, since the large fall in unemployment has reduced the scope for further growth in output per person that can come from employment growth alone.

---

277 Among recent years, the year 2004 did exhibit a notably better productivity growth rate than this average.

278 Quoted in *JMCB* (1982, p. 141).

10 Conclusions

In this paper, we have provided a retrospective on U.K. macroeconomic policy in the last 50 years. As we stressed in the introduction, the U.K. economy over this period is of special interest because of the multiplicity of monetary policy regimes that have been deployed. We have, however, not arranged our discussion strictly by regime. In large part, this is because subsequent developments often diminish the significance of what initially appears to be a major regime change. For example, the adoption of domestic credit targets in 1969 and monetary targets in 1976 proved not to be major regime changes, because the U.K. authorities continued to emphasize incomes policy and to carry out easy monetary policy after the targets were adopted. The 1972 floating of the exchange rate was not a major break in policy behavior because it was simply a by-product of a domestic monetary expansion that had already been in place for over a year. The Thatcher Government's announcement of a "Medium-Term Financial Strategy" in 1980 was not an important regime change because it enshrined a link between monetary and fiscal policy which was fallacious and which the Government did not let determine its subsequent decisions, and because the Government within a year shifted its emphasis from broad money to the monetary base as the measure of money.

The 1992 shift to inflation targeting does qualify as a major regime change, but it is nevertheless undesirable to divide the U.K. policy record into two eras, inflation targeting and pre-inflation targeting. This is because changing views by policymakers about the importance of monetary policy, a process which took place roughly from 1970 onward, made possible the eventual adoption of inflation targeting. There were essentially three steps to this process in the U.K. The first was the acceptance of monetary policy as the key tool for managing aggregate demand; this acceptance took place in the early 1970s. The second was the shaking-off of cost-push views of inflation in favor of a monetary view, allowing monetary policy to become the government's anti-inflationary weapon; this shift occurred in 1979. The third was the discarding of ineffective monetary policy instruments, which had given U.K. policymakers the false notion that they could alter the stance of monetary policy without affecting short-term interest rates or the monetary base. This process culminated with the abandonment of overfunding in 1985. And as the role of monetary policy became clearer and more coherent in the U.K., the role of central bankers also shifted, from the "City Syndrome" era emphasis on responsibility for financial-market psychology, to the ability to make technical judgments on macroeconomic developments.

The abandonment of nonmonetary views of aggregate demand and inflation determination also had important ramifications for the conduct of U.K. fiscal policy. The nonmonetary approach not only led to a misplaced confidence in fiscal activism in the 1950s and 1960s, but to the use of fiscal measures as remedies for cost-push inflation: for example, the attempts to hold down prices via subsidies in 1970-74 and attempts at wage/tax trade-offs over 1974-79. The casting-off of cost-push views of inflation was a precondition for fiscal policy to be assigned a longer-term role, while the acceptance of the importance of monetary policy for demand management has also diminished policymakers' interest in short-term fiscal adjustments.

Acknowledgements

We thank Jason Buol, Nathalie Carcenac, and Justin Hauke for research assistance. The views expressed in this paper are those of the authors and should not be interpreted as those of the Federal Reserve Bank of St. Louis, the Federal Reserve System, the Board of Governors, or the International Monetary Fund.

REFERENCES

[1] Allen, William A. (1982). "Recent Developments in Monetary Control in the United Kingdom." In L.H. Meyer (ed.), *Improving Money Stock Control: Problems, Solutions and Consequences*. Boston: Kluwer-Nijhoff. 97-123.

[2] Allsopp, Christopher J. (1981). "*The Economics of Public Borrowing*." Manuscript, Oxford University.

[3] Allsopp, Christopher J. (1991). "Macroeconomic Policy: Design and Performance." In M.J. Artis and D. Cobham (eds.), *Labour's Economic Policies* 1974-1979. Manchester, U.K.: Manchester University Press. 19-37.

[4] Allsopp, Christopher J., and David G. Mayes (1985). "Demand Management in Practice." In D. Morris (ed.), *The Economic System in the U.K.* 3rd edition. Oxford, U.K.: Oxford University Press. 398-443.

[5] Andrés, Javier, David López-Salido, and Edward Nelson (2004). "Tobin's Imperfect Asset Substitution in Optimizing General Equilibrium," *Journal of Money, Credit, and Banking,* Vol. 36(4), 665-690.

[6] Artis, Michael J. (1961). "Liquidity and the Attack on Quantity Theory," *Oxford Bulletin of Economics and Statistics*, Vol. 23(4), 343-366.

[7] Artis, Michael J. (1974). "Monetary Policy in the 1970s in Light of Recent Developments." In H.G. Johnson and A.R. Nobay (eds.), *Issues in Monetary Economics: Proceedings of the 1972 Money Study Group Conference*. Oxford, U.K.: Oxford University Press. 517-566.

[8] Artis, Michael J., and Zenon G. Kontolemis (1996). "Inflation in the U.K. in the 1980s." In P. De Grauwe, S. Micossi and G. Tullio (eds.), *Inflation and Wage Behaviour in Europe*. Oxford, U.K.: Clarendon Press. 58-90.

[9] Artis, Michael J., and Mervyn K. Lewis (1981). *Monetary Control in the United Kingdom*. London: Philip Allan.

[10] Artis, Michael J., and Mervyn K. Lewis (1991). *Money in Britain: Monetary Policy, Financial Innovation and Europe*. London: Phillip Allan.

[11] Backhouse, Roger (1983). *Macroeconomics and the British Economy*. London: Martin Robertson.

[12] Bain, A.D. (1983). "The Wilson Report—Three Years On," *Three Banks Review*, Vol. 31(138), 3-19.

[13] Ball, Laurence and Niamh Sheridan (2005). "Does Inflation Targeting Matter?" In B.S. Bernanke and M. Woodford (eds.), *The Inflation Targeting Debate*. Chicago: University of Chicago Press. 249-276.

[14] Balls, Ed, and Gus O'Donnell (2001). *Reforming Britain's Economic and Financial Policy*. London: Palgrave Macmillan.

[15] Balogh, Thomas (1958). "Productivity and Inflation," *Oxford Economic Papers*, Vol. 10(2), 220-245.

[16] Bank of England (1984). "Monetary Targets." In Bank of England, *The Development and Operation of Monetary Policy*, 1960-1983. Oxford, U.K.: Oxford University Press. 45-48.

[17] *The Banker* (1960). "Monetary Policy in Action: The Radcliffe Evidence," *The Banker*, Vol. 110(410), 223-240.

[18] Barro, Robert J. (1982). "United States Inflation and the Choice of Monetary Standard." In R.E. Hall (ed.), *Inflation: Causes and Effects*. Chicago: University of Chicago Press. 99-110.

[19] Batini, Nicoletta, Brian Jackson, and Stephen Nickell (2005). "An Open Economy New Keynesian Phillips Curve for the U.K.," *Journal of Monetary Economics*, Vol. 52(6), 1061-1071.

[20] Batini, Nicoletta, and Edward Nelson (2000). "Optimal Horizons for Inflation Targeting." *Bank of England Working Paper No*. 120. (Version without appendix published in *Journal of Economic Dynamics and Control*, Vol. 25(6-7), 2001, 891-910.)

[21] Batini, Nicoletta, and Edward Nelson (2001). "The Lag from Monetary Policy Actions to Inflation: Friedman Revisited," *International Finance*, Vol. 4(3), 381-400.

[22] Bean, Charles R., and James Symons (1989). "Ten Years of Mrs. T.," *NBER Macroeconomics Annual*, Vol. 4(1), 13-61.

[23] Beckhart, B.H. (1964). "Review: *Banking in Western Europe*," *Economica*, Vol. 31(121), 94-96.

[24] Beenstock, Michael (1979). "Taxation and Incentives in the U.K.," *Lloyds Bank Review*, Vol. 34(134), 1-15.

[25] Beenstock, Michael (1980). "The Debate about Monetary Policy," *London Business School Economic Outlook*, Vol. 5(October), 23-30.

[26] Bell, Geoffrey (1970). "Competing for Deposits," *The Banker*, Vol. 120(529), 286-293.

[27] Bernanke, Ben S. (2004). "The Great Moderation." Remarks at the meetings of the Eastern Economic Association, Washington, DC. February 20.

[28] Bernanke, Ben S., Thomas Laubach, Frederic S. Mishkin, and Adam S. Posen (1999). *Inflation Targeting: Lessons from the International Experience*. Princeton, N.J.: Princeton University Press.

[29] Bernanke, Ben S. and Vincent R. Reinhart (2004). "Conducting Monetary Policy at Very Low Short-Term Interest Rates," *American Economic Review* (*Papers and Proceedings*), Vol. 94(2), 85-90.

[30] Bernstein, George (2004). *The Myth of Decline: The Rise of Britain Since 1945*. London: Pimlico.

[31] Bindseil, Ulrich (2004). "The Operational Target of Monetary Policy and the Rise and Fall of Reserve Position Doctrine." *ECB Working Paper No*. 372.

[32] Birchenhall, Chris R., Denise R. Osborn, and Marianne Senser (2000). "Predicting U.K. Business Cycle Regimes." *CHBC Discussion Paper Series* No. 002, University of Manchester.

[33] Blanchard, Olivier, and John Simon (2001). "The Long and Large Decline in U.S. Output Volatility," *Brookings Papers on Economic Activity*, Vol. 32(1), 135-174.

[34] Blinder, Alan S. (1984). "Ruminations on Karl Brunner's Reflections." In R.W. Hafer (ed.), *The Monetary Versus Fiscal Policy Debate.* Totowa, N.J.: Rowman and Allanheld. 117-126.

[35] Bootle, R.P. (1985). "Monetary Policy." In D. Morris (ed.), *The Economic System in the U.K.* 3rd edition. Oxford, U.K.: Oxford University Press. 295-332.

[36] Brittan, Samuel and Peter Lilley (1977). *The Delusion of Incomes Policy.* London: Maurice Temple Smith.

[37] Brown, Roger (1981). *Monetary Control in Britain 1971-1981.* London: Banking Information Service.

[38] Brunner, Karl (1981). "The Case Against Monetary Activism," *Lloyds Bank Review*, Vol. 36(139), 20-39.

[39] Brunner, Karl, and R.L. Crouch (1967). "Money Supply Theory and British Monetary Experience," *Methods of Operations Research*, Vol. 3(1), 77-112.

[40] Brunner, Karl, and Allan H. Meltzer (1973). "Mr. Hicks and the 'Monetarists,'" *Economica*, Vol. 40(157), 44-59.

[41] Budd, Alan (1979). "Economic Viewpoint: Monetary Targets and a Financial Plan," *London Business School Economic Outlook*, Vol. 4(2) (November), 11-14.

[42] Budd, Alan (1999). "Learning from the Wise People," *Manchester School*, Vol. 67 (Supplement), 36-48.

[43] Budd, Alan, and Terence Burns (1981). "The Relationship Between Fiscal and Monetary Policy in the London Business School Model." In M.J. Artis and M.H. Miller (eds.), *Essays in Fiscal and Monetary Policy.* Oxford, U.K.: Oxford University Press. 136-163.

[44] Budd, Alan, and Sean Holly (1986). "Economic Viewpoint: Does Broad Money Matter?," *London Business School Economic Outlook*, Vol. 10 (June), 16-22.

[45] Campbell, John (1993). *Edward Heath: A Biography.* London: Jonathan Cape.

[46] Campbell, John (2003). *Margaret Thatcher, Volume 2: The Iron Lady.* London: Jonathan Cape.

[47] Capie, Forrest, and Alan Webber (1985). *A Monetary History of the United Kingdom, 1870–1982, Volume I: Data, Sources, Methods.* London: George Allen and Unwin.

[48] Carter, C.F. (1960). "Problems and Prospects of the Economic Position of Great Britain," *Three Banks Review*, Vol. 12(45), 3-13.

[49] Caves, Richard E. (1980). "Productivity Differences among Industries." In R.E. Caves and L.B. Krause (eds.), *Britain's Economic Performance.* Washington, D.C.: Brookings Institution. 135-192.

[50] Chrystal, K. Alec (1999). "Comment: Government Debt, the Composition of Bank Portfolios, and the Transmission of Monetary Policy." In K.A. Chrystal (ed.), *Government Debt Structure and Monetary Conditions.* London: Bank of England. 194-198.

[51] Cobham, David (1984). "Convergence, Divergence and Realignment in British Macroeconomics," *Banca Nazionale del Lavoro Quarterly Review*, Vol. 149(2), 1591-76.

[52] Cobham, David (1991). "Monetary Policy." In M.J. Artis and D. Cobham (eds.), *Labour's Economic Policies 1974-1979.* Manchester, U.K.: Manchester University Press. 38-55.

[53] Cobham, David (2002). *The Making of Monetary Policy in the U.K., 1975-2000*. Sussex, U.K.: Wiley.

[54] Cockerell, Michael (1989). *Live from Number 10: The Inside Story of Prime Ministers and Television*. Suffolk, U.K.: Richard Clay.

[55] Congdon, Tim (1978). *Monetarism: An Essay in Definition*. London: Centre for Policy Studies.

[56] Congdon, Tim (1980). "The Incomes Policy Cycle in Britain: An Attempt at Explanation," *The Banker*, Vol. 130(648), 27-32.

[57] Congdon, Tim (1982). *Monetary Control in Britain*. London: Macmillan.

[58] Congdon, Tim (1992). *Reflections on Monetarism: Britain's Vain Search for a Successful Economic Strategy*. Cheltenham, U.K.: Edward Elgar.

[59] Congdon, Tim (1995). "Broad Money vs. Narrow Money," *Review of Policy Issues*, Vol. 1(5), 13-27.

[60] Craven, B.M., and R. Gausden (1991). "How Best to Measure Inflation? The U.K. and Europe," *Royal Bank of Scotland Review*, Vol. 39(170), 26-37.

[61] Crick, Bernard (1988). "An Englishman Considers His Passport," *Irish Review*, Vol. 5(1), 1-10.

[62] Crouch, R.L. (1964). "The Inadequacy of 'New-Orthodox' Methods of Monetary Control," *Economic Journal*, Vol. 74(296), 916-934.

[63] Crouch, R.L. (1967). "Special Deposits: Their Perverse Nature." In R.L. Crouch, *A Model of the United Kingdom's Monetary Sector*. Ph.D. Dissertation, University of Essex. Chapter 4.

[64] Currie, Lauchlin (1934). *The Supply and Control of Money in the United States*. Cambridge, MA: Harvard University Press.

[65] Dacey, W. Manning (1960). *Money under Review*. London: Hutchinson.

[66] Darby, Michael R., and James R. Lothian (1983). "British Economic Policy Under Margaret Thatcher: A Midterm Examination," *Carnegie-Rochester Conference Series on Public Policy*, Vol. 18(1), 157-208.

[67] Davis, Richard (1982a). "Comments by the Author." In *Interest Rate Deregulation and Monetary Policy: Alisomar Conference Sponsored by the Federal Reserve Bank of San Francisco*. San Francisco: Federal Reserve Bank of San Francisco. 52-59.

[68] Davis, Richard (1982b). "Monetary Targeting in a Zero Balance World." In *Interest Rate Deregulation and Monetary Policy: Alisomar Conference Sponsored by the Federal Reserve Bank of San Francisco*. San Francisco: Federal Reserve Bank of San Francisco. 20-51.

[69] Davis, Richard G. (1983). "Comment on Papers Presented by Messrs. Fforde and Coleby." In P. Meek (ed.), *Central Bank Views on Monetary Targeting*. New York: Federal Reserve Bank of New York. 68-69.

[70] Davis, William (1972). *Money Talks—William Davis Translates*. London: André Deutsch.

[71] Dean, James W. (1975). "The Secondary Reserve Requirement as an Instrument of Monetary Policy," *Manchester School*, Vol. 43(1), 68-88.

[72] Debelle, Guy, and Stanley Fischer (1994). "How Independent Should a Central Bank Be?" In J.C. Fuhrer (ed.), *Goals, Guidelines and Constraints Facing Monetary Policymakers*. Boston: Federal Reserve Bank of Boston. 195-225.

[73] Dell, Edmund (1996). *The Chancellors: A History of the Chancellors of the Exchequer 1945-1990*. London: HarperCollins.

[74] Dennis, G.E.J. (1981a). "Rationale of Monetary Policy." In D.T. Llewellyn (ed.), *The Framework of U.K. Monetary Policy*. London: Heinemann. 138-165.

[75] Dennis, G.E.J. (1981b). "Monetary Policy and Debt Management." In D.T. Llewellyn (ed.), *The Framework of U.K. Monetary Policy*. London: Heinemann. 244-293.

[76] Dotsey, Michael (1991). "Monetary Policy and Operating Procedures in New Zealand," *Federal Reserve Bank of Richmond Economic Review*, Vol. 77(5), 13-19.

[77] Dow, J.C.R. (1964). *The Management of the British Economy, 1945-60*. Cambridge, U.K.: Cambridge University Press.

[78] Dow, J.C.R., and Iain D. Saville (1988). *A Critique of Monetary Policy*. Oxford, U.K.: Clarendon Press.

[79] Fforde, John (1983). "The United Kingdom—Setting Monetary Objectives." In P. Meek (ed.), *Central Bank Views on Monetary Targeting*. New York: Federal Reserve Bank of New York.

[80] Fleming, Ian (1959). *Goldfinger*. London: Jonathan Cape.

[81] Foster, John (1979). "Interest Rates and Inflation Expectations: The British Experience," *Oxford Bulletin of Economics and Statistics*, Vol. 41(2), 145-164.\

[82] Friedman, Milton (1956). "The Quantity Theory of Money: A Restatement." In M. Friedman (ed.), *Studies in the Quantity Theory of Money*. Chicago: University of Chicago Press. 3-21.

[83] Friedman, Milton (1960). *A Program for Monetary Stability*. Fordham, N.J.: Fordham University Press.

[84] Friedman, Milton (1977). "Discussion of 'The Monetarist Controversy,'" *Federal Reserve Bank of San Francisco Economic Review* (*Supplement*), Vol. 3(1), 12-19.

[85] Friedman, Milton (1980). "Memorandum: Response to Questionnaire on Monetary Policy, June 11, 1980." In Treasury and Civil Service Committee, *Memoranda on Monetary Policy*. London: HMSO. 55-61.

[86] Friedman, Milton, and Anna J. Schwartz (1963). *A Monetary History of the United States, 1867–1960*. Princeton, N.J.: Princeton University Press.

[87] Friedman, Milton, and Anna J. Schwartz (1970). *Monetary Statistics of the United States*. New York: Columbia University Press.

[88] Friedman, Milton, and Anna J. Schwartz (1982). *Monetary Trends in the United States and the United Kingdom: Their Relation to Income, Prices, and Interest Rates, 1867-1975*. Chicago: University of Chicago Press.

[89] Gibson, N.J. (1964). "Special Deposits as an Instrument of Monetary Policy," *Manchester School*, Vol. 32(3), 239-259.

[90] Gilbody, John (1988). *The U.K. Monetary & Financial System: An Introduction*. London: Routledge.

[91] Goodhart, Charles A.E. (1972). "The Gilt-Edged Market." In H.G. Johnson *et al* (eds.), *Readings in British Monetary Economics*. Oxford, U.K.: Clarendon Press. 452-469.

[92] Goodhart, Charles A.E. (1973). "British Monetary Policy." In K. Holbik (ed.), *Monetary Policy in Twelve Industrial Countries*. Boston: Federal Reserve Bank of Boston. 465-524.

[93] Goodhart, Charles A.E. (1983). "Review: *Money and Inflation*," *Economic Journal*, Vol. 93(369), 217-219.

[94] Goodhart, Charles A.E. (1984a). "Introduction." In C.A.E. Goodhart, *Monetary Theory and Practice: The U.K. Experience*. London: Macmillan. 1-19.

[95] Goodhart, Charles A.E. (1984b). "Problems of Monetary Management: The U.K. Experience." In C.A.E. Goodhart, *Monetary Theory and Practice: The U.K. Experience*. London: Macmillan. 91-121.

[96] Goodhart, Charles A.E. (1992). "The Objectives for, and Conduct of, Monetary Policy in the 1990s." In A. Blundell-Wignall (ed.), *Inflation, Disinflation and Monetary Policy*. Sydney: Ambassador Press. 314-334.

[97] Goodhart, Charles A.E. (1997). "Book Review: Sir Alec Cairncross, *Managing the British Economy in the 1960s: A Treasury Perspective*," *Economic Journal*, Vol. 107(442), 852-854.

[98] Goodhart, Charles A.E. (1999). "Monetary Policy and Debt Management in the United Kingdom: Some Historical Viewpoints." In K.A. Chrystal (ed.), *Government Debt Structure and Monetary Conditions*. London: Bank of England. 43-97.

[99] Goodhart, Charles A.E. (2004). "The Bank of England, 1970-2000." In R. Michie and P. Williamson (eds.), *The British Government and the City of London in the 20th Century*. Cambridge, U.K.: Cambridge University Press.

[100] Gordon, Robert J. (1984). "Comments on Karl Brunner's 'Fiscal Policy in Macro Theory: A Survey and Evaluation.'" In R.W. Hafer (ed.), *The Monetary Versus Fiscal Policy Debate*. Totowa, N.J.: Rowman and Allanheld. 127-136.

[101] Griffiths, Brian (1974). "Two Monetary Inquiries in Great Britain: Comment," *Journal of Money, Credit and Banking*, Vol. 6(1), 101-114.

[102] Griffiths, Brian, and Geoffrey E. Wood (1984). "Introduction." In B. Griffiths and G.E. Wood (eds.), *Monetarism in the United Kingdom*. New York: St. Martin's Press. 3-12.

[103] Grossman, Herschell I. (1984). "Book Review: Frank Hahn, *Money and Inflation*," *Journal of Political Economy*, Vol. 92(2), 337-340.

[104] Gurley, John G., and Edward S. Shaw (1960). *Money in a Theory of Finance*. Washington, D.C.: Brookings Institution.

[105] Hahn, Frank (1983). *Money and Inflation*. Cambridge, MA: MIT Press.

[106] Haldane, Andrew, and Danny Quah (1999). "U.K. Phillips Curves and Monetary Policy," *Journal of Monetary Economics*, Vol. 44(2), 259–278.

[107] Hall, Maximilian J.B. (1983). *Monetary Policy Since 1971: Conduct and Performance*. New York: St. Martin's Press.

[108] Harris, Kenneth (1988). *Thatcher*. Boston: Little Brown.

[109] Harrod, Roy (1958). *Policy Against Inflation*. London: Macmillan.

[110] Harrod, Roy (1972). "Prospects for the British Economy," *The Bankers' Magazine*, Vol. 208(1535), 59-62.

[111] Hawtrey, Ralph (1959). "The Report of the Radcliffe Committee," *The Bankers' Magazine*, Vol. 188(1387), 253-261.

[112] HM Treasury (1980). "The Stability of the Income Velocity of Circulation of Money Supply." In *Third Report from the Treasury and Civil Service Committee, Session 198̃081: Monetary Policy*. London: HMSO. 126-128.

[113] HM Treasury and the Bank of England (1980). *Monetary Control*. Cmnd 7858. London: HMSO.

[114] Hodgman, Donald R. (1971). "British Techniques of Monetary Policy: A Critical Review," *Journal of Money, Credit, and Banking*, Vol. 3(4), 760-779.

[115] Holtrop, M.W. (1957). "Method of Monetary Analysis Used by De Nederlandische Bank," *IMF Staff Papers*, Vol. 5(3), 303-316.

[116] Holtrop, M.W. (1958). "Memorandum of Evidence Submitted by the President of the Netherlands Bank, 5th November 1958." In *Principal Memoranda of Evidence Submitted to the Committee on the Working of the Monetary System, Volume 1*. London: HMSO, 1960. 260-268.

[117] Howard, David H., and Karen H. Johnson (1982). "Financial Innovation, Deregulation and Monetary Policy: The Foreign Experience." In *Interest Rate Deregulation and Monetary Policy: Alisomar Conference Sponsored by the Federal Reserve Bank of San Francisco*. San Francisco: Federal Reserve Bank of San Francisco. 139-181.

[118] Howe, Geoffrey (1994). *A Conflict of Loyalty*. London: Macmillan.

[119] Jenkins, Roy (1969). "The Chancellor on the State of the U.K. Economy," *The Banker*, Vol. 119(525), 1212-1215.

[120] Johnson, Harry G. (1956). "The Revival of Monetary Policy in Britain," *Three Banks Review*, Vol. 8(30), 1-20.

[121] Johnson, Harry G. (1971a). "Harking Back to Radcliffe," *The Bankers' Magazine*, Vol. 203(1530), 115-120.

[122] Johnson, Harry G. (1971b). *Macroeconomics and Monetary Theory*. London: Gray-Mills.

[123] Johnson, Harry G., *et al* (eds.) (1972). *Readings in British Monetary Economics*. Oxford, U.K.: Clarendon Press.

[124] Joint Economic Committee (1981). *Monetarism in the United States and the United Kingdom: Hearings Before the Joint Economic Committee, Congress of the United States, Ninety-Seventh Congress, First Session, October 6, 1981*. Washington, D.C.: Government Printing Office.

[125] Joint Economic Committee (1982). *Monetarism and the Federal Reserve's Conduct of Monetary Policy: Compendium of Views Prepared for the Use of the Subcommittee on Monetary and Fiscal Policy*. Washington, D.C.: Government Printing Office.

[126] Jonson, P.D. (1976). "Money and Economic Activity in the Open Economy: The United Kingdom, 1880-1970," *Journal of Political Economy*, Vol. 84(5), 979-1012.

[127] *Journal of Money, Credit, and Banking* (1982). "Money, Credit, and Banking Debate: Is the Federal Reserve's Monetary Control Policy Misdirected?," *Journal of Money, Credit, and Banking* , Vol. 14(1), 119-147.

[128] Kaldor, Nicholas (1982). *The Scourge of Monetarism*. Oxford, U.K.: Oxford University Press.

[129] Kara, Amit, and Edward Nelson (2003). "The Exchange Rate and Inflation in the U.K.," *Scottish Journal of Political Economy*, Vol. 50(5), 585-608.

[130] Kara, Amit, and Edward Nelson (2004). "International Evidence on the Stability of the Optimizing IS Equation," *Oxford Bulletin of Economics and Statistics*, Vol. 66 (Supplement), 687-712.

[131] Kareken, John H. (1968). "Monetary Policy." In R.E. Caves (ed.), *Britain's Economic Prospects*. Washington, D.C.: Brookings Institution. 68-103.

[132] Kay, J.A., and D.J. Thompson (1986). "Privatisation: A Policy in Search of a Rationale," *Economic Journal*, Vol. 96(381), 18-32.

[133] Keegan, William (1985). *Mrs. Thatcher's Economic Experiment*. 2nd edition. London: Penguin.

[134] Keegan, William (1989). *Mr. Lawson's Gamble*. London: Hodder and Stoughton.

[135] Kern, David (1972). "Monetary Policy and CCC," *National Westminster Bank Review* (November) 34-49.

[136] King, Mervyn A. (1977). *Public Policy and the Corporation*. London: Chapman and Hall.

[137] Kissinger, Henry (1999). *Years of Renewal*. New York: Simon and Schuster.

[138] Laidler, David (1981). "Comments: Monetary Targets and the Public Sector Borrowing Requirement." In B. Griffiths and G.E. Wood (eds.), *Monetary Targets*. New York: St. Martin's Press. 176-179.

[139] Laidler, David (1989). "Radcliffe, the Quantity Theory, and Monetarism." In D. Cobham, R. Harrington, and G. Zis (eds.), *Money, Trade and Payments: Essays in Honour of Dennis Coppock*. Manchester, U.K.: Manchester University Press. 17-27.

[140] Lamont, Norman (1992). "Chancellor's Mansion House Speech," *Treasury Bulletin*, Vol. 3(3), 46-50.

[141] Lamont, Norman (1999). *In Office*. London: Little Brown.

[142] Lawson, Nigel (1992). *The View from No. 11*. London: Bantam.

[143] Levin, Andrew T., Fabio M. Natalucci, and Jeremy M. Piger (2004). "The Macroeconomic Effects of Inflation Targeting," *Federal Reserve Bank of St. Louis Review*, Vol. 86(4), 51-80.

[144] Lewis, Mervyn K. (1980). "Is Monetary Base Control Just Interest Rate Control in Disguise?," *The Banker*, Vol. 130(655), 35-38.

[145] Llewellyn, David T. (1981). "Money Supply in the U.K." In D.T. Llewellyn (ed.), *The Framework of U.K. Monetary Policy*. London: Heinemann. 73-121.

[146] Lothian, James R. (1976). "The Demand for High-Powered Money," *American Economic Review*, Vol. 66(1), 56-68.

[147] Macleod, Iain (1969). "Taxation: Planning for Office," *The Banker*, Vol. 119(518), 306-311.

[148] Major, John (1999). *John Major: The Autobiography*. London: HarperCollins.

[149] McConnell, Margaret M., and Gabriel Perez-Quiros (2000). "Output Fluctuations in the United States: What Has Changed since the Early 1980's?," *American Economic Review*, Vol. 90(5), 1464-1476.

[150] McRae, Hamish (1969). "Gilt-Edged in Perspective," *The Banker*, Vol. 119(525), 1168-1175.

[151] Meade, J.E. (1951). *The Theory of International Economic Policy, Volume 1: The Balance of Payments*. London: Oxford University Press.

[152] Meltzer, Allan H. (1976). "Statement on Monetary Policy, June 24, 1976." In House Committee on Banking, Currency, and Housing, *Ending Inflation: The Next Steps*. Washington, DC: Government Printing Office. 178-180.

[153] Meltzer, Allan H. (1981). "Tests of Inflation Theories from the British Laboratory," *The Banker*, Vol. 131(665), 21–27.

[154] Meltzer, Allan H. (2001). "Money and Monetary Policy: An Essay in Honor of Darryl Francis," *Federal Reserve Bank of St. Louis Review*, Vol. 83(4), 23-31.

[155] Miles, David K., and Joe Wilcox (1991). "The Money Transmission Mechanism." In C.J. Green and D.T. Llewellyn (eds.), *Surveys in Monetary Economics, Volume 1: Monetary Theory and Policy*. Oxford, U.K.: Basil Blackwell. 225-262.

[156] Minford, Patrick (1980). "A Rational Expectations Model of the United Kingdom under Fixed and Floating Exchange Rates," *Carnegie-Rochester Conference Series on Public Policy*, Vol. 12(1), 293-355.

[157] Minford, Patrick (1993). "Monetary Policy in the Other G-7 Countries: The United Kingdom." In M.U. Fratianni and D. Salvatore (eds.), *Monetary Policy in Developed Economies* (*Handbook of Comparative Economic Policies, Volume 3*). Westport, CT: Greenwood Press. 405-431.

[158] Mishkin, Frederic S. (2001). "From Monetary Targeting to Inflation Targeting: Lessons from the Industrialized Countries." Manuscript, Columbia University.

[159] Mishkin, Frederic S., and Klaus Schmidt-Hebbel (2001). "One Decade of Inflation Targeting in the World: What Do We Know and What Do We Need to Know?" NBER Working Paper No. 8397.

[160] Morgan, Kenneth O. (1997). *Callaghan: A Life*. Oxford, U.K.: Oxford University Press.

[161] Morgan, Kenneth O. (2001). *Britain Since 1945: The People's Peace*. Oxford, U.K.: Oxford University Press.

[162] Morrell, James (1987). "Whatever Happened to Velocity?," *Royal Bank of Scotland Review*, Vol. 35(153), 25-35.

[163] Neiss, Katharine S., and Edward Nelson (2003). "The Real Interest Rate Gap as an Inflation Indicator," *Macroeconomic Dynamics*, Vol. 7(3), 239-262.

[164] Nelson, Edward, and Kalin Nikolov (2003). "U.K. Inflation in the 1970s and 1980s: The Role of Output Gap Mismeasurement," *Journal of Economics and Business*, Vol. 55(4), 353-370.

[165] Nelson, Edward (2004). "The Great Inflation of the Seventies: What Really Happened?" Federal Reserve Bank of St. Louis Working Paper 2004-001A.

[166] Nelson, Edward, and Kalin Nikolov (2004). "Monetary Policy and Stagflation in the U.K.," *Journal of Money, Credit and Banking*, Vol. 36(3), 293-318.

[167] Newlyn, W.T. (1955). "The Credit Squeeze in the Light of Basic Principles," *The Bankers' Magazine*, Vol. 190(1339), 287-290.

[168] Newlyn, W.T. (1962). *Theory of Money*. Oxford, U.K.: Clarendon Press.

[169] Newton, Maxwell (1983). *The Fed*. New York: Crown Publishing.

[170] Nickell, Stephen (2003). "Employment and Taxes." Manuscript, London School of Economics.

[171] Norton, W.E. (1969). "Debt Management and Monetary Policy in the United Kingdom," *Economic Journal*, Vol. 79(315), 475-494.

[172] OECD (1982). *Budget Financing and Monetary Control*. Paris: OECD.

[173] Orphanides, Athanasios (2003). "The Quest for Prosperity without Inflation," *Journal of Monetary Economics*, Vol. 50(3), 633-663.

[174] Orphanides, Athanasios (2004). "Monetary Policy Rules, Macroeconomic Stability, and Inflation: A View from the Trenches," *Journal of Money, Credit, and Banking*, Vol. 36(2), 151-175.

[175] Parkin, Michael (1982). "Discussion." In L.H. Meyer (ed.), *Improving Money Stock Control: Problems, Solutions and Consequences*. Boston: Kluwer-Nijhoff. 124-132.

[176] Parsons, Wayne (1989). *The Power of the Financial Press: Journalism and Economic Opinion in Britain and America*. Cheltenham, U.K.: Edward Elgar.

[177] Pechman, Joseph A. (1980). "Taxation." In R.E. Caves and L.B. Krause (eds.), *Britain's Economic Performance*. Washington, D.C.: Brookings Institution. 199-253.

[178] Pepper, Gordon (1994). *Money, Credit and Asset Prices*. London: St. Martin's Press.

[179] Pepper, Gordon, and Michael Oliver (2001). *Monetarism under Thatcher: Lessons for the Future*. Cheltenham, U.K.: Edward Elgar.

[180] Prescott, Edward C. (2004). "Why Do Americans Work So Much More Than Europeans?," *Federal Reserve Bank of Minneapolis Quarterly Review*, Vol. 28(1), 2-13.

[181] Prest, A.R., 1968, "Sense and Nonsense in Budgetary Policy," *Economic Journal*, Vol. 78(1), 1-18.

[182] Radcliffe Committee (1959). *Report of the Committee on the Working of the Monetary System*. Cmnd. 827. London: HMSO.

[183] Ridley, Nicholas (1991). *'My Style of Government': The Thatcher Years*. London: Hutchinson.

[184] Robbins, Lionel (1954). "The Control of Inflation." In L. Robbins, *The Economist in the Twentieth Century*, London: Macmillan. Reprinted in L. Robbins, *Money, Trade, and International Relations*. London: Macmillan, 1971. 69-89.

[185] Robbins, Lionel (1961). "Monetary Theory and the Radcliffe Report." In L. Robbins, *Politics and Economics*. London: St. Martin's Press. Reprinted in L. Robbins, *Money, Trade, and International Relations*. London: Macmillan, 1971. 90-119.

[186] Robbins, Lionel (1979). *Against Inflation: Speeches in the Second Chamber, 1965-1977*. London: Macmillan.

[187] Robertson, Donald (1992). "Term Structure Forecasts of Inflation," *Economic Journal*, Vol. 102(414), 1083̃1093.

[188] Romer, Christina D., and David H. Romer (2002a). "A Rehabilitation of Monetary Policy in the 1950's," *American Economic Review* (*Papers and Proceedings*), Vol. 92(2), 121-127.

[189] Romer, Christina D., and David H. Romer (2002b). "The Evolution of Economic Understanding and Postwar Stabilization Policy." In *Rethinking Stabilization Policy*. Kansas City: Federal Reserve Bank of Kansas City. 11-78.

[190] Rowan, D.C. (1973). "The Monetary System in the Fifties and Sixties," *Manchester School,* Vol. 41(1), 19-42.

[191] Sayers, R.A. (1957). *Central Banking after Bagehot*. Oxford, U.K.: Oxford University Press.

[192] Schwartz, Anna J. (1969). "Short-Term Targets of Some Foreign Central Banks." In K. Brunner (ed.), *Targets and Indicators of Monetary Policy*. San Francisco: Chandler. 27-65.

[193] Schwartz, Anna J. (1985). "Where the Bank Went Wrong," *The Banker*, Vol. 135(708), 100-101.

[194] Select Committee on Nationalized Industries (1970). *First Report: Bank of England*. London: HMSO.

[195] Smith, David (1987). *The Rise and Fall of Monetarism*. London: Penguin.

[196] Taylor, John B. (1999). "A Historical Analysis of Monetary Policy Rules." In J.B. Taylor (ed.), *Monetary Policy Rules*. Chicago: University of Chicago Press. 319-341.

[197] Temperton, Paul (1986). *A Guide to U.K. Monetary Policy*. New York: St. Martin's Press.

[198] Tew, J.H.B. (1979). "Monetary Policy, Part I." In F.T. Blackaby (ed.), *British Economic Policy, 1960-74: Demand Management*. Cambridge, U.K.: Cambridge University Press. 218-257.

[199] Tew, J.H.B. (1981). "The Implementation of Monetary Policy in Post-War Britain," *Midland Bank Review* (Spring), 5-14.

[200] Thatcher, Margaret (1993). *The Downing Street Years*. London: HarperCollins.

[201] Thatcher, Margaret (1995). *The Path to Power*. London: HarperCollins.

[202] Thatcher, Margaret (2002). *Statecraft: Strategies for a Changing World*. London: HarperCollins.

[203] Thompson, Grahame (1986). *The Conservatives' Economic Policy*. London: Croom Helm.

[204] Thorpe, D.R. (2003). *Eden: The Life and Times of Anthony Eden, First Earl of Avon, 1897-1977*. London: Chatto and Windus.

[205] Throop, Adrian W. (1980). "Managed Floating and the Independence of Interest Rates," *Federal Reserve Bank of San Francisco Economic Review*, Vol. 6(3), 6-23.

[206] Treasury and Civil Service Committee (1981). *Monetary Policy, Volume II: Minutes of Evidence*. London: HMSO.

[207] Wadsworth, J.E. (ed.) (1973). *The Banks and the Monetary System in the U.K., 1959-1971*. London: Methuen.

[208] Walters, Alan A. (1965). "Bank Rate," *The Bankers' Magazine*, Vol. 200(1456), 7-12.

[209] Walters, Alan A. (1969). "Money Supply and the Gilt-Edged Market," *The Banker*, Vol. 119(525), 1179-1184.

[210] Walters, Alan A. (1970). "The Radcliffe Report, Ten Years After—A Survey of Empirical Evidence." In D.R. Croome and H.G. Johnson (eds.), *Money in Britain, 1959-1969*. Oxford, U.K.: Oxford University Press. 39-68.

[211] Walters, Alan A. (1986). *Britain's Economic Renaissance: Margaret Thatcher's Reforms, 1979-1984*. Oxford, U.K.: Oxford University Press.

[212] Walters, Alan A. (1990). *Sterling in Danger: The Economic Consequences of Pegged Exchange Rates*. London: Fontana.

[213] Walters, Alan A. (1995). "Money, Narrow or Broad?," *Review of Policy Issues*, Vol. 1(5), 29-34.

[214] Watkins, Alan (1992). *A Conservative Coup: The Fall of Margaret Thatcher*. 2nd edition. London: Duckworth.

[215] *Whitaker's Almanack 1979* (1978). "Parliamentary Summary Lords and Commons, 1977-78." London: William Clowes and Sons. 347-366.

[216] *Whitaker's Almanack 1980* (1979). "Parliamentary Summary Lords and Commons, 1978-79." London: William Clowes and Sons. 355-367.

[217] Wilson Committee (1980). *Committee to Review the Functioning of Financial Institutions, Report, Chairman: The Rt Hon Sir Harold Wilson KG, OBE, FRS, MP, Presented to Parliament by the Prime Minister by Command of Her Majesty, June 1980*. Cmnd. 7937. London: HMSO.

[218] Wood, John (ed.) (1970). *Powell and the 1970 Election*. Surrey, U.K.: Elliot Right Way.

[219] Woodford, Michael (2001). "Monetary Policy in the Information Economy." In *Economic Policy for the Information Economy*. Kansas City: Federal Reserve Bank of Kansas City. 297-370.

In: Trends in Inflation Research
Editor: Barbara T. Credan, pp. 87-141
ISBN: 1-59454-825-0
© 2006 Nova Science Publishers, Inc.

Chapter 2

VALUATING CASH FLOWS IN AN INFLATIONARY ENVIRONMENT:[1] THE CASE OF WORLD BANK

Ignacio Vélez–Pareja*
Politécnico Grancolombiano
Bogotá, Colombia

ABSTRACT

This chapter shows that when valuating cash flows they should be based on estimates of free cash flows at nominal prices. In particular, we show that results from the valuation of cash flows with the constant and real price methods are biased upwards and there is a risk that in practice, bad projects will be accepted as good projects or that the valuation of free cash flows for valuing firms is overstated. Generally speaking, inflation has a negative impact on the Net Present Value, NPV of a project. When expected inflation rates over the cash flow horizon are high, which is a typically case in emerging and transitional markets, the use of the real and constant prices methodology could lead to serious mistakes in valuation.

There is no doubt that some decades ago, before the advent of the powerful computing capacity of personal computers, modeling the impacts of inflation in investment appraisal was an insurmountable task. Today, conducting investment appraisal by constructing financial statements with nominal prices is a simple and straightforward task. In this chapter, we would like to persuade the reader (if indeed there is need for persuasion) that conducting investment appraisal based on financial statements with real or constant prices is potentially misleading and under some conditions, the adverse effects of inflation could result in the selection of the "wrong" projects.

Estimated financial statements (i.e. Income Statement, Balance Sheet, cash budgets and free cash flows) are managerial tools that help the manager to control and follow up any activity. Financial statements at constant or real prices will be of no use when the project is implemented because what occurs in reality (that is what we are interested in) is very different from what is written in the final report of a project evaluation. Some items are deflated while others (say depreciation charges and interest payments) are in nominal prices. Hence, for managerial purposes, it is useless to have this mixed information in the financial statements.

We present some examples where we show that the value of a cash flow should be based on estimates of free cash flows at nominal prices. It is an accepted practice to evaluate

---

[1] This work is based on Vélez-Pareja 1999 and Vélez-Pareja, Tham 2002 and Vélez-Pareja, 2004b.

* E-mail adddress: ivelez@poligran.edu.co

projects at constant or real prices. These days, the use of constant or real prices is an unnecessary oversimplification of reality. In particular, we present an example where the results from the constant and real price methodologies are biased upwards and there is a risk that in practice, bad projects will be accepted as good projects. It is a third party and near real life example (an example presented in the training material on economic regulation of public utilities developed by the World Bank Institute) we compare the results of the constant prices methodology with results of the nominal prices methodology. World Bank (WB) has played a crucial role in the development of the economies of the world, especially in the emerging countries. We recognize the leadership it has shown and the intellectual authority it has on planning offices, practitioners and consultants. For this reason it is critical whatever improvements made in the methodologies it uses in assessing the feasibility of infrastructure projects. This influence affects private practice in valuation and project appraisal as well.

Vélez-Pareja in 1999 warned: "constant price methodology implies some assumptions and a mixture of items, some deflated, and some others not deflated". Vélez-Pareja 1999 and Vélez Pareja and Tham, 2002, warn about the overvaluation of a project when appraised at constant prices. On the other hand Tham and Vélez-Pareja 2004 mentioned the most frequent (and avoidable) mistakes when valuing cash flows.

We show how in the case based on the example from WB where they use some current practices several improvements to some areas of the model can be made, such as valuation at constant prices, mixing deflated and non-deflated items in a financial statements, using constant leverage when in the forecasted financial statements it is not constant, inconsistency in the cash flow and value calculations and some other irregularities that will be described in the body of the chapter. This analysis shows an overvaluation of more than 21% when the constant prices methodology is compared with the current prices methodology and using market values to calculate the WACC. This is a dramatic number.

Keywords: World Bank, regulatory policy for infrastructure, developing countries, project evaluation, project appraisal, firm valuation, cost of capital, cash flows, free cash flow, capital cash flow

JEL Classification: M21, M40, M46, M41, G12, G31, J33

> Setting up the cash flow of a project in nominal prices requires an inflation forecast. This is a difficult, if not impossible, task. (pg 42)
> Belli, P. et al.

> The difficult can be done immediately,
> the impossible takes a little longer.
> Army Corp of Engineers

INTRODUCTION

This chapter shows that when valuating cash flows they should be based on estimates of free cash flows at nominal prices. In particular, we show that results from the constant and real price methods are biased upwards and there is a risk that in practice, bad projects will be accepted as good projects or that the valuation of free cash flows for valuing firms is overstated. Generally speaking, inflation has a negative impact on the Net Present Value, NPV of a project. When expected inflation rates over the cash flow horizon are high, which is a typically case in emerging and transitional markets, the use of the real and constant prices methodology could lead to serious mistakes in valuation.

There is no doubt that some decades ago, before the advent of the powerful computing capacity of personal computers, modeling the impacts of inflation in investment appraisal was an insurmountable task. Today, conducting investment appraisal by constructing financial statements with nominal prices is a simple and straightforward task.[3]. In this chapter, we would like to persuade the reader (if indeed there is need for persuasion) that conducting investment appraisal based on financial statements with real or constant prices is potentially misleading and under some conditions, the adverse effects of inflation could result in the selection of the "wrong" projects.

Estimated financial statements (i.e. Income Statement, Balance Sheet, cash budgets and free cash flows) are managerial tools that help the manager to control and follow up any activity. Financial statements at constant or real prices will be of no use when the project is implemented because what occurs in reality (that is what we are interested in) is very different from what is written in the final report of a project evaluation. Some items are deflated while others (say depreciation charges and interest payments) are in nominal prices. Hence, for managerial purposes, it is useless to have this mixed information in the financial statements.

We present some examples where we show that the value of a cash flow should be based on estimates of free cash flows at nominal prices. It is an accepted practice to evaluate projects at constant or real prices. These days, the use of constant or real prices is an unnecessary oversimplification of reality. In particular, we present an example where the results from the constant and real price methodologies are biased upwards and there is a risk that in practice, bad projects will be accepted as good projects. It is a third party and near real life example (an example presented in the training material on economic regulation of public utilities developed by the World Bank Institute) we compare the results of the constant prices methodology with results of the nominal prices methodology. World Bank (WB) has played a crucial role in the development of the economies of the world, especially in the emerging countries. We recognize the leadership it has shown and the intellectual authority it has on planning offices, practitioners and consultants. For this reason it is critical whatever improvements made in the methodologies it uses in assessing the feasibility of infrastructure projects. This influence affects private practice in valuation and project appraisal as well.

Vélez-Pareja in 1999 warned: "constant price methodology implies some assumptions and a mixture of items, some deflated, and some others not deflated". Vélez-Pareja 1999 and Vélez Pareja and Tham, 2002, warn about the overvaluation of a project when appraised at constant prices. Some reactions to these assertions were that it was the construction of a straw man to destroy it. We wish that the constant and real prices approaches were a straw man. We have a very special case where the constant prices methodology is fully at work: the Financial Modeling of Regulatory Policy by the World Bank.

On the other hand Tham and Vélez-Pareja 2004 mentioned the most frequent (and avoidable) mistakes when valuing cash flows.

We show how in the case based on the example from WB where they use some current practices several improvements to some areas of the model[4] can be made, such as valuation at constant prices, mixing deflated and non-deflated items in a financial statements, using

[3] However, the proponents of investment appraisal with real and/or constant prices continue to preach the merits of their approach and the continued acceptance of the "real prices" approach to investment appraisal is puzzling, indefensible and inexcusable.

[4] This is an example included in the training material on economic regulation of public utilities developed by the World Bank Institute and it includes an interactive CD and various books. This material is used to train on the use of economic and financial models used in regulatory processes developed by the World Bank Institute.

constant leverage when in the forecasted financial statements it is not constant, inconsistency in the cash flow and value calculations and some other irregularities that will be described in the body of the chapter. This analysis shows an overvaluation of more than 21% when the constant prices methodology is compared with the current prices methodology and using market values to calculate the WACC. This is a dramatic number.

The analysis of the model is done based on the Excel file titled model.xls for electric infrastructure that is in a CD from International Bank for Reconstruction and Development – The World Bank 2002. In that reference we can find the paper by Estache et. al. 2002. We find some differences between what is said in the paper and what is done in the Excel file. For instance, they say that the weights in the calculation for the weighted average cost of capital WACC are based on the market values, but that is not reflected in the Excel file.

In this chapter we point out those areas where improvement can be made and suggest some refinements to improve the model and the practice.

The chapter is organized as follows. Section One describes the different approaches to valuation in the presence of inflation: nominal prices, real prices and constant prices methodologies. In Section Two we review the literature in the finance textbooks Also we discuss the common arguments for using the constant and real prices methodologies. In Section Three we analyze and present some conditions that have to be satisfied in order that the results by the three methods are the same. In Section Four we present the concept of tax savings, TS, and its relevance for the valuation of cash flows. In Section Five we present and critically analyze in detail the above mentioned example used by the World Bank for training purposes. In Section Six we reconstruct the WB example to properly calculate the value using nominal prices (assuming neutral inflation) and market values to calculate the WACC and compare it with the value calculated in the example at constant prices In Section Seven we conclude.

SECTION ONE: APPROACHES TO VALUATION IN AN INFLATIONARY ENVIRONMENT

There are three main approaches to project evaluation under inflation.

a. Nominal or current prices (actual estimated prices)
b. Real prices (non-neutral inflation, with estimates of changes in relative prices)
c. Constant prices (neutral inflation)

In the first method, the nominal prices approach, we estimate the actual prices for inputs and outputs over the cash flow horizon, construct the financial statements in nominal terms, and discount the nominal free cash flows with the nominal discount rate. In the second method, the real prices approach, we estimate the changes in relative prices for the inputs and outputs over the cash flow horizon, construct the financial statements in real terms, taking into account the changes in relative prices, and discount the real free cash flows with the real discount rate. The third method, the constant prices approach, is a special case of the real prices approach. It assumes that the changes in relative prices are zero, and discounts the real free cash flows with the real discount rate.

In the presence of inflation, the project analyst is faced with two formidable tasks. First, she must estimate the changes in relative prices for the inputs and outputs over the cash flow horizon. Second, she must estimate the expected inflation rates over the cash flow horizon. It is generally believed that estimating the expected inflation rates is more difficult than estimating changes in relative prices[5]. Without easy availability of computing power, it is understandable that analysts made simplifying assumptions to tackle the equally difficult tasks.

The constant price approach "solves" both of the difficult tasks by making one key assumption. Actually, it avoids the difficult tasks of estimating changes in relative prices and the expected inflation rates by assuming that there are no changes in relative prices and that there is no inflation. With this assumption, there are no changes in the real prices, and consequently, the financial statements are constructed in constant terms, and the free cash flows are discounted with the real discount rate. On the other hand, interest rates have to be considered without the inflationary component and hence, the discount rate will be the real rate of interest. This methodology sets an initial price for inputs and outputs and keeps them constant during the planning horizon. All this is equivalent to say that there is a neutral inflation.

The real prices approach recognizes that relative prices may change and solves the "easier" of the two tasks by estimating the changes in relative prices over the cash flow horizon and no inflation rates estimates. The analyst constructs the financial statements in real terms, taking into account the estimated changes in relative prices and discounts the real free cash flows with the real discount rate. The *constant dollar or real prices approach* estimates the increases in relative prices and discount future free cash flows at the real discount rate. This means that the financial model assumes that the actual prices will be modified in the future, but only in the differences between the inflation rates and the nominal increases in price. This means non-neutral inflation. As price increases do not include the inflationary component, interest rates have to be considered without the inflationary component and hence, the discount rate will be the real rate of interest. This methodology sets an initial price for inputs and outputs and applies the real increases to the initial prices, during the planning horizon.

The nominal prices approach tackles the two tasks head-on. It estimates the nominal prices for the inputs and outputs and the expected inflation rates over the planning horizon. In the days before personal computers, estimating changes in relative prices and the expected inflation rates required enormous computing resources. These days, with data and easily available computing power, both of these tasks are still difficult and should not be under-estimated. However, with computing power, we can conduct sensitivity and scenario analyses and examine the impacts of different scenarios for the expected inflation rates on the outcomes of the project. The *nominal or current prices approach* estimates prices for inputs and outputs and discount future free cash flows at the nominal discount rate. This means that the financial analyst tries to estimate the actual prices and interest rates that will occur in the future and based on the estimates, specifies and conducts the relevant scenario analyses.

---

[5] In many graduate and executive courses it is heard that if the discounting of the free cash flows is made with current prices, then the NPV will be inflated. This statement is wrong. When the free cash flows are discounted with a current or nominal rate of interest, the inflation effect is included in the discount rate. Then, when the discount procedure is applied to nominal figures the inflation effect is discounted. And the NPV is deflated in terms of inflation.

Next, we briefly discuss the appeal and some weaknesses of the constant prices and real prices methodologies. First, many analysts believe that all three approaches give the same results. Second, analysts believe that even if the results are not identical, the error in using the real or constant prices methods is sufficiently small and acceptable. Third, analysts believe that the "simplicity" of real or constant prices outweigh any marginal benefits of using the nominal prices approach. Fourth, analysts believe that it is too difficult to "forecast" future inflation rates and consequently, they prefer to do the analysis in real or constant terms. In Vélez-Pareja and Tham, 2002, they briefly comment on the strength of these reasons.

SECTION TWO: A REVIEW

The three methods look similar, and one would be tempted to assume that all three methods should give the same results. In fact, the authors of many textbooks assert that the nominal prices and real and constant prices approach give the same results, with one important caveat: The methods will give the same results as long as the nominal free cash flows are discounted with the nominal discount rate, and the real and constant free cash flows are discounted with the real discount rate. The cash flows and discount rates must be consistent, they say. If the free cash flows are nominal, then the discount rate must be nominal, and if the free cash flows are real, the discount rate must be real. The nominal cash flows should not be discounted with real discount rates[6]. However, simple consistency between the cash flows and the discount rate is not enough as will be proved in this chapter. The result is that in practice, -and this is more critical in economies with relative high rates of inflation- practitioners conduct project evaluation in the wrong manner.

For instance, Canada and White, 1996, suggest that it is necessary to be careful and to be consistent: discount nominal free cash flows with nominal discount rate, and discount real free cash flows with real discount rate. However, they recognize that taxes and depreciation introduce bias into the analysis.

Brealey, Myers and Marcus, 1996, say that the same NPV is obtained either with nominal free cash flows, discounted with the nominal discount rate, or real free cash flows discounted with the real discount rate. Again, they warn the reader not to mix real rates and nominal free cash flows and vice versa. They suggest that using real free cash flows, discounted with the real discount rate is equivalent to using nominal free cash flows discounted with the nominal discount rate. Furthermore, Brealey and Myers, 1995 and 2003, say it is not an error to discount the real free cash flows at the real discount rate even if it is not a usual procedure. They present an example where they show the equivalence between real and nominal prices and obtain the same NPV.

---

[6] It is useful to state the relationships between the nominal and real rates of interest. Nominal interest rates are observed in the economy. For instance, the nominal interest rates are the rates that are quoted when we go to the bank. There is a strong relationship between the expected inflation rates and nominal interest rates. We can say that the higher the expected inflation rate, the higher the nominal interest rate. The mathematical relationship, disregarding the risk premium included in any commercial interest rate, is 1 + nominal interest rate = (1 + real rate)(1 + inflation rate)

What is a real rate of interest? Imagine an economy with zero inflation and an investment with zero risk. The interest rate for the investment should be the real interest rate. If we know the nominal interest rate and the inflation rate (not risk premium), we could calculate the real rate of interest as follows by rearranging the above equation. *Real rate = (1 + nominal rate)/(1 + inflation rate) -1*

Ross et al. 1999, stress that nominal cash flows should be discounted with nominal rates and real cash flows with real rates. They use a very simple example to prove that the discounting process give the same results. Grinblatt and Titman, 2002, say the same.

Levy and Sarnat, 1995, say that the right answer is obtained with either approach (real or nominal) and the only caution required is not to mix up rates of interest and free cash flows. Again, this gives the impression that real prices and nominal prices give the same answer. However, they devote some effort to show that when taxes exist, depreciation introduces an upward bias when working with the constant approach.

Weston and Copeland, 1992, present a very detailed example to show that when there is no inflation (or there is neutral inflation) the results are the same. When inflation is not neutral, the results differ; however the reader may wrongly assume that the same decision is obtained. The example shows two positive NPV's and does not warn the reader that the final decision could be reversed with non-neutral inflation. In other words, a positive NPV project with neutral inflation could be a negative NPV project under non-neutral inflation.

Damodaran, 1996, presents an example that shows that it is equivalent to work with either approach (nominal and real) and warns the reader not to mix up rates and free cash flows.

Dixon and Hufschmidt, 1986, recognize that neutral inflation cannot be assumed (when working with constant prices) and they work with the increase in relative price or real prices. They think that the results are identical once the increases in relative prices are included.

Copeland, Koller and Murrin, 2000, say, "when done properly, the resulting value should be identical. (Nominal cash flows discounted at a nominal rate should equal the corresponding real cash flow discounted at the corresponding real rate.)" Again, this leaves the impression that the two methods are equivalent.

Belli et al, 2001 state that it is an impossible task to work with inflation rates forecasts.

Very few authors (Arzac[7], 2005, Van Horne, 1997, Vélez-Pareja, 1983, 1987, 1998, 1999, 2004a, Vélez-Pareja and Tham, 2002, and 2004 and Tham and Vélez-Pareja 2002, 2004a and 2004b) clearly commit to the right approach: future estimates for the free cash flows have to be made at nominal or current prices, and future free cash flows have to be discounted with the nominal rate of return. Mills 1996 tackle the issue of the bias for using constant cash flows and real discount rates.

The later positions are very significant. And they are important because practitioners have the idea (at least as it can be seen from the recommendations of financial institutions such as, the Inter American Development Bank, IADB and the World Bank, (WB) and domestic central banks) that the right procedure is the constant or the real price approach (in fact, the example we analyze is the one the WB uses for training purposes). The IADB and the WB support the constant dollar or constant price approach. Some economists argue that the constant price methodology could imply an increase in prices! ... relative prices. Obviously, this is contradictory and this alternative is analyzed below.[8]

---

[7] This author offers a website where inflation forecasts can be found (http://www.phil.frb.org/econ/spf/ index.html). However, he "shows" that valuating at nominal cash flows we obtain the same result as valuating with real cash flows; this is true as long as the cash flows are in nominal terms and then they are deflated as well as the discount rate. Of course it gives the same result because it means that we are dividing and multiplying every cash flow by the same amount, this is, $(1 + i_f)^j$, where i_f is inflation rate and j is the period. This is neither constant nor real prices methodology; this is just deflation of cash flows and discount rates.

[8] We wish to say, for the record, that some colleagues, economists, insist that constant price methodology does not imply increases in prices equals to 0%; they say that it should be called constant dollar methodology and not

On the other hand, there are many papers that have dealt with the issue since 1971. Van Horne, (1971) shows the bias when real cash flows are discounted with nominal discount rates (there are some rounding errors explained by the lack of tools like we have today). Cooley, Roenfeldt and Chew, (1975) consider that not introducing inflation in the analysis leads to suboptimal decisions and some bias will be encountered. Findlay, 1976 says "there is not theoretical justification to conduct to conduct analysis at the level of the firm in real terms". Nelson (1976) mentions that in an ideal world, with no taxes, introducing inflation in the analysis does not affect the calculated value. The NPV for ranking will depend on inflation. Bailey and Jensen (1977) show how when adjusting discount rates by inflation, the result of choosing among mutually exclusive alternatives is affected. Levy and Sarnat (1982) identify the bias from the tax savings generated by depreciation charges. Rappaport and Taggart, (1982) recognize three approaches: Gross profit per unit approach (constant prices?), nominal prices, and real prices. If there are no taxes, then the three are the same because there is not TD. They recognize that the value of tax savings from depreciation when calculated using the nominal prices approach is lower than the one calculated using the constant prices approach. They consider that real prices approach consists of forecasting nominal cash flows and deflating them by inflation. This is a similar view as Arzac's. They recognize as well, the declining value of TD with inflation. Ezzell and Kelly 1984, criticize the "rule" that all we need to find identical results among the different methods is consistency between cash flows and discount rates. They mention the effect of taxes on depreciation, this is, the tax savings. Mehta, Curley and Fung, 1984 say that given the presence o inflation, the nominal is more expedient that the constant. They also say that when we have neutral inflation all methods give identical results. Howe, (1992) recognizes that we have to include inflation in the analysis. He said that discounting real cash flows with real discount rates is seldom done (¡!). Mills, (1996) shows that when discounting with real and nominal (the proper cash flows) a bias arises. This bias occurs with the depreciation charges and the working capital.

There are slight and subtle differences among the three methods and as we will show in the subsequent sections, the three methods do not always give the same results. Under certain restrictive conditions and assumptions, it may be possible to derive the same results for all three methods. However, the special conditions and assumptions rarely hold in practice, and it would be unrealistic to assume that they do.

SECTION THREE: IMPLICIT ASSUMPTIONS FOR IDENTICAL NPVS

Next, we state and examine the conditions under which the three methods give the same values. (For details see Vélez-Pareja, 1999 and Vélez-Pareja and Tham 2002).

---

constant price methodology. And therefore, the analyst could consider changes in prices, relative prices. We insist: constant prices methodology implies to keep prices constant and constant dollars implies to deflate prices using a deflator, such as the Consumer Price Index. And this procedure might leave implicit the increase in relative prices. Also, we insist there has been a worldwide and generalized use of the constant price approach. We think this is wrong. In this chapter we study the problem associated to the use of these wrong procedures. It has to be said again, that *constant price methodology implies that initial -year 0- prices do not change*; *constant dollar methodology* is different from the former and it *assumes that prices do change* and this change is reflected in what is called, *relative prices. We do emphasize on the analysis and criticism of the constant price methodology, because it is well spread and its use is very common. This use is privileged not only in social project evaluation, but also in private or financial project evaluation.*

1. *No taxes.*
2. *All cash excess* is distributed to the equity and debt holders.
3. *Price increases that actually occur (current or nominal) will be equal to the inflation rate,* included in the current or nominal discount rate.
4. *Income and payments* for goods and services are in cash, *no credit.*
5. *No salvage or terminal value.*
6. There is no *price-demand elasticity* effect.
7. The *discount rate* at current or nominal prices is exactly equal to *(1+ real rate of interest)(1+ inflation rate)-1* and at constant or real prices, the discount rate has to be equal to ir, the real rate of interest.
8. The cost of debt, Kd must be *deflated.*

Now, each of these assumptions or conditions necessary to guarantee that the NPV calculated by the three methodologies, constant, real and nominal price will be identical will be reviewed.

1. No taxes

When taxes are included in the analysis, depreciation and interest charges give rise to a tax shield[9], TS, which affects the project. The depreciation charges would be identical -in absolute values- for both methodologies, *but* the relative value is greater with constant prices than with current or nominal prices. Hence, the project would be overvalued, because earnings before taxes are undervalued and then taxes will be lower. If it is assumed that there are taxes, then in order to match the NPV's values, it has to be assumed that there is no depreciation and no interest is paid for the financing of the project. Conversely, if there is depreciation and the project is financed with debt, in order to obtain identical results between the NPVs for each methodology, we have to assume that there are no taxes. Some people have realized this and then they propose to deflate the *depreciation*! This procedure lacks any economic meaning and cannot be implemented unless the future inflation rates are estimated and that is the main feature of the method: to avoid the estimation of inflation rates.

No taxes imply also that any effect of losses carried forward is null in the analysis. When the law allows carrying losses forward there is a recovery of tax shield or tax savings. In this case, with the assumption of no taxes, those benefits are lost. In the analysis with constant prices, the taxes are calculated with a mix of constant and non- constant figures and the tax savings recovered with the losses carried forward is also distorted.

Also, the distortions in the magnitude of revenues and expenses affect taxes. These distortions are created by several factors, among which are the depreciation and the difference in revenues and expenses that were mentioned previously. The value of the upward bias favoring real or constant valuation is as follows.

Depreciation charges are a deducible expense; hence they generate a TS of T × Dep. But the value of the depreciation charge is not affected by the methodology of constant or nominal prices. The present value PV is quite different if we use constant or nominal prices. This difference is one of the sources of overvaluation found in a constant price methodology appraisal.

Next we show how the difference in the value of TS arises.

---

[9] Some special effects and consequences of tax shields will be discussed in a next section.

$$PV(TS_{dep})_{const} = \sum_{j=1}^{N} \frac{T \times D}{(1+i_{real})^j} \tag{1a}$$

$$PV(TS_{dep})_{nom} = \sum_{j=1}^{N} \frac{T \times D}{(1+i_{nominal})^j} \tag{1b}$$

Since $i_{nominal} > i_{real}$, then

$$PV(TS_{dep})_{const} \rangle PV(TS_{dep})_{nom} \tag{1c}$$

and

$$PV(TS_{dep})_{const} - PV(TS_{dep})_{nom} \rangle 0 \tag{1d}$$

As

$$(1 + i_{nominal}) = (1 + i_{real})(1 + i_f) \tag{1e}$$

Then

$$PV(TS)_{constant} - PV(TS)_{nominal} = \sum_{t=1}^{n} \frac{T \times D_t}{(1+i_{real})^t} - \sum_{t=1}^{n} \frac{T \times D_t}{(1+i_{real})^t (1+i_f)^t} \tag{1f}$$

where $PV(TS_{dep})$ is the value of the tax savings for depreciation at constant prices and nominal prices (according to the subindex), $i_{nominal}$ is the nominal interest rate, i_{real} is the real interest rate, i_f is the inflation rate.

With non-neutral inflation, the difference between the PV(TS)'s is higher than with neutral inflation. Here it can be seen that in this case a project valued at constant prices is overvalued compared with the same project valued at current or nominal prices. It is possible to accept bad projects as good projects. Many times, we do not know why a project that was seen as attractive, becomes a failure when implemented. The use of constant prices might be one explanation for this. We believe, without formal empirical data[10], that many projects, both public and private, become failures because they have been accepted with a NPV calculated with the constant or real prices methodology, and if they had been evaluated with current or nominal prices information, they might have been rejected.

[10] We have some informal, anecdotal evidence about this. In 1986 the author taught a course in an in-company graduate program for the major ironworks factory in Colombia and tested this hypothesis with two real projects that became failures. They reconstructed the analysis with the data that were available at the time the study was made with constant and nominal prices. The final results at nominal prices showed that the project should be rejected whereas the analysis with constant prices was positive. In this chapter we show the case of World Bank example.

The expression for the difference is very simple and elegant, but it is valid in a very restricted context, as mentioned previously. One could try to make an adjustment to the constant prices result, subtracting the amount defined above, but the problem is that it only could be made if the result at current prices -NPV_I- is known! In fact, beforehand, it is not known whether the firm will get the tax savings (the tax shield at constant and/or current prices). This is known only when the pro-forma financial statements with constant and current prices are estimated. And in order to know this, we have to estimate inflation and the financial pro-forma statements. It is necessary to know if the project (the firm) has enough revenues to offset the depreciation charges. And to avoid this was one of the purposes of the methodology at constant prices or dollars.

The effect of depreciation charges upon the NPV at constant prices compared with nominal prices can be seen in the next table.

If real interest rate is 6%, inflation rate is 10% and the relative increase in prices and costs is 1%, then the discount rate is 16.6%. The price and cost increase in nominal terms is 11.1%. Taxes are 40%. A simplified Income statement is shown below.

Table 1a. Income Statement at Constant and Nominal Prices.

	Constant prices		**Nominal prices**		**Increase for each item**
Sales	100.00	100.0%	111.10	100.0%	11.1%
Expenses	50.00	50.0%	55.55	50.0%	11.1%
Depreciation	10.00	10.0%	10.00	9.0%	0.0%
Earnings before taxes	40.00	40.0%	45.55	41.0%	13.9%
Taxes	16.00	16.0%	18.22	16.4%	13.9%
Net Income	24.00	24.0%	27.33	24.6%	13.9%

Observe how the relative weight of depreciation is greater for constant prices and hence the earnings before taxes is relatively less at constant prices than at nominal prices. And taxes have a lower proportion or weight in constant than in nominal prices. This is the reason for the bias.

If we assume that all transactions are made in cash and taxes are paid the same year, the cash flow will be as follows.

Table 1b. Comparison of Cash Flows.

Cash flow	**Constant prices**	**Nominal prices**
Year 1	34.00	37.33
Present value at the proper discount rate	$32.08	$32.02

The cash flow for constant prices is Net income plus depreciation charges, 34.00 (24 + 10) and the present value of it at real rate is 32.08 (34/1.06) The case of real prices (constant dollars) is similar.

Table 2a. Income Statement at Real and Nominal Prices.

	Real prices		Nominal prices		Increase for each item
Sales	101.00	100.00%	111.1	100.00%	10.00%
Expenses	50.50	50.00%	55.55	50.00%	10.00%
Depreciation	10.00	9.90%	10.00	9.00%	0.00%
Earnings before taxes	40.50	40.10%	45.55	41.00%	12.47%
Taxes	16.20	16.04%	18.22	16.40%	12.47%
Net Income	24.30	24.06%	27.33	24.60%	12.47%

Observe the different weights of depreciation and taxes. Again, if all transactions are on a cash basis and taxes are paid in the same period, then, the cash flow will be as follows:

Table 2b. Comparison of Cash Flows.

Cash flow	Real prices	Nominal prices
Year 1	34.3	37.33
Present value at the proper discount rate	$32.36	$32.02

Observe in both cases that the relative weight of the depreciation charges is larger for constant prices or dollars and that is directly related to the lower tax payments, and hence, the present value is affected.

Adjustments for inflation in the financial statements intend to correct this bias. Part of this difference could be offset if the evaluation is made at constant prices with taxes calculated *without* taking into account the adjustment for inflation in the financial statements *and* the evaluation at current or nominal prices is made *taking into account* those adjustments. However, this adjustment might not be enough. If the projects to be compared are different in fixed assets capital intensity, then the difference *increases*. As we suggest below, the practice of adjustment for inflation to the financial statements is decreasing and is discretional in many countries.

2. All cash excess is distributed to the equity and debt holders.

There is huge evidence that firms hold cash in hand and invested in market securities and there are many reasons that explain this behavior. [11]. In reality, this is not always possible and in the general case, it is not. When the evaluation of a cash flow is worked out with a spreadsheet, the cash surpluses are invested at the market rates[12]. To ensure that the reinvestment is at the "correct" discount rate, we have to eliminate the option to invest cash surpluses. In this way, when the future free cash flows are discounted, the discount procedure automatically assumes that reinvestment rates are equal to discount rates when in fact the excess cash is distributed.

---

[11] There is strong evidence on this; see the most cited and known authors in the area (Almeida et al, Baumol, Blanchard, Bruner, Faulkender et al. Fazzari, et al, Jensen et al., La Porta et al., Mikkelson et al., Myers, et al., Opler et al., Ozkan et al, Pinkwitz et al.).

[12] This can be seen in the discount procedure as follows: when cash flows are paid to equity holders and debt holders, they invest these cash flows minimum at their required discount rate. The discounting process assumes that they invest the cash flows at the same rate they require for their investment (this means, at their cost of capital).

In general, the interest rate at which the cash surpluses can be invested is different from $(1+i_f)(1+i_r)-1$[13], which is the discount rate that should be applied when working at current or nominal prices.

This assumption also means that there is no minimum cash requirement (MCR) has to be zero or if there is some MCR, then the following relationship has to hold:

$$\frac{MCR_K}{MCR_{nom}} = \frac{1}{(1+i_f)^n} \tag{6}$$

where MCR is the minimum cash requirement at constant or real prices or at nominal prices (nom), i_f is the inflation rate and n is the period.

3. The price increases that actually occur (current or nominal) will be equal to the inflation rate or the relative or real increases are zero, included in the current or nominal discount rate.

This situation is known as neutral inflation, in which all prices and costs increase at the same rate and it is the inflation rate. This situation is completely unrealistic. Everyday we observe that the changes in the price are different from changes in inflation. In fact, the inflation rate, measured by the Consumer Price Index, CPI, is a weighted average of the increases of a great variety of products and services. Some authors, as mentioned above, recognize this fact and they propose to work with the *increase in relative prices.* This solution is not sufficient to solve the problem, because it is not the only source of discrepancy between the two methodologies.

Now we explain why it is believed that valuing with constant prices is identical with valuing at real prices, given that we do not mix real rates with nominal cashflows and viceversa. We have to bear in mind the Fisher Equation that relates the nominal interest rate, the real interest rate and the inflation rate (see footnote).

Where i_c is the nominal interest rate, i_r, is the real interest rate, and i_f, is the inflation rate.

Then two inflows, one at nominal prices and the other one at constant prices (or what is the same, *with* 0% increase in prices) will satisfy this relationship, given that the price increases are equal to the inflation rate:

$$Ic_{t+1} = Ik_t(1+i_a) \tag{2a}$$

$$Ik_t = \frac{Ic_{t+1}}{1+i_f} = \frac{Ik_t(1+i_a)}{1+i_f} \tag{2b}$$

When discounted,

$$\frac{Ik_t}{(1+i_r)} = \frac{Ic_{t+1}}{(1+i_f)(1+i_r)} = \frac{Ik_t(1+i_a)}{(1+i_r)(1+i_f)} \tag{2c}$$

[13] It has to be remembered that the relationship between the nominal or current interest rate and the real rate is given by $(1+i_c) = (1+i_r)(1+i_f)$. This is known as the Fisher Equation.

Then, the equality holds, if and only if $i_a=i_f$ and $Ik_{(t)} = Ik_{(t+1)}$ (this means constant prices), this is.

$$\frac{Ic_{t+1}}{(1+i_f)(1+i_r)} = \frac{Ik_t(1+i_a)}{(1+i_r)(1+i_f)} = \frac{Ik_t}{(1+i_r)} \quad (2.d)$$

Donde Ik es el ingreso neto a precios constantes; Ic, el ingreso neto a precios corrientes o nominales; i_f, la tasa de inflación; i_a, la tasa de aumento en los precios, e i_c, la tasa de interés corriente o nominal.
where:

Ik	= Net cash inflow at constant prices
Ic	= Net cash inflow at current or nominal prices
i_f	= Inflation
i_a	= Rate of increase in prices
i_c	= nominal or current rate of interest

This is the typical "proof" we find in financial textbooks and is the reason why some authors claim the NPV at constant prices is identical to NPV at current or nominal prices. If the inflation rate and the rate of increase of prices are not equal, then there will be some gains or some losses that are not taken into account when the NPV is computed with the constant price methodology.[14]

4. *Income and payments for goods and services are in cash and there are no credit transactions.*

This is an ideal situation. If there is some credit given or received, the firm has to adjust for inflation the constant price figures (the amount of credit received from the suppliers or given to the customers). This implies that we must estimate inflation rates and to avoid this was one of the reasons to use the constant prices methodology.

Let us analyze what happens when payments and/or income (or part of them) are on credit. *Any* firm in its regular operation registers accounts receivable and accounts payable. If in the estimated cash flow those amounts are not adjusted by inflation, the two NPV (calculated at constant and at current prices) will not be identical.

Simple algebra operations explain this. It can be shown that when a firm grants credit, the present value of the total sales (on credit and on cash) is the same (with constant or nominal price analysis) when the following conditions are met:

1. No credit or no nominal discount rate, but real discount rate and hence there would not be a nominal price situation, or
2. The firm grants credit for 100% and all the funds are received in the future and there is an adjustment of (1+inflation rate) for one year that cancels out with the discount

[14] Gains in the case that the increase of income be greater than inflation and/or that the increase of expenses be lower than inflation and losses in the case that the increase of expenses be greater than inflation and/or that the increase of income be lower than inflation.

rate equal to (1+real rate of interest)(1+inflation rate)-1. Or there is no inflation or price increase in price at nominal prices (it means then constant prices).

Assume we have an amount today (say, the actual invoicing), Io. This amount will be receiveed as follows: today we receive Io(1–λ) and the remaining in the next period. λ is the fraction of the invoicing sold on a credit basis. Its present value is as follows.

At constant prices:

$$PV_K = Io \times (1 - \lambda) + \frac{Io \times \lambda}{(1 + i_r)} \tag{11.12}$$

At nominal or current prices:

$$PV_C = Io \times (1 - \lambda) + \frac{Io \times \lambda}{(1 + i_r)(1 + i_f)} \tag{11.13}$$

The inflation rate is i_f, the real discount rate is i_r, PV_C and PV_k are the nominal and constant present values. The difference is:

$$PV_K - PV_C = \frac{Io \times \lambda}{(1 + i_r)} - \frac{Io \times \lambda}{(1 + i_r)(1 + i_f)} \tag{11.14}$$

$$PV_K - PV_C = \frac{Io \times \lambda}{(1 + i_r)} \times \left(1 - \frac{1}{1 + i_f}\right) = \frac{Io \times \lambda}{(1 + i_r)} \times \left(\frac{i}{1 + i_f}\right) \tag{11.15}$$

This difference is the overvaluation. In the case of accounts payable the result will be an undervaluation. The net result will depend on the working capital structure.

A very simple example illustrates how the PVs under the two methods do not match:

Table 3a. Effect of Sales on Cash in the Present Value.

Sales 100% in cash	Year 1
Real rate of interest	12%
Inflation rate	20%
Current or nominal prices	$120
Current discount rate	1.12x 1.2 - 1 = 34.4%
Present Value at current prices	$120/1.344 = $89.286
Constant prices	$100
Constant discount rate	12%
Present Value at constant prices	$100/1.12 = $89.286

The present value is identical because the increase in prices is equal to the inflation rate, i. e. 20%. If a fraction of sales were on credit, we will have:

Table 3b. Effect of Sales on Credit in the Present Value.

Sales 90% in cash	Year 1	Year 2
Current prices	$108	$12
Present value at current prices	$108/1.344 = $80.357	$12/(1.344)^2 = $6.643
Total present value	87.0	
Constant prices	$90	$10
Present value at constant prices	$90/1.12= 80.357	10/(1.12)^2 = 7.972
Total present value	88.329	

The two present value figures do not coincide.

As it was said above, if the adjustment for *inflation* is made to the cash budget, then the two figures are identical. With the same example,

Table 3c. Comparison of Present Value.

	Year 1	Year 2
Current prices	$108	$12
Present value at current prices	$108/1.344 = $80.357	$12/(1.344)^2 = $6.643
Total present value	$87.000	
Constant prices	$90	$10/(1.20) = $8.333
Present value at constant prices	$90/1.12= 80.357	$8.333/(1.12)^2 = $6.643
Total present value	$87.000	

In this example the adjustment was done with the inflation rate. In strict sense, those adjustments should be made with the estimated changes in prices. In this example it is assumed that the changes in prices are equal to the inflation rate.

In Vélez-Pareja 1999 and Vélez-Pareja and Tham 2002, they mention an extensive example, where the NPV is calculated at constant and at current or nominal prices and all the assumptions and conditions mentioned here are included. The unique case in which the three NPV are identical is when those conditions are fulfilled.

To see how important the policy for the management of accounts receivable might be consider the following. If in the example mentioned in the previous paragraph the proportion of accounts receivable collected in the same year of invoicing increases 1% (goes from 95% to 95.95%), the NPV increases 1.3% and in the case for the accounts payable, the NPV will be reduced in –1.17%. A similar analysis could be made for a very important item: salvage value.

5. No salvage value.

Depending on the cash flow horizons, terminal value might account for a relevant fraction of total value, it might range from 25% to 90% or more. In case the terminal or salvage value is included, the relationship between the terminal or salvage value at current or nominal prices and constant prices should be equal to $(1+i_f)^n$, *where* if is equal to the inflation rate. In general, that proportion should be the cumulative effect of the inflation, taking into account the fact that those inflation rates might be different for each period.

The relationship between terminal values should be at any time n, $TV_{nominal}/TV_{constant} = (1+i_f)^n$

6. There is no price-demand elasticity effect.

If the analyst works with constant prices and the elasticity is defined as the sensitivity of the demand to price variations, there is no real increase in prices and the model will not catch those variations (favorable or not).

In order to adjust the figures for this situation, the elasticity function has to consider zero inflation for the constant price case and the increases in relative prices should be equal to

$$\frac{1+\text{price increase at current prices}}{1+\text{inflation rate}} - 1 \tag{3}$$

If relative increase in prices is calculated as in equation (3), the elasticity adjustment factor will be equal with both methodologies, for *instance*, as follows[15]:

For current prices:

$$1-\beta\left[\frac{(1+\text{increase in current prices})}{(1+i_f)}-1\right] \tag{4a}$$

$$1-\beta\left[\frac{(1+(1+i_f)(1+\text{increase in relative prices})-1)}{(1+i_f)}-1\right] \tag{4b}$$

$$=1-\beta[(1+\text{increase in relative prices})-1] \tag{4c}$$

$$=1-\beta\times\text{increase in relative prices} \tag{4d}$$

where β is the elasticity for the output and i_f is the inflation rate.

For constant prices this adjustment factor is 1, because the increase in relative prices is zero.

7. The discount rate at current or nominal prices has to be exactly equal to (1+ ir)(1+ if)-1 and at constant and real prices the discount rate has to be equal to ir, the real rate of return.

We could offset this assumption by noting that the current or nominal *discount* rates should be deflated with the inflation rate. And those discount rates include the risk perceived by others, namely, the creditors and stockholders. Then, the discount rate at constant prices would not be ir, but,

---

[15] This is the hypothetical elasticity function utilized in the extensive example (mentioned in Vélez-Pareja, 1999 and in Tham and Vélez-Pareja, 2004)).

$$i_{df} = \frac{1+i_{cr}}{1+i_f} - 1 \quad (5)$$

where idf is the deflated discount rate and *icr* is the current discount rate, risk premium included and i_f is the inflation rate.

This disregards what has been said near 50 years ago by Modigliani and Miller that the cost of capital depends on the market value of the firm or project and the risk of the equity holder depends on the leverage at market prices.

8. The cost of debt Kd, has to be deflated. The cost of debt might be linked to the inflation rate. In any case, when the cost of debt is not constant, the inflation rate for future years has to be forecasted.

These eight *conditions* have to be included in all the analyses –constant, real and current or nominal prices- in order to obtain identical values with all methodologies[16]. And the adjustments to be made are of such complexity that the supposed simplification of the constant price methodology is eliminated. In addition, the adjustments require the estimation of the expected inflation rate and one of the reasons for using the constant price approach was to "avoid" the estimation of the expected inflation rate! The conclusion is that when evaluating projects the current prices have to be estimated and the constant price and constant dollar methodologies have to be rejected.

SECTION FOUR: TAX SAVINGS (TS) AND ITS RELEVANCE IN VALUATION

The tax savings are a subsidy that the government gives to the firm (or individual, depending on the tax law) every time an expense is listed in the Income Statement. In the case of a firm there is a particular interest in the financial expenses because they affect the discount rate. The TS are the difference between taxes paid without the expense and the taxes paid with the expense. In general, an expense after taxes is the expense before taxes (E) times (1-T) and the tax savings are E×T. In the case of financial expenses the expense is (in the most general and simple case) TKdD; in the case of depreciation charge it is T × Dep. When a firm earns a tax saving on interest charges? Only when there are enough earnings (Earnings Before Interest and Taxes, EBIT) to offset the interest expense and when the firm pays the taxes.

It might seem that the tax savings are earned if the firm pays taxes or not. No. It is misleading. The critical value is if there is enough EBIT to offset the financial expense. We can explain this idea with two simple situations:

1. EBIT > Interest payments
2. EBIT < Interest payments

---

[16] For the numerical example where this holds see Vélez-Pareja 1999 and Vélez-Pareja and Tham 2002.

Table 4a. Tax savings when EBIT > Interest payments.

	Levered	Not levered
EBIT	200	200
Interest payments	150	0
Net Income before taxes	50	200
Tax rate 40%	20	80
Net Income	30	120
TS = difference in taxes	60	0

In this case the TS is TKdD. TS are earned if there is enough EBIT and when taxes are paid. The difference in taxes is 60, so it is the tax savings. Observe that the TS is T × Interest payments = 40% × 150 = 60, as well.

As the financial expenses increased in 150 the first reaction of the reader might be that the Net Income will be reduced by 150. However, a close look to the previous table tells us the reduction in Net income is only 90. What happened? The answer is very simple. The firm received a subsidy from the Government. The expense after taxes is E×(1-T) = 150(1−40%) = 90. This means that there are tax savings for the amount of 60.

An expense in a firm with enough income generates tax savings equal to the expense E times the tax rate, this is, the tax savings are T × E. If expenses are increased by 150 that amount results in 90 after taxes because the tax savings of 40%×150 and 150 – 60 is 90.

In the second case we have:

Table 4b. Tax savings when EBIT < Interest payments.

	Levered	Not levered
EBIT	100	100
Interest payments	150	0
Net Income before Taxes	-50	100
Tax rate 40%	0	40
Net Income	-50	60
TS = difference between tax payments	40	0

Observe now that the tax savings are not T × Interest payments = 40% × 150 = 60 but 40. This happens because there is not enough EBIT to offset the financial expense. In this case the TS earned in the year is T × EBIT = 40% × 100.

It should be said that this is a very important issue. When EBIT is less than the interest charges the tax savings are not the tax rate times the interest. The rule for this situation is:

If EBIT > Interest payments, then TS = T × Interest payments (7a)

If 0 < EBIT < Interest payments Then TS = T × EBIT (7b)

If EBIT < 0 then TS = 0 (7c)

The TS "lost" in one period can be recovered in future periods if losses carried forward are allowed (as they are in the WB example we study below).

The traditional Weighted Average Cost of Capital, WACC = Kd × D% × (1 − T) + Ke × E% applies only to case 1 if taxes are paid the same year as they are accrued. This is a very special and particular case. It is a particular case of a more general formulation (see Vélez-Pareja and Burbano 2003 and Tham y Vélez-Pareja, 2004):

$$WACC_{adjusted} = Ku_i - \frac{TS_i}{V^L_{i-1}} - (Ku_i - \psi_i)\frac{V^{TS}_{i-1}}{V^L_{i-1}} \tag{8}$$

Where TS is the tax savings, ψ is the discount rate for the TS, Ku is the unlevered cost of equity, V is the total value and V^{TS} is the value of the future tax savings.

Let us explain how the (1−T) factor in the traditional WACC works. Assume a loan of 1,000 at year 0 to be paid at year 1 at a rate of 30% per annum. The tax rate is 40%.

Table 5a. A loan with taxes paid the same year as accrued.

Year	Loan	TS	Net Cash Flow
0	1,000		1,000
1	-1,300	120	-1,180
Kd (Before Taxes)	30%	Kd (After Taxes)	18%

If the tax rate T is 40%, then TS is 120 (300 × 40%). In the previous table we have taxes paid the same year and the TS is totally earned in the same year. Then Kd after taxes is Kd(1-T) = 30% × 60% = 18%. In this case the use of the factor (1−T) is straightforward.

If the taxes are paid the next year we will have the following:

Table 5b. A loan with taxes paid the next year as accrued.

Year	Loan	TS	Net Cash Flow
0	1,000		1,000
1	−1,300		−1,300
2		120	120
Kd before tax	30%	Kd after tax	20%

In this case Kd after taxes is not Kd(1-T). Hence in cases such the one we have presented in the previous table the traditional WACC formulation cannot be used.

The widespread use of the traditional formula for WACC, without taking into account this fact, ends in an underestimation of WACC and hence, in an overvaluation of the value of the cash flows.

In the next section, using the WB example, it will be shown that the constant price approach changes the decision: a bad project becomes a good project, just by changing the methodology of analysis.

SECTION FIVE: THE WORLD BANK CASE

In this section we present and critically analyze the example the World Bank has published for training purposes.

Description of the Model

Regarding the WB example we briefly describe the characteristics of the example used to train in valuation. This model deals with the calculation of a proper value for the tariff for the distribution of electric energy in such a way that the net present value of the cash flow for twenty years is zero.

In this model they use the constant prices methodology and discount the cash flows with a real (deflated) constant weighted average cost of capital (WACC). They construct the forecasted Income Statement and the Balance Sheet. From these financial statements they derive the free cash flow FCF and the cash flow to equity CFE.

Common Practice

Tham and Vélez-Pareja 2004 show the most frequent, unnecessary and avoidable mistakes in valuation and Vélez-Pareja and Burbano-Perez 2003 show the required consistency in cash flows and values when valuing a firm. We will examine the above mentioned case of the World Bank pointing out some common practices that contradict or confirm what is said in these two papers and in other theoretical texts such as the work of Modigliani and Miller (1958, 1959 and 1963). In the body of this chapter we show the issue and the reader should go to the appendix where we present the numbers that support our assertion.

In order to gain insight into the relevance of including the forecasted inflation rate in the analysis we have to ask a simple question: does inflation create or destroy value?

1. If it creates value we should encourage it.
2. If it is innocuous, then we should not worry about it.
3. If it destroys value, we should combat it.

It is not difficult to accept that inflation destroys value. When valuing at constant prices value is not affected by inflation because it is out of the analysis. When valuing at nominal prices inflation is taken into account in the cash flows and the discount rates.

Most authors warn that the only care it has to be taken is to be consistent. This is, use nominal discount rates if the cash flows are nominal and real discount rate if cash flows are real, as mentioned above. If that is true, then inflation will not affect value because it is taken into account in that rule. However, inflation destroys value: the greater the inflation rate, the lower the value. Then, when valuing at constant prices (that does not take into account the inflation) there is an overvaluation because the value at nominal prices (that takes into account the inflation) decreases as long as the inflation rate increases (and in constant prices the value is invariable with inflation). This means that when inflation is present the difference between the value at constant prices and nominal prices is different from zero and that difference will increase with the inflation rate.

Valuation with Constant Prices Methodology

When using the constant prices methodology we can incur in some typical practices that distort the calculated value: the amount of the depreciation charge is not affected by the constant price methodology and it undervalues the tax charges and hence overvalues the value calculation. The same effect occurs when we have accounts receivable AR, as it is the case in the WB example. The overvaluation due to the depreciation is 6.61% and the overvaluation due to the AR is 6.37%. As there are no accounts payable (AP) in the case and hence, we have not estimated the over or undervaluation due to AP. (See Appendix 1).

We have calculated the overvaluation due to the depreciation charges using the tax savings from that item (this is, T × Dep) and discounted it using the nominal cost of capital (WACCN) and using the real cost of capital (WACC). The difference is the overvaluation.

In the case of AR we included inflation to adjust the sales for every year (this means that we assumed neutral inflation as is implicit in the constant prices methodology) and discounted the real AR and the nominal AR with the WACC and the WACCN respectively. The difference in the discounted values is the overvaluation.

When adjustments for inflation are included in the financial statements the effect of the tax savings for depreciation charges might be modified and eventually the overvaluation might disappear. In the case of AR if some interest is charged to the AR, then the overvaluation might disappear if the interest is identical to the inflation rate[17]. If not, the differences will persist. In the next table we show the over (under)valuation given the "interest" charged to AR. Inflation in the WB example is 3.5%.

Table 6. Over(under)valuation for an "interest" charged on AR.

"Interest" charged on AR	Over(under)valuation due to AR
0.0%	6.37%
0.5%	5.47%
1.0%	4.57%
1.5%	3.67%
2.0%	2.76%
2.5%	1.84%
3.0%	0.92%
3.5%	0.00%
4.0%	−0.93%
4.5%	−1.86%
5.0%	−2.80%
5.5%	−3.75%

[17] It is possible that in many regulatory situations the charge of some interest (or some sort of indexation) is allowed. However, it has to be defined (in the model) if the indexation is based on an amount lower or higher or equal to the inflation rate.

In the case of accounts payable AP, the result might be the opposite.

In general we should say that neutral inflation does not occur in reality. There is some real increase (positive and in some cases negative) that is not captured when constant prices methodology is used. And the net result will depend on the magnitude of and the items affected by them. This means that constant prices methodology might disguise the positive or negative effects of the real change in prices for inputs and outputs.

It has to be said that when applying adjustments for inflation to the financial statements there might be some charges related to the equity (all this might depend on the way the adjustments are designed) and these charges generate a tax savings associated to the equity[18]. In addition, it has to be said that not all the countries allow the adjustments for inflation to the financial statements. Usually these adjustments are done when hyperinflation is present. In a working paper from the World Bank by Goldschmidt and Yaron, 1991, it is said that " The Bank's draft Operational Directive on Financial Sector Operations requires the adjustment of financial statements in countries where the cumulative inflation rate over three years approaches or exceeds 100 percent."[19] This means that some or many countries might not allow inflation adjustments to the financial statements. More, the fact that the WB "requires the adjustment of financial statements" does not mean that the country where the valuation is performed will adopt the inflation adjustments and the distorting effects disappear. The distorting effects exist because reality is different of what is modeled when constant prices methodology is used. The adjustments reduce the distorting effects only if they really happen when the project is operating.

In fact, some of the criteria for defining hyperinflation (one of the conditions to adopt adjustment of the financial statements) are (According to international accounting standards)[20]:

1. In general the people prefer to keep non monetary assets or foreign exchange.
2. In general, the people have as reference in prices not the local currency, but the foreign exchange.
3. Sales and purchases on credit have prices that compensate the loss in purchasing power of the local currency.
4. Interest rates, wages and prices are linked directly to the price index, and
5. The cumulated inflation rate during 3 years is near or above 100%.

It can be predicted that financial statements adjusted for inflation will disappear in the near future and will be replaced by an accounting system not based on historical prices but based on fair values. In fact, some countries like Argentina and Colombia eliminated or will eliminate the inflation adjustments to financial statements in the near future. Right now the practice of inflation adjustments is not homogeneous and some countries do not apply them; others use integral adjustments and other use partial adjustments. Clearly the case we are studying in this chapter does not comply with the general criteria where inflation adjustments are expected.

[18] See Vélez-Pareja and Tham, 2004.

[19] In the example we work out, inflation rate is 3.5%, and the cumulative for even 10 years is far away from the standard stated by the WB.

[20] From private correspondence with Professor Samuel Mantilla at Universidad Javeriana, Bogotá.

It might be argued that converting initial costs and prices to a foreign currency makes it correct to work in constant prices (using U.S. dollars, for instance). That is true if the revenues and costs occur in the foreign currency or if there is perfect purchasing power parity and the inflation rate in the foreign economy is zero. In other words, that the increase in price of the item is equal to the change in price of the foreign exchange. It is easy to show that if some costs are denominated in local currency (say payroll expenses) and increase say, 25% per annum and the change in price for the foreign currency is 15% per annum, then considering constant prices in foreign currency the costs might be underestimated. This is shown in the next table.

Table 7. Items in foreign currency and domestic currency.

Year	1	2	3
Payroll expenses in domestic currency	10,000,000.00	12,500,000.00	15,625,000.00
Foreign exchange rate	1,000.00	1,150.00	1,322.50
Payroll expenses in constant foreign currency	10,000.00	10,000.00	10,000.00
Payroll expenses in nominal foreign currency	10,000.00	10,869.57	11,814.74
Increase of payroll expenses in foreign currency		8.70%	8.70%

For instance, the payroll payment for year 2 in nominal foreign exchange is derived as 12,500,000/1,1150 = 10,869.57. Observe that payroll expenses in constant foreign exchange have no increase (constant prices) while the same expense converted from domestic currency to foreign exchange has an increase of 8.7%.

This simple numerical example shows how when using constant foreign exchange when some items are spent in local currency, might generate critical distortions. Hence, assuming a foreign currency and constant prices might produce some divergence in values if not considered the relationship between devaluation and domestic inflation.

We agree with, Coello, et. al. (2003) when they say: "In reality, a firm will base its investment decisions on expected prices, which may or may not be realized, and thus an investment that is optimal ex ante can appear to be suboptimal ex post". The proper methodology for valuation is nominal or current prices. This implies expected inflation rates and real changes in prices. Indications from several explorations on this subject suggest that constant prices methodology tends to overvalue the valuation of cash flows and as we will show in the appendix this generates tariff sets (or price set)[21] for regulated firms that are lower than the required. We wonder if this fact is one of the causes that some (or many) projects become a failure.

On the other hand it is very easy to mix nominal items and constant prices items in the financial statements. In this case, for example, they use a nominal cost of debt, Kd and calculate the interest charges with that nominal Kd. The interest charges are listed as an

[21] For regulated firms the tariffs are defined as those which make the NPV equal to zero.

expense in the income statement distorting the taxes, the cash flow to debt, CFD and the cash flow to equity, CFE.[22]

Using Constant Leverage in the WACC Calculation when It Is Not Constant

When valuing the cash flows they use constant WACC based on constant leverage, calculated with the initial book values. When we observe the market value calculated with their constant price methodology and calculate the leverage or even when we calculated the leverage with book values, we find that leverage is not constant. The leverage using their market value has a maximum value of 0.71 and a minimum of 0.20. On the other hand, the maximum value for leverage with book value is 0.61 and the minimum is 0.04. If constant leverage is assumed as a target leverage, then this fact has to be reflected in the financial statements increasing or decreasing debt in order to keep D% (using market values) constant. See Appendix 2.

In this appendix it can be observed that the market value for the cash flows is 92.8 and this is the reference value we use to compare our proposed methodology.

Inconsistency in the Cash Flows

Since the late 50's and early 60's Modigliani and Miller M&M, in seminal and illuminating papers defined the relationship that must hold between the different values when valuing a firm. That relationship is the same for the different cash flows. These cash flows are the free cash flow, FCF, the cash flow to debt, CFD, the cash flow to equity, CFE and the tax savings, TS. The relationship is

$$FCF + TS = CFD + CFE \tag{9}$$

The consistency among the cash flows has to be maintained even when each of the elements is calculated independently. For instance, the CFD and the CFE are derived from the cash budget where it is shown exactly the value of these cash flows (see Tham and Vélez-Pareja, 2004, Vélez Pareja 2004b and 2005). On the other hand, the TS are derived taking into account the timing and the amount of the TS and the FCF is derived indirectly departing, for instance, from EBIT.

Equation (9) does not hold in the case we are analyzing. This happens because they calculate the operating FCF and derive from it the CFE as

$$CFE = OCF - CFD^{23} = FCF + T \times EBIT - CFD \tag{10}$$

[22] The typical reaction to this is that the calculation of FCF is not affected if we use nominal or real interest rates. However, given that the FCF calculated indirectly with the well known approach that departs from EBIT is not affected by interest charges, it is true that some conditions regarding the size of EBIT might require that tax savings be calculated very precisely. As we mentioned in Section Four, when EBIT is negative or less than the interest charges, the formulation of WACC requires the determination of the tax savings in a very precise manner. Negative EBIT or EBIT lower than the financial expenses is a typical situation in new projects or firms.

[23] See Estache et al 2002 p. 22. In private correspondence with the consultant that constructed the model he says that it should has been CFE = OCF – Taxes – CFD and that it is a typo not included in the calculations.

$$\text{OCF} = \text{EBITDA} - \text{Investments} - \text{Provision for unrecoverable} \quad (11)$$

Where OCF is the operating cash flow and EBITDA is the earnings before interest, taxes, depreciation and amortization.

This means that the equity holder receives some funds that are still tied in the firm and on top of that the result includes the TS. If we examine equation (9) we find that defining CFE as in (10) what we get is

Replacing (10) in equation (9) we have

$$\text{FCF} + \text{TS} = \text{CFD} + \text{FCF} + \text{T} \times \text{EBIT} - \text{CFD} \quad (12)$$

Simplifying

$$\text{TS} = \text{T} \times \text{EBIT} \quad (13)$$

And this cannot be true unless, as shown above, that EBIT is less than interest charges. See Appendix 10.

The different cash flows and the dividends paid are

Table 8. Cash flows in the original model.

Year	**1**	**2**	**3**	**…**	**12**	**13**	**14**	**15**	**16**	**17**	**18**	**19**	**20**
FCF	−6.1	−2.9	3.0	…	14.8	17.3	18.1	19.0	18.2	18.0	20.8	23.5	45.4
CFD	−5.6	−2.4	4.3	…	8.5	9.9	9.4	7.9	4.6	3.6	3.4	2.2	2.4
Tax on EBIT	0.0	0.8	1.3	…	5.5	5.9	6.2	6.6	8.3	8.7	8.4	7.2	4.5
FCF + T × EBIT	−6.1	−2.0	4.2	…	20.3	23.2	24.3	25.5	26.6	26.8	29.1	30.7	49.8
CFE = OCF - CFD = FCF + T × EBIT – CFD	−0.4	0.4	−0.1	…	11.8	13.2	14.8	17.6	22.0	23.2	25.7	28.5	47.5
TS with Kd nominal	–	0.8	1.3	…	1.1	1.0	0.8	0.5	0.4	0.3	0.2	0.1	0.1
Dividends	0.0	0.0	0.0	…	7.7	8.6	9.7	10.7	14.0	14.9	14.5	12.6	7.8
FCF+TS	−6.1	−2.0	4.2	…	15.9	18.3	18.8	19.5	18.6	18.3	20.9	23.6	45.4
CFD+CFE	−6.1	−2.0	4.2	…	20.3	23.2	24.3	25.5	26.6	26.8	29.1	30.7	49.8
Check= difference of the previous two lines		0.0	0.0	…	−3.5	−4.3	−4.9	−5.5	−6.0	−7.9	−8.5	−8.2	−7.1

We calculated the tax savings recognizing the fact that not all of them are earned in the same year they are accrued (because the presence of operational losses or EBIT less than interest charges). (See Appendix 3).

This means that the equity holders "invest" some funds that NEVER get out of their pockets[24] or "receive" funds that never show up. In fact if we observe the BS we will find that some net income is accumulated and never paid.

We can easily check that there is no consistency in the cash flows. See Table above and Appendix 3.[25]

However, this shows the importance of the proper calculation of CFD. If we do the same operation of using the revised definition we obtain a counter evident result: TS = EBIT – Taxes + EBIT × T.

[24] That fact is not reflected in the Balance Sheet.

Calculation of the Cost of Capital

On the other hand, the cost of the levered equity, Ke, is calculated using the CAPM as Ke = Kd + β_{lev} × MRP[26]. The proper calculation should be Ke = $R_f + \beta_{lev} \times$ MRP + CR where R_f is the risk free rate and CR is the country risk. The Kd is calculated assuming implicitly that β for debt is zero and hence Kd = R_f + CR.

The proper cost of capital to discount the FCF varies depending of the market value of the firm and the value of TS. We define market value of firms or projects not traded in the market as the present value of the cash flows discounted at the proper discount rate. For instance, the present value of the FCF discounted at the correct WACC calculated with weights based on market values (this generates a circularity). For a proper discount rate we understand the following (in the most general formulation):

1. If we use the FCF, we should discount it with[27]

$$WACC_{adjusted} = Ku_i - \frac{TS_i}{V^L_{i-1}} - (Ku_i - \psi_i)\frac{V^{TS}_{i-1}}{V^L_{i-1}} \quad (14)$$

2. If we use the Capital Cash Flow CCF

$$CCF = CFD + CFE = FCF + TS \quad (15)$$

we should discount it with

$$WACC_{for\ CCF} = Ku_i - (Ku_i - \psi_i)\frac{V^{TS}_{i-1}}{V^L_{i-1}} \quad (16)$$

3. If we use CFE we should discount it with (in this case we have to add the value of debt to obtain the total value)

$$Ke_i = Ku_i + (Ku_i - Kd_i)\frac{D_{i-1}}{E^L_{i-1}} - (Ku_i - \psi_i)\frac{V^{TS}_{i-1}}{E^L_{i-1}} \quad (17)$$

where E is the market value of equity and D is the market value of debt; other variables have been defined previously.

Of course we have to make explicit the assumption on ψ, the discount rate for the TS. We have assumed the ψ is the unlevered cost of equity, Ku.

When the discount rate for the tax savings ψ is Ku the previous expressions are

---

[25] The derivation of the CFE is affected by the way CFD is calculated. If in the CFD the interest rate is the nominal Kd, then CFE will be distorted as it might be in this case.

[26] This seems to be a typo that is compensated by the fact that Kd includes the Rf and the CR.

[27] We will use the name $WACC_{adjusted}$ to distinguish the general formulation from the traditional one defined as WACC = Kd(1 – T)D% +KeE%.

$$WACC_{\text{for CCF}} = Ku_i \quad (18a)$$

$$WACC_{\text{adjusted}} = Ku_i - \frac{TS_i}{V^L_{i-1}} \quad (18b)$$

and

$$Ke_i = Ku_i + (Ku_i - Kd_i)\frac{D_{i-1}}{E^L_{i-1}} \quad (19)$$

In the example we are analyzing, this cost of equity, Ke is held constant from year 1 up to the last year. As we show above, the leverage is not constant and hence the Ke should change accordingly. In a world where the discount rate for tax savings is Ku, the calculation for the cost of levered equity is

$$Ke = Ku + (Ku - Kd) \times D/E \quad (20)$$

Where Ke is the cost of levered equity, Ku is the cost of unlevered equity, Kd is the cost of debt, D is the market value of the debt and E is the market value of equity.

When there are negative EBIT or EBIT less than interest charges, the TS are not earned in the period. If there is the possibility of losses carried forward then we can recover the TS not earned during the loss period. However, this means that the traditional WACC cannot be used. The traditional WACC is,

$$WACC = Kd \times D\% \times (1 - T) + Ke \times E\% \quad (21)$$

The assumptions in the WACC formula are not met by the example we are dealing with because they have some years with negative EBIT and losses carried forward (LCF).

In this case we have to use the more general formulation of WACC assuming (in this case) that the discount rate for the tax savings, ψ, is Ku and then WACC is

$$WACC_t = Ku_t - \frac{TS_t}{V^L_{t-1}} \quad (22)$$

where TS is the tax savings of the period t and V_{t-1} is the market value of the firm for the previous period, Ku is the unlevered cost of equity and WACC is the weighted average cost of capital. This formulation implies circularity between value and WACC.

The traditional WACC is a special case of this general formulation and is only valid when taxes are paid the same year and TS are fully earned the same year as accrued.

In the next table we show some selected values

Table 9. Calculation of value at constant prices using proper WACC.

	0	1	2	3	...	17	18	19	20
FCF		-6.1	-3.2	3.0	...	18.0	20.8	23.5	45.4
TS		0.0	0.8	1.3	...	0.1	0.1	0.1	0.0
WACC adj = Ku-TS_t/V_{t-1}		8.61%	7.76%	7.45%	...	8.44%	8.47%	8.51%	8.53%
V = PV(FCF at WACCadj)	84.5	97.8	108.5	113.7	...	74.6	60.2	41.8	-

As can be seen the cost of capital changes depending on the value of the firm. See Appendix 5. As can be seen in Appendix 9, the value calculated with the FCF and with the adjusted WACC matches the one calculated with the capital cash flow (CCF) in the same Appendix. Observe that there is a difference in value when calculated with constant WACC and assuming constant prices (92.82 as shown in Appendix 2).

Inconsistency in the Values

As we mentioned above, M&M stated the relationship that must hold between the different values when valuing a firm. These values are the unlevered market value of the firm, derived from the FCF, the market value of the TS derived from the TS, the market value for debt, derived from the CFD and the market value for the levered equity derived from the CFE. The relationship is

$$V^{un} + V^{TS} = V^{D} + V^{E} \tag{23}$$

where V^{un} is the unlevered value of the firm calculated with the FCF and Ku, the unlevered cost of equity, V^{TS} the present value of the TS discounted at a proper discount rate, V^{D} the market value of debt and V^{E} the market levered value of equity calculated with the CFE at the levered cost of equity, Ke.

As with the cash flows, equation (21) does not hold in the WB example.

When we calculate the levered equity value using the Ke they use in their WACC calculation, we find that the value is 36.2 and when subtracted from the total value they obtain from the valuation of the FCF that is 92.8 we obtain 56.6 as the debt at year zero. The actual debt at year zero is 48.1. If we subtract the market value of debt from the total value (PV(FCF)) we obtain 44.7 as the value of equity.

The different values are

Table 10a. Inconsistency in values.

V = PV(FCF)	92.8
Equity= PV(CFE)	36.2
Debt from BS	48.1
Debt = PV(CFD)	48.1
Debt = PV(FCF) – PV(CFE)	56.6
Equity = PV(FCF) - debt from BS	44.7
Equity = PV(FCF) – PV(CFD)	44.7

As can be seen there is not consistency on the values. See Appendix 6.

Overestimation of the "Correct" Value

We recalculate the value using a "proper" methodology to introduce the effect of the actual leverage using market values. We calculate value using the capital cash flow[28], CCF, approach and assuming that the discount rate for the TS is Ku. Using this assumption the value calculated in this way is lower than the one calculated assuming Kd as the discount rate for the TS.

We calculate the CCF as

$$CCF = CFD + CFE = FCF + TS \tag{24}$$

We perform the calculations of the CCF and the value using real (deflated) Kd to calculate the interest charges (deflated) with Kd, in order to make this calculation comparable with the one performed in the WB example. This, on the other hand, affects the CFE and that was adjusted as well. We have to recognize that when changing the interest charges, the amount of financing might change to the downside, but we did not perform that adjustment.

Using the CCF defined as above with real Kd to calculate the CFD we found a difference in value of 9.87% (84.5 compared with 92.8, taking care of decimals). We have to remind the reader that this difference in value is just due to the use of the proper calculation of the cash flows and the proper use of market value to estimate leverage and hence cost of capital. This difference does not include the overestimation due to the use of the constant prices methodology; this is, it does not include, for example, the overvaluation due to depreciation and AR mentioned above. See Appendix 7.

SECTION SIX

In this section we reconstruct the valuation using nominal prices (neutral inflation). We compare this result with the original result found in the example at constant prices.

A "Proper" Solution

We have reconstructed the example and calculated the tax savings TS taking into account two facts: one that TS are not earned the same period they are accrued and the second fact is that to be consistent, the interest payments has to be calculated in real terms. At last, we calculated the cash flow to equity in the proper way, this is calculated as

$$CFE = FCF + TS - CFD \tag{25}$$

---

[28] Although the CCF is the essence of part of the M&M propositions, Ruback 2000 popularized its use.

To calculate values we assumed that the discount rate for TS is Ku, the cost of unlevered equity. In this scenario we calculate the CCF as FCF + TS and discount it with Ku_r (Ku_r = real Ku); the CFE was discounted with the proper formula for Ke, this is

$$Ke_r = Ku_r + (Ku_r - Kd_r)D/E \qquad (26)$$

where Ke_r is the real Ke, Ku_r is the real Ku, Kd_r, D is the market value of the debt and E is the market value of the equity.

When we do this we find a complete consistency in values as follows (See Appendixes 5 and 7):

Table 10b. Consistency in value with constant prices using proper WACC[29] at constant prices.

Ku_r	8.61%
V = PV(CCF)	84,5
Debt (BS)	48.1
Equity = PV(CCF) – Debt (BS)	36.4
V = PV(CFE at Ke_r)	36.4

This means an overvaluation (using the constant prices methodology for this revised calculation) of 9.87% as we mentioned above. This figure does not include nor pretend to measure the differences in values that arise due to the valuation in constant prices compared with nominal prices. In other words, it does not include the overvaluation due to AR and tax savings for depreciation mentioned in Section Five (6.61% for depreciation and 6.37% for AR).

As a double check, see Table 9, above, where the total value has been calculated using the FCF and the proper WACC at constant prices. The two values match.

Tariffs Recalculated

With these values we recalculate the tariffs to be applied to the project and we find that there is an underestimation of the tariffs by 6.8% and 8.2% respectively. See Appendix 8. We have to remind that tariffs for regulated firms are defined as those which makes the NPV equal to zero.

Value Using Nominal Prices

We have updated the revenues, expenses and investments using the inflation rate. We assumed no real increases in prices; hence we deal with neutral inflation as is implicit in the constant prices methodology. Done this, we found that the overvaluation of the constant prices methodology compared with the nominal prices approach (and using the proper cost of

[29] By proper WACC we understand that it has been calculated using market values and the proper TS.

capital based on market values) is 21.2%. This implies an underestimation of tariffs by 15.2% and 18.0%. See Appendix 9.

The correct value can be calculated using three different approaches: using the FCF, the CFE and the CCF. In the next tables we show a partial view of those calculations. The underlying assumptions in the next tables is that the discount rate for the TS, ψ, is Ku. The complete tables are in the Appendix 9.

When calculating value using the CCF we discount it with the nominal Ku, in this case, 12.4%.

Table 11a. Calculation of value using the CCF.

	0	**1**	**2**	**3**	**4**	**...**	**17**	**18**	**19**	**20**
Ku		12.4%	12.4%	12.4%	12.4%	...	12.4%	12.4%	12.4%	12.4%
CCF		−6.1	−2.6	4.4	6.7	...	31.7	36.2	42.4	81.3
V=PV(CCF)	76.5	92.2	106.2	115.0	122.5	...	123.0	102.0	72.3	
Equity = PV(CCF) − Debt	28.4	34.6	41.4	49.5	59.2	...	91.7	76.8	56.5	

For the calculation of the equity values (and total value adding the market value of the debt) we use Ku=12.4% to derive Ke and it is adjusted according to the proper market leverage.

Table 11b. Calculation of value using the CFE.

	0	**1**	**2**	**3**	**4**	**...**	**17**	**18**	**19**	**20**
CFE		−0.5	0.1	−0.2	−0.6	...	24.8	27.6	31.0	64.2
Ke=Ku+−Ku-KdD/E		19.9%	19.8%	19.3%	18.2%	...	13.9%	13.9%	13.9%	13.6%
PV(CFE)	28.4	34.6	41.4	49.5	59.2	...	91.7	76.8	56.5	-
Debt	48.1	57.6	64.8	65.4	63.3	...	31.3	25.2	15.8	0.0
V = PV(CFE) + Debt	76.5	92.2	106.2	115.0	122.5	...	123.0	102.0	72.3	

When calculating total value using the FCF, note that we do not use the traditional formulation for the WACC. Instead, we use the adjusted WACC mentioned above (see equation 18b).

Table 11c. Calculation of value using the FCF and WACC.

	0	1	2	3	4	...	17	18	19	20
FCF		-6.1	-3.6	2.7	4.9	...	30.8	35.3	41.7	80.8
TS		0.0	1.1	1.7	1.8	...	1.0	0.9	0.7	0.4
$WACC_{adjusted}$		12.4%	11.2%	10.8%	10.8%	...	11.7%	11.7%	11.7%	11.8%
V	76.5	92.2	106.2	115.0	122.5	...	123.0	102.0	72.3	0

In the next table we show the consistency among the different values.

Table 11d. Consistency in value using nominal prices and proper WACC.

V = PV(CCF) = PV(FCF)	76.5
Debt	48.1
PV(CCF)-Debt	28.4
PV(CFE)	28.4

There is consistency in values.
The leverage using correct market values ranges from 0.22 to 0.63. See Appendix 9.
With this value the tariffs to obtain an NPV of zero are shown in the next table.

Table 11e. Tariffs calculated with the correct value.

Residential users		
-First block	($/KWh)	0.0590
-Second block	($/KWh)	0.0490
Underestimation of tariffs (First block)		6.8%
Underestimation of tariffs (Second block)		8.2%

The overestimation of value can be seen in the next table.

Table 11f: A summary of overestimation of value

	Absolute Value	**As % WB value**	**As % of nominal value**
Improper WACC	7.91	8.53%	10.34%
AR	5.91	6.37%	7.72%
Depreciation	3.32	3.57%	4.33%
Total	17.14	18.47%	22.39%
Constant – Nominal	**16.23**	**17.50%**	**21.21%**

Although when calculating independently and isolated way the elements of the overvaluation they give a different value than the one we obtain when the overvaluation is calculated in an integrated manner, the correct one is the later. This means that 17.50% of the value calculated using the constant prices methodology and constant WACC, is an overvaluation. Or the other way around, the value calculated in the WB example is 21.21% larger than the one calculated with nominal prices and correct WACC. As can be seen, in any case, differences are relevant and larger than the traditional ±5%.

A Summary

We have analyzed two different methods to value a firm or a project in an inflationary context: constant prices and nominal or current prices. We mentioned some conditions that have to be met in order to have identical NPV's for the three methods. We analyzed as well, that these conditions where unrealistic.

We have shown several areas in the methodology proposed by the World Bank where some improvement can be done in the task of valuing cash flows. There are several areas of improvement:

1. Regarding the methodology of valuation (constant prices instead of nominal prices)
2. Use of constant leverage, constant WACC and constant Ke when leverage is not constant
3. Improper determination of cash flows such as the CFE and the CFD
4. Inconsistency among calculated cash flows
5. Inconsistency among calculated values
6. Overestimation of values and
7. Underestimation of tariffs.

The magnitude of the overestimation is shown in the following table

Table 12a. A measure of overestimation of value using constant prices.

Source	Amount
Overestimation in value due to assume constant D% and improper WACC	9.87%
Overestimation of value due to tax savings for depreciation	6.61%
Overestimation of value due to AR	6.37%
Underestimation of tariffs (First block)	6.8%
Underestimation of tariffs (Second block)	8.2%

The overestimation of value due to depreciation and AR do not cancel each other and do not cancel with the overestimation due to the wrong use of WACC and cash flows. These overestimations give a total of 22.85% (9.87% + 6.61% + 6.37%)

These numbers are consistent in magnitude with the figures we obtain when we calculate the values using the nominal prices methodology (assuming neutral inflation) and the proper calculation of WACC taking into account market values and variable leverage.

Table 12b. A measure of overestimation of value using nominal prices.

Total overestimation of value (using constant versus nominal prices)	21.21%
Underestimation of tariffs (First block) using nominal prices	15.2%
Underestimation of tariffs (Second block) using nominal prices	18.0%

We can observe that the overestimation when nominal prices methodology is used is quite similar to the partial overestimations calculated above. The difference of 1.64% (22.85% − 21.21%) might arise for several reasons:

1. The overestimations for AR and depreciation charges were calculated using nominal WACCN constant.
2. Depreciation was assumed the same for constant and nominal prices and it is not because there are capital expenditures during all the years the project is analyzed and when we use nominal prices capital investments are adjusted with the inflation rate.

3. When using nominal prices and correct leverage the nominal and correct WACC is not constant in comparison with the WACCN that was set in the WB example as constant.

The consequences of this type of mistakes might result in acceptance of bad projects as good and in a misspecification of tariffs. This fact might imply the failure of the project because tariffs might not be enough to make the project achieve the goals in economic terms.

SECTION SEVEN: CONCLUDING REMARKS

The major failure of the constant price methodology is that the implicit assumptions distort the reality we wish to represent through the model. Hence, the validation of the model (the free cash flow) with reality is impossible. We have seen that it is possible to assign scarce resources to the wrong activities if they are evaluated at constant or real prices. Scarcity of resources is critical in emerging economies where usually inflation rates are high. Care has to be taken by financial analysts from international and domestic agencies in the process of project selection in those countries. We have shown that the magnitude of the errors when the wrong methodologies are applied might be considerable. It is not a small ±5%; it can mean that we accept a bad project as desirable.

It is not true that it is equivalent to evaluate projects with constant and real price or current or nominal price methodologies. The constant and real price methodologies produce an upward bias and overvalue a project. These methodologies are an oversimplification of reality and produce adverse results.

The proposal is very simple. The right approach is the current or nominal prices one and any other approach that does not represent the reality as closer as possible, should be discarded, right away. On the other hand, the discount rate (WACC) should reflect the changing leverage (and effects such as a changing forecasted inflation) and the use of market values when calculating any of the proper formulations for WACC or Ke.

The WB example is a case where several refinements can be made to improve some areas of analysis in a complex model such as the one we have studied in the WB example. The practice presented by the World Bank in that example supports a tradition of doing project appraisal and firm valuation with conceptual limitations. The critical issue here is the intellectual authority that represents the World Bank among practitioners and governmental agencies that support their practices. This practice has to be improved to reduce the probability to accept bad projects as good projects and miscalculate the proper tariffs in regulated infrastructure projects for developing countries.

More, what is at risk is the enormous amount of funds that goes to emerging countries supported by appraisals that might favor inconvenient projects and the determination of tariffs for public services like water and electricity distribution. All these decisions are made in detriment of the less developed countries and their population.

APPENDIX 1

In this appendix we show the numbers that support the comments in the body of the chapter.

Table A1.1 Overestimation of value due to Tax savings on depreciation.

	0	1	2	3	4	5	6	7	8	9	10	11	12	13	14	15	16	17	18	19	20
Depreciation charge		8.8	6.9	7.2	7.4	7.6	8.1	8.4	8.6	8.8	8.9	8.9	8.3	8.4	8.5	8.6	4.9	3.9	4.0	4.0	3.9
TS for dep = T x Deprec charge		3.1	2.4	2.5	2.6	2.7	2.8	2.9	3.0	3.1	3.1	3.1	2.9	3.0	3.0	3.0	1.7	1.4	1.4	1.4	1.4
PV TS Dep at nominal	21.4	20.7	20.6	20.3	20.0	19.5	18.8	18.0	16.9	15.7	14.3	12.8	11.3	9.6	7.6	5.4	4.3	3.4	2.4	1.2	
PV TS Dep at real	27.5	26.5	26.0	25.4	24.6	23.7	22.6	21.3	19.9	18.2	16.4	14.5	12.6	10.6	8.4	6.0	4.7	3.6	2.5	1.3	
Difference	6.1																				
% of total val	6.61%																				

Table A1.2 Structure of collectible and uncollectible.

		Collection					
	Uncollectible	**1**	**2**	**3**	**4**	**5**	**6**
0	11.00%	85.0%	8.0%	4.0%	2.0%	1.0%	
1	10.31%	76.2%	7.2%	3.6%	1.8%	0.9%	
2	9.66%		76.8%	7.2%	3.6%	1.8%	0.9%
....							

The collection pattern is shown in line for year 0 and it applies to the net collectible AR.

Table A1.3 Total Collected Income at real and nominal.

	0	1	2	3	4	5	6	7	8	9	10	11	12	13	14	15	16	17	18	19	20
Real	-	54.3	61.6	66.5	70.4	73.7	76.4	79.2	82.1	85.0	88.1	90.2	92.5	94.9	97.2	99.5	101.9	104.3	106.9	109.3	111.8
Total Collected Income adjusted by inflation rate		56.2	65.8	73.4	80.2	86.8	93.2	99.9	107.2	114.9	123.2	130.6	138.6	147.2	156.0	165.3	175.3	185.7	196.8	208.5	220.6

The only year where the reader can check the inflation adjustment is at year 1 because the AR for years 2 to 20 include AR with previous inflation adjustments. For instance, at years 2 to 5 there are AR calculated with sales from previous years and in those years sales have been adjusted by $(1+\text{inflation rate})^{\text{previous years}}$ where previous years are 1, 2, 3, ….

This gives some differences as follows

Table A1.4 Overestimation due to AR.

PV of AR at real	840.2
PV of AR at nominal	834.3
Difference	5.9
Value (WB)	92.8
Difference on value (WB)	6.37%

APPENDIX 2

Table A2.1 Leverage D% using WB book and market value.

Year	0	1	2	3	4	5	6	7	8	9	10	11	12	13	14	15	16	17	18	19	20
Debt	48.1	57.6	64.6	65.5	63.9	60.2	64.6	60.5	56.2	51.5	47.0	39.4	34.0	26.8	19.5	13.2	9.7	6.9	4.0	2.2	0.0
MV (WB)	92.82	98.5	101.0	98.6	94.8	90.2	91.3	86.9	81.0	74.9	68.8	61.4	55.0	48.1	41.3	34.7	28.7	23.3	17.4	11.2	
D% MV (WB)	0.52	0.58	0.64	0.66	0.67	0.67	0.71	0.70	0.69	0.69	0.68	0.64	0.62	0.56	0.47	0.38	0.34	0.30	0.23	0.20	0.71
BV assets	97.5	102.5	107.4	106.9	105.1	102.5	109.0	107.5	103.5	99.2	95.1	88.0	83.2	76.6	70.0	64.3	61.7	59.8	57.9	56.8	55.2
D% BV	0.49	0.56	0.60	0.61	0.61	0.59	0.59	0.56	0.54	0.52	0.49	0.45	0.41	0.35	0.28	0.20	0.16	0.12	0.07	0.04	0.61

MV = Market value BV = Book value D% = leverage

Assumed constant value of Leverage by WB 0.50

APPENDIX 3

Table A3.1 Cash Flow to Debt CFD and TS at nominal Kd.

Year	0	1	2	3	4	5	6	7	8	9	10	11	12	13	14	15	16	17	18	19	20
Debt (BS)	48.1	57.6	64.6	65.5	63.9	60.2	64.6	60.5	56.2	51.5	47.0	39.4	34.0	26.8	19.5	13.2	9.7	6.9	4.0	2.2	0.0
Plus Real Interest on Financial Debts	0.0	3.8	4.6	5.2	5.2	5.1	4.8	5.2	4.8	4.5	4.1	3.8	3.1	2.7	2.1	1.6	1.1	0.8	0.5	0.3	0.2
Plus Total amortizations		12.3	12.5	14.0	14.6	15.5	16.4	20.3	15.1	15.0	13.8	12.6	10.7	10.0	8.6	6.4	4.5	3.7	2.8	1.9	2.2
Minus Loans Long term		15.2	13.7	10.4	9.1	8.2	14.5	11.4	7.5	7.2	6.5	3.5	3.8	2.0	0.9	0.0	0.7	0.6	0.0	0.0	-
Minus Loans short term		6.5	5.9	4.5	3.9	3.5	6.2	4.9	3.2	3.1	2.8	1.5	1.6	0.8	0.4	0.0	0.3	0.3	0.0	0.0	-
Total CFD		-5.6	-2.4	4.3	6.8	8.8	0.5	9.2	9.2	9.2	8.6	11.4	8.5	9.9	9.4	7.9	4.6	3.6	3.4	2.2	2.4
PV(CFD at Kd nominal)	48.1	57.6	64.6	65.5	63.9	60.2	64.6	60.5	56.2	51.5	47.0	39.4	34.0	26.8	19.5	13.2	9.7	6.9	4.0	2.2	
TS		-	0.8	1.3	1.7	1.8	2.5	2.5	2.8	1.7	1.4	1.3	1.1	1.0	0.8	0.5	0.4	0.3	0.2	0.1	0.1

Table A3.2 CFD and TS with real Kd.

Year	0	1	2	3	4	5	6	7	8	9	10	11	12	13	14	15	16	17	18	19	20
Debt (BS)	48.1	57.6	64.6	65.5	63.9	60.2	64.6	60.5	56.2	51.5	47.0	39.4	34.0	26.8	19.5	13.2	9.7	6.9	4.0	2.2	0.0
Plus Real Interest on Financial Debts		2.1	2.5	2.8	2.8	2.8	2.6	2.8	2.6	2.4	2.2	2.0	1.7	1.5	1.2	0.8	0.6	0.4	0.3	0.2	0.1
Plus Total amortizations		12.3	12.5	14.0	14.6	15.5	16.4	20.3	15.1	15.0	13.8	12.6	10.7	10.0	8.6	6.4	4.5	3.7	2.8	1.9	2.2
Minus Loans Long term		15.2	13.7	10.4	9.1	8.2	14.5	11.4	7.5	7.2	6.5	3.5	3.8	2.0	0.9	0.0	0.7	0.6	0.0	0.0	0.0
Minus Loans short term		6.5	5.9	4.5	3.9	3.5	6.2	4.9	3.2	3.1	2.8	1.5	1.6	0.8	0.4	0.0	0.3	0.3	0.0	0.0	0.0
Total CFD		−7.4	−4.6	2.0	4.4	6.5	−1.7	6.8	7.0	7.1	6.7	9.7	7.0	8.7	8.5	7.2	4.1	3.2	3.1	2.0	2.3
PV(CFD at real Kd	48.1	57.6	64.6	65.5	63.9	60.2	64.6	60.5	56.2	51.5	47.0	39.4	34.0	26.8	19.5	13.2	9.7	6.9	4.0	2.2	
TS		0.0	0.8	1.3	1.4	1.1	0.9	1.0	0.9	0.9	0.8	0.7	0.6	0.5	0.4	0.3	0.2	0.1	0.1	0.1	0.0

Table A3.3 Tax savings TS, With nominal interest payment.

	1	2	3	4	5	6	7	8	9	10	11	12	13	14	15	16	17	18	19	20
EBIT	−0.8	2.4	3.6	4.8	6.1	7.2	8.4	9.8	11.2	12.8	13.8	15.6	16.7	17.8	18.8	23.8	24.9	24.0	20.7	12.8
Interest	3.8	4.6	5.2	5.2	5.1	4.8	5.2	4.8	4.5	4.1	3.8	3.1	2.7	2.1	1.6	1.1	0.8	0.5	0.3	0.2
TS at nominal Kd accrued	1.3	1.6	1.8	1.8	1.8	1.7	1.8	1.7	1.6	1.4	1.3	1.1	1.0	0.8	0.5	0.4	0.3	0.2	0.1	0.1
TS earned	0.0	0.8	1.3	1.7	1.8	1.7	1.8	1.7	1.6	1.4	1.3	1.1	1.0	0.8	0.5	0.4	0.3	0.2	0.1	0.1
Net income	−4.7	−2.2	−1.6	−0.4	1.0	2.3	2.1	3.2	4.3	5.7	6.5	8.1	9.1	10.2	11.2	14.8	15.7	15.2	13.2	8.2
Cumulative net income		−6.9	−8.5	−8.9	−7.9	−5.6	−3.5	−0.3	4.1	9.7	16.3	24.3	33.4	43.6	54.8	69.6	85.3	100.5	113.7	121.9
TS recovered	0.0	0.8	1.3	1.7	1.8	2.5	2.5	2.8	1.7	1.4	1.3	1.1	1.0	0.8	0.5	0.4	0.3	0.2	0.1	0.1

Table A3.4 Tax savings TS, With real interest payment.

	1	2	3	4	5	6	7	8	9	10	11	12	13	14	15	16	17	18	19	20
EBIT	−0.8	2.4	3.6	4.8	6.1	7.2	8.4	9.8	11.2	12.8	13.8	15.6	16.7	17.8	18.8	23.8	24.9	24.0	20.7	12.8
Interest	2.1	2.5	2.8	2.8	2.8	2.6	2.8	2.6	2.4	2.2	2.0	1.7	1.5	1.2	0.8	0.6	0.4	0.3	0.2	0.1
TS at nominal Kd accrued	0.7	0.9	1.0	1.0	1.0	0.9	1.0	0.9	0.9	0.8	0.7	0.6	0.5	0.4	0.3	0.2	0.1	0.1	0.1	0.0
TS earned	0.0	0.8	1.0	1.0	1.0	0.9	1.0	0.9	0.9	0.8	0.7	0.6	0.5	0.4	0.3	0.2	0.1	0.1	0.1	0.0
Net income	−2.9	−0.1	0.8	2.0	3.3	4.5	5.6	5.3	6.3	7.4	8.1	9.4	10.2	11.0	11.8	15.1	15.9	15.4	13.3	8.2
Cumulative net income		−3.0	−2.2	−0.3	3.0	7.6	13.1	18.5	24.7	32.2	40.3	49.7	60.0	71.0	82.8	98.0	113.9	129.3	142.5	150.7
TS recovered	0.0	0.8	1.3	1.4	1.1	0.9	1.0	0.9	0.9	0.8	0.7	0.6	0.5	0.4	0.3	0.2	0.1	0.1	0.1	0.0

Table A3.5 Inconsistency in cash flows.

	1	2	3	4	5	6	7	8	9	10	11	12	13	14	15	16	17	18	19	20
FCF	−6.1	−2.9	3.0	4.9	6.6	−1.7	7.2	10.4	11.5	12.3	15.9	14.8	17.3	18.1	19.0	18.2	18.0	20.8	23.5	45.4
CFD	−5.6	−2.4	4.3	6.8	8.8	0.5	9.2	9.2	9.2	8.6	11.4	8.5	9.9	9.4	7.9	4.6	3.6	3.4	2.2	2.4
TX on EBIT	0.0	0.8	1.3	1.7	2.1	2.5	2.9	3.4	3.9	4.5	4.8	5.5	5.9	6.2	6.6	8.3	8.7	8.4	7.2	4.5
FCF + Tx EBIT	−6.1	−2.0	4.2	6.6	8.7	0.8	10.1	13.8	15.4	16.8	20.8	20.3	23.2	24.3	25.5	26.6	26.8	29.1	30.7	49.8
Dividends	0.0	0.0	0.0	0.0	0.0	0.0	0.0	3.1	4.1	5.4	6.2	7.7	8.6	9.7	10.7	14.0	14.9	14.5	12.6	7.8
CFE = OCF - CFD = FCF + T× (EBIT) - CFD	−0.4	0.4	−0.1	−0.1	−0.2	0.3	0.9	4.6	6.2	8.2	9.4	11.8	13.2	14.8	17.6	22.0	23.2	25.7	28.5	47.5
TS with Kd nominal	–	0.8	1.3	1.7	1.8	2.5	2.5	2.8	1.7	1.4	1.3	1.1	1.0	0.8	0.5	0.4	0.3	0.2	0.1	0.1
FCF+TS	−6.1	−2.0	4.2	6.6	8.4	0.8	9.7	13.2	13.1	13.8	17.2	15.9	18.3	18.8	19.5	18.6	18.3	20.9	23.6	45.4
CFD+CFE	−6.1	−2.0	4.2	6.6	8.7	0.8	10.1	13.8	15.4	16.8	20.8	20.3	23.2	24.3	25.5	26.6	26.8	29.1	30.7	49.8
Check		0.0	0.0	0.0	0.0	−0.3	0.0	−0.4	−0.6	−2.2	−3.0	−3.5	−4.3	−4.9	−5.5	−6.0	−7.9	−8.5	−8.2	−7.1

APPENDIX 4

Cost of Capital Calculation.

From the Excel file we have:

Table A4.1 Information for cost of capital calculations.

Cost of Debt	8.0%
Liabilities/Assets Ratio (%)	50.00
Beta of Equity	0.79
Market risk premium	11.2%
WACC (real)	7.3%
WACC (nominal)	11.01%
Pre-devaluation expected inflation	3.5%
Risk-free Rate	4.0%
Country Risk (in basis points)	400
Income Tax	35%

Kd = Rf + CR = 4% + 400/10,000 = 8%

Ke = Rf + β_{lev} × PRM + CR = 4% + 0.79 × 11.2% + 400/10.000 = 16.83%

After tax (traditional WACC) = WACCN = Kd(1 − T) × D% + Ke × (1 − D%)
= 8%×50%×(1 − 35%) + 16.83% × (1 − 50%) = 11.01%

Deflated WACC:

WACC = (1+WACCN)/(1 + Inflation rate) = 1.1101/1.035 − 1 = 7.26%

Real cost of debt = (1+Kd)/(1+ Inflation rate) = 1.08/1.035 − 1 = 4.35%

Calculation of Ku, the unlevered cost of equity:

The value of Ku can be calculated (and in fact we calculate it to value the CCF as we mentioned above), as

$$Ku = Rf + \beta_{unlev} \times MRP + CR \qquad (A4.1)$$

Where β_{unlev} is the β for the unlevered cost of equity, Ku.

The unlevered β was calculated using the following expression:

$$\beta_{unlev} = \frac{\beta_{lev}}{1+\frac{D}{E}} \qquad (A4.2)$$

Although we know that it is an example, used by the WB, we assumed the initial leverage and the β_{lev} proposed by the model is good enough approximation for the reality. This can be checked with the β's for emerging countries found at Professor Damodaran website (http://pages.stern.nyu.edu/~adamodar/).

From that web site we found the following

Table A4.2. β_{unlev} values from Damodaran.

Industry	No. of firms	β_{lev}	D/E	Unlevered[1] β
Electric-Distribution	21	1.26	191.80%	0.43060907
Electric-Generation	34	0.83	159.63%	0.31960147

The proposed leverage in the model is 50% and the β_{lev} is 0.79. This means that D/E is 1 and the unlevered β is 0.395 which compares with the 0.431 from the information from Damodaran. With this β_{unlev} the calculated Ku is 12.41% using (A1).

It can be shown as it is in this case, that Ku calculated by the CAPM is the same as the Ku calculated as Kd×D% + Ke×E%. In this case we have Ku = 8% × 50% + 16.83% × (1 – 50%) = 12.41%.

If we use the FCF to calculate value then we have to use a different version of the WACC. In this case, assuming that the discount rate for the TS is Ku we have to use a formulation for WACC that takes into account the fact that TS is not always earned the year it is accrued due to the losses carried forward, LCF. The adjusted and more general formulation is

$$WACC_t = Ku_t - \frac{TS_t}{V^L_{t-1}} \tag{A4.3}$$

where TS is the tax savings of the period t and V_{t-1} is the market value of the firm for the previous period.

[1] This unlevered β's has been calculated by the authors.

APPENDIX 5

Table A5.1 Calculation of correct FCF[1].

	1	2	3	4	5	6	7	8	9	10	11	12	13	14	15	16	17	18	19	20
EBIT	−0.8	2.4	3.6	4.8	6.1	7.2	8.4	9.8	11.2	12.8	13.8	15.6	16.7	17.8	18.8	23.8	24.9	24.0	20.7	12.8
Tax	–	−0.8	−1.3	−1.7	−2.1	−2.5	−2.9	−3.4	−3.9	−4.5	−4.8	−5.5	−5.9	−6.2	−6.6	−8.3	−8.7	−8.4	−7.2	−4.5
Depreciation	8.8	6.9	7.2	7.4	7.6	8.1	8.4	8.6	8.8	8.9	8.9	8.3	8.4	8.5	8.6	4.9	3.9	4.0	4.0	3.9
Investment	−5.2	−7.7	−5.2	−5.5	−5.6	−14.8	−7.3	−5.2	−5.1	−5.4	−2.6	−4.2	−2.7	−2.7	−2.6	−2.8	−3.8	−2.9	−2.7	−2.9
Change in WC	−8.8	−3.9	−1.3	−0.1	0.6	0.4	0.7	0.5	0.5	0.5	0.7	0.6	0.7	0.6	0.7	0.6	1.7	4.0	8.7	18.4
Asset base	–	–	–	–	–	–	–	–	–	–	–	–	–	–	–	–	–	–	–	17.6
FCF	−6.1	−3.2	3.0	4.9	6.6	−1.7	7.2	10.4	11.5	12.3	15.9	14.8	17.3	18.1	19.0	18.2	18.0	20.8	23.5	45.4

Table A5.2 Calculation of value at constant prices and "correct" constant prices WACC.

	0	1	2	3	4	5	6	7	8	9	10	11	12	13	14	15	16	17	18	19	20
FCF		−6.1	−3.2	3.0	4.9	6.6	−1.7	7.2	10.4	11.5	12.3	15.9	14.8	17.3	18.1	19.0	18.2	18.0	20.8	23.5	45.4
TS		0.0	0.8	1.3	1.4	1.1	0.9	1.0	0.9	0.9	0.8	0.7	0.6	0.5	0.4	0.3	0.2	0.1	0.1	0.1	0.0
WACC adj = Ku−TS/V		8.61%	7.76%	7.45%	7.38%	7.70%	7.85%	7.86%	7.92%	7.97%	8.02%	8.07%	8.14%	8.19%	8.25%	8.33%	8.40%	8.44%	8.47%	8.51%	8.53%
PV(FCF at WACCadj)	84.5	97.8	108.5	113.7	117.1	119.6	130.7	133.8	134.0	133.2	131.6	126.3	121.7	114.4	105.8	95.6	85.4	74.6	60.2	41.8	–

[1] There is a small discrepancy between the value of FCF from WB and the calculated by the author at year 2 of about 0.3.

APPENDIX 6

Table A6.1 Inconsistency in values: Calculation of market value of debt using different sources in WB approach.

	0	1	2	3	4	5	6	7	8	9	10	11	12	13	14	15	16	17	18	19	20
FCF		−6.1	−2.9	3.0	4.9	6.6	−1.7	7.2	10.4	11.5	12.3	15.9	14.8	17.3	18.1	19.0	18.2	18.0	20.8	23.5	45.4
CFD		−5.6	−2.4	4.3	6.8	8.8	0.5	9.2	9.2	9.2	8.6	11.4	8.5	9.9	9.4	7.9	4.6	3.6	3.4	2.2	2.4
TX on EBIT		0.0	0.8	1.3	1.7	2.1	2.5	2.9	3.4	3.9	4.5	4.8	5.5	5.9	6.2	6.6	8.3	8.7	8.4	7.2	4.5
FCF + Tx EBIT		−6.1	−2.0	4.2	6.6	8.7	0.8	10.1	13.8	15.4	16.8	20.8	20.3	23.2	24.3	25.5	26.6	26.8	29.1	30.7	49.8
CFE = OCF − CFD = FCF + T× (EBIT) − CFD		−0.4	0.4	−0.1	−0.1	−0.2	0.3	0.9	4.6	6.2	8.2	9.4	11.8	13.2	14.8	17.6	22.0	23.2	25.7	28.5	47.5
PV(FCF)	92.8	98.5	101.0	98.6	94.8	90.2	91.3	86.9	81.0	74.9	68.8	61.4	55.0	48.1	41.3	34.7	28.7	23.3	17.4	11.2	
PV(CFE)	36.2	41.3	46.2	52.2	59.1	66.9	75.2	83.9	90.2	95.5	99.6	103.1	104.5	104.7	103.4	99.1	89.8	78.2	62.5	42.1	
Debt = PV(FCF) − PV(CFE)	56.6	64.3	70.0	69.4	66.4	61.2	63.9	58.1	51.8	45.2	39.0	29.7	23.1	14.8	6.8	0.1	−1.7	−1.7	−1.2	0.2	
Debt = PV(CFD)	48.1	57.6	64.6	65.5	63.9	60.2	64.6	60.5	56.2	51.5	47.0	39.4	34.0	26.8	19.5	13.2	9.7	6.9	4.0	2.2	
debt from BS	48.1	57.6	64.6	65.5	63.9	60.2	64.6	60.5	56.2	51.5	47.0	39.4	34.0	26.8	19.5	13.2	9.7	6.9	4.0	2.2	
Equity = PV(FCF) − debt from BS	44.7	48.0	51.5	56.2	61.6	67.8	74.5	81.4	85.8	89.3	91.6	93.4	93.5	92.7	90.6	86.0	78.5	69.6	57.3	40.1	
Equity = PV(FCF) − PV(CFD)	44.7	40.9	36.3	33.1	30.9	30.0	26.8	26.4	24.9	23.4	21.8	22.1	21.0	21.2	21.8	21.5	19.1	16.4	13.3	9.0	

Appendix 7

Table A7.1 Calculation of correct CFE with nominal and real interest payments (CFE = FCF + TS – CFD).

	0	1	2	3	4	5	6	7	8	9	10	11	12	13	14	15	16	17	18	19	20
FCF		−6.1	−3.2	3.0	4.9	6.6	−1.7	7.2	10.4	11.5	12.3	15.9	14.8	17.3	18.1	19.0	18.2	18.0	20.8	23.5	45.4
CFD		−5.6	−2.4	4.3	6.8	8.8	0.5	9.2	9.2	9.2	8.6	11.4	8.5	9.9	9.4	7.9	4.6	3.6	3.4	2.2	2.4
TS		–	0.8	1.3	1.7	1.8	2.5	2.5	2.8	1.7	1.4	1.3	1.1	1.0	0.8	0.5	0.4	0.3	0.2	0.1	0.1
CFE (nominal)		-0.4	0.1	-0.1	-0.1	-0.4	0.3	0.5	4.0	4.0	5.2	5.9	7.5	8.3	9.4	11.6	14.0	14.7	17.6	21.4	43.1
CCF = FCF + TS(nominal)		−6,1	−2,0	4,2	6,6	8,4	0,8	9,7	13,2	13,1	13,8	17,2	15,9	18,3	18,8	19,5	18,6	18,3	20,9	23,6	45,4
CFD		−7.4	-4.6	2.0	4.4	6.5	−1.7	6.8	7.0	7.1	6.7	9.7	7.0	8.7	8.5	7.2	4.1	3.2	3.1	2.0	2.3
TS		0.0	0.8	1.3	1.4	1.1	0.9	1.0	0.9	0.9	0.8	0.7	0.6	0.5	0.4	0.3	0.2	0.1	0.1	0.1	0.0
CFE (real)		1.3	2.2	2.2	2.0	1.1	0.9	1.3	4.3	5.2	6.4	7.0	8.4	9.1	10.0	12.0	14.4	15.0	17.7	21.5	43.1
CCF = FCF + TS(real)		-6.1	-2.3	4.2	6.3	7.6	-0.8	8.1	11.3	12.3	13.1	16.6	15.4	17.8	18.5	19.3	18.4	18.2	20.9	23.5	-6.1

Now we calculate the PV of the "correct" CCF using real Ku

Table A7.2 PV of the "correct" CCF using real Ku.

	0	1	2	3	4	5	6	7	8	9	10	11	12	13	14	15	16	17	18	19	20
CCF = CFD + CFE		-6.1	-2.3	4.2	6.3	7.6	-0.8	8.1	11.3	12.3	13.1	16.6	15.4	17.8	18.5	19.3	18.4	18.2	20.9	23.5	45.4
Ku real		8.61%	8.61%	8.61%	8.61%	8.61%	8.61%	8.61%	8.61%	8.61%	8.61%	8.61%	8.61%	8.61%	8.61%	8.61%	8.61%	8.61%	8.61%	8.61%	8.61%
PV(CCF)	84.5	97.8	108.5	113.7	117.1	119.6	130.7	133.8	134.0	133.2	131.6	126.3	121.7	114.4	105.8	95.6	85.4	74.6	60.2	41.8	

Compared with 92.8 (the total value obtained by the WB exercise the later is overestimated by 9.87%. Note that this is the same value we obtained using the FCF and the adjusted version of WACC.

Now we calculate the equity value as total value minus debt and compare it with the present value of the CFE.

Table A7.3 PV of the "correct" CFE using real Ke.

	0	1	2	3	4	5	6	7	8	9	10	11	12	13	14	15	16	17	18	19	20
PV(CCF) −debt	36.4	40.2	43.9	48.2	53.2	59.4	66.1	73.3	77.9	81.7	84.6	86.9	87.7	87.5	86.2	82.4	75.7	67.7	56.1	39.6	
CFE		1.3	2.2	2.2	2.0	1.1	0.9	1.3	4.3	5.2	6.4	7.0	8.4	9.1	10.0	12.0	14.4	15.0	17.7	21.5	43.1
Ke= Ku+(Ku−Kd)D/E		14.2%	14.7%	14.9%	14.4%	13.7%	12.9%	12.8%	12.1%	11.7%	11.3%	11.0%	10.5%	10.3%	9.9%	9.6%	9.3%	9.2%	9.0%	8.9%	8.8%
PV(CFE)	36.4	40.2	43.9	48.2	53.2	59.4	66.1	73.3	77.9	81.7	84.6	86.9	87.7	87.5	86.2	82.4	75.7	67.7	56.1	39.6	-
Debt(BS)	48.1	57.6	64.6	65.5	63.9	60.2	64.6	60.5	56.2	51.5	47.0	39.4	34.0	26.8	19.5	13.2	9.7	6.9	4.0	2.2	-

Contrasting with the values calculated with the WB approaches, there is absolute consistency in the values.

APPENDIX 8

Setting the NPV equal to zero we could use the following set of tariffs.

Table A8.1a Tariffs recalculated.

Residential users		
-Fixed Charge	($/month)	2.550
-First block	($/KWh)	0.0590
-Second block	($/KWh)	0.0490

Instead of the tariffs proposed by the case.

Table A8.1b Original tariffs.

Residential users		
-Fixed Charge	($/month)	2.550
-First block	($/KWh)	0.055
-Second block	($/KWh)	0.045

This means that the tariffs set for the NPV = 0 when the total value of the project was 92.8 were underestimated, (this is just an example because we could change others or include in the change additional input tariffs or variables).

APPENDIX 9

When we calculate the financial statements including the inflation rate as the increase in prices for revenues, expenses (OPEX) and investments (CAPEX) (neutral inflation and hence nominal prices) and recalculate the FCF, use the CFD with nominal Kd, use the TS derived with nominal Kd and derive the CFE we have

Table A9.1 Consistency in nominal cash flows.

	1	2	3	4	5	6	7	8	9	10	11	12	13	14	15	16	17	18	19	20
FCF	−6.1	−3.6	2.7	4.9	6.7	−4.2	6.8	11.1	12.9	14.5	20.2	19.2	23.6	25.5	27.7	29.6	30.8	35.3	41.7	80.8
TS	0.0	1.1	1.7	1.8	2.5	3.0	3.6	4.2	-2.3	1.9	1.8	1.7	1.6	1.4	1.3	1.1	1.0	0.9	0.7	0.4
FCF+TS	−6.1	−2.6	4.4	6.7	9.2	−1.3	10.4	15.3	10.6	16.4	22.1	20.8	25.2	26.9	29.0	30.7	31.7	36.2	42.4	81.3
CFD	−5.6	−2.6	4.6	7.3	9.1	-6.5	4.7	7.6	7.5	7.1	11.5	7.5	10.0	9.5	9.4	8.5	6.9	8.6	11.4	17.1
CFE	−0.5	0.1	−0.2	−0.6	0.1	5.2	5.7	7.7	3.1	9.3	10.6	13.4	15.2	17.4	19.6	22.2	24.8	27.6	31.0	64.2
CCF=CFD+CFE	−6.1	−2.6	4.4	6.7	9.2	-1.3	10.4	15.3	10.6	16.4	22.1	20.8	25.2	26.9	29.0	30.7	31.7	36.2	42.4	81.3

With the CCF we can find the value of the firm using the nominal Ku and the value of equity either subtracting the debt from the total value. We calculate the market value of equity as the present value of CFE at the proper Ke.

Table A9.2 Calculation of value at nominal prices and correct WACC.

	0	1	2	3	4	5	6	7	8	9	10	11	12	13	14	15	16	17	18	19	20
Ku		12.4%	12.4%	12.4%	12.4%	12.4%	12.4%	12.4%	12.4%	12.4%	12.4%	12.4%	12.4%	12.4%	12.4%	12.4%	12.4%	12.4%	12.4%	12.4%	12.4%
CCF		−6.1	−2.6	4.4	6.7	9.2	−1.3	10.4	15.3	10.6	16.4	22.1	20.8	25.2	26.9	29.0	30.7	31.7	36.2	42.4	81.3
PV(CCF)	76.5	92.2	106.2	115.0	122.5	128.5	145.7	153.5	157.2	166.1	170.3	169.3	169.5	165.4	159.0	149.7	137.6	123.0	102.0	72.3	
PV(CCF)-Debt	28.4	34.6	41.4	49.5	59.2	69.2	75.2	82.0	87.6	98.4	104.3	109.6	112.4	113.7	112.7	109.1	102.2	91.7	76.8	56.5	
CFE		−0.5	0.1	−0.2	−0.6	0.1	5.2	5.7	7.7	3.1	9.3	10.6	13.4	15.2	17.4	19.6	22.2	24.8	27.6	31.0	64.2
Ke=Ku+−Ku-KdD/E		19.9%	19.8%	19.3%	18.2%	17.1%	16.2%	16.6%	16.3%	15.9%	15.4%	15.2%	14.8%	14.7%	14.4%	14.2%	14.1%	13.9%	13.9%	13.9%	13.6%
PV(CFE)	28.4	34.6	41.4	49.5	59.2	69.2	75.2	82.0	87.6	98.4	104.3	109.6	112.4	113.7	112.7	109.1	102.2	91.7	76.8	56.5	-
Debt	48.1	57.6	64.8	65.4	63.3	59.3	70.5	71.5	69.6	67.7	66.0	59.8	57.1	51.7	46.3	40.6	35.4	31.3	25.2	15.8	0.0

As a double check we calculate the total value using the FCF but as we mentioned above, we cannot use the traditional formulation of the WACC. Hence we use the WACC formulation stated in equation (7). In this case we have.

Table A9.3 Calculation of value using FCF and adjusted WACC.

	0	1	2	3	4	5	6	7	8	9	10	11	12	13	14	15	16	17	18	19	20
FCF		-6.1	-3.6	2.7	4.9	6.7	-4.2	6.8	11.1	12.9	14.5	20.2	19.2	23.6	25.5	27.7	29.6	30.8	35.3	41.7	80.8
TS		0.0	1.1	1.7	1.8	2.5	3.0	3.6	4.2	-2.3	1.9	1.8	1.7	1.6	1.4	1.3	1.1	1.0	0.9	0.7	0.4
WACC		12.4%	11.2%	10.8%	10.8%	10.3%	10.1%	10.0%	9.7%	13.9%	11.3%	11.3%	11.4%	11.5%	11.5%	11.6%	11.7%	11.7%	11.7%	11.7%	11.8%
V	76.5	92.2	106.2	115.0	122.5	128.5	145.7	153.5	157.2	166.1	170.3	169.3	169.5	165.4	159.0	149.7	137.6	123.0	102.0	72.3	0

As before the consistency is complete. The overvaluation of the value calculated using the WB methodology is 21.2%.
For this case the tariffs would be

Table A9.4 Tariffs recalculated at nominal prices.

RESIDENTIAL USERS		
-Fixed Charge	($/month)	2.550
-First block	($/KWh)	0.0649
-Second block	($/KWh)	0.0549

This means an undervaluation of those tariffs of 15.2% and 18.0% respectively.
The leverage using market values is shown in Table A9.5

Table A9.5 Leverage using correct market values.

	0	1	2	3	4	5	6	7	8	9	10	11	12	13	14	15	16	17	18	19
Total value	76.5	92.2	106.2	115.0	122.5	128.5	145.7	153.5	157.2	166.1	170.3	169.3	169.5	165.4	159.0	149.7	137.6	123.0	102.0	72.3
Debt(BS)	48.1	57.6	64.8	65.4	63.3	59.3	70.5	71.5	69.6	67.7	66.0	59.8	57.1	51.7	46.3	40.6	35.4	31.3	25.2	15.8
D%	0.63	0.62	0.61	0.57	0.52	0.46	0.48	0.47	0.44	0.41	0.39	0.35	0.34	0.31	0.29	0.27	0.26	0.25	0.25	0.22

Appendix 10

In this appendix we show the inconsistencies in the definition of CFE presented in the WB example.

$$\text{CFE} = \text{OCF} - \text{Taxes} - \text{CFD} \tag{1}$$

$$\text{FCF} + \text{TS} = \text{CFE} + \text{CFD} \tag{2}$$

Replacing (1) in (2)

$$\text{FCF} + \text{TS} = \text{OCF} - \text{Taxes} - \text{CFD} + \text{CFD} \tag{3}$$

On the other hand,

$$\text{OCF} = \text{EBITDA} - \text{Investments} - \text{Provision for unrecoverable} \tag{4}$$

Then

$$\begin{aligned}&\text{FCF} + \text{TS}\\ &= \text{EBITDA} - \text{Investments} - \text{Provision for unrecoverable}\\ &- \text{Taxes} - \text{CFD} + \text{CFD}\end{aligned} \tag{5}$$

But

$$\text{FCF} = \text{EBIT}(1-\text{T}) + \text{Depreciation} - \text{Investments} - \text{Provision for unrecoverable} \tag{6}$$

and

$$\text{EBITDA} = \text{EBIT} + \text{Depreciation} \tag{7}$$

Replacing (7) in (5) we have

$$\begin{aligned}&\text{FCF} + \text{TS}\\ &= \text{EBIT} + \text{Depreciation} - \text{Investments} - \text{Provision for unrecoverable}\\ &- \text{Taxes} - \text{CFD} + \text{CFD}\end{aligned} \tag{8}$$

Replacing (6) in (8), we have

$$\begin{aligned}&\text{EBIT}\times(1-\text{T}) + \text{Depreciation} - \text{Investments} - \text{Provision for unrecoverable} + \text{TS}\\ &= \text{EBIT} + \text{Depreciation} - \text{Investments} - \text{Provision for unrecoverable}\\ &- \text{Taxes} - \text{CFD} + \text{CFD}\end{aligned} \tag{9}$$

Simplifying

EBIT−EBIT × T + Depreciation − Investments − Provision for unrecoverable + TS = EBIT + Depreciation − Investments − Provision for unrecoverable – Taxes – CFD + CFD −EBIT × T + TS = EBIT – Taxes

Then

−EBIT × T + TS = EBIT – Taxes

If Taxes are taxes on EBIT, then

TS = EBIT

If Taxes are the taxes paid by the firm, then

TS = EBIT – Taxes + EBIT ×T

TS = EBIT×(1+T) − Taxes

REFERENCES

[1] Almeida, H., Campello, M., and Weisbach, M. S., 2002, *Corporate Demand for Liquidity*, New York University, working paper.

[2] Almeida H., M. Campello, and M. Weisbach, 2003, *The cash flow sensitivity of cash*, *Journal of Finance* **59**, 1777-1804.

[3] Almeida, H., M. Campello, and M. S. Weisbach. 2002 "*The Demand for Corporate Liquidity: A Theory and Some Evidence.*" Working Paper, University of Illinois and New York University.

[4] Arzac, Enrique R., 2005, *Valuation for Mergers*, Buyouts and Restructuring, Wiley.

[5] Bailey, A. D. & Jensen, D. L. (1977), 'General price level adjustments in the capital budgeting decision', *Financial Management Spring*, **26**—31.

[6] Baum, Christopher (Kit) F., Caglayan, Mustafa, Ozkan, Neslihan and Talavera, Oleksandr, 2004, "The Impact of Macroeconomic Uncertainty on Cash Holdings for Non-Financial Firms". *ZEW Discussion Paper* No. **04**-10. *http://ssrn.com/abstract=555952*

[7] Baumol, W. J., 1952, "The transactions demand for cash: An inventory theoretic approach", *Quarterly Journal of Economics* (November), 545-556.

[8] Belli, P., J. Anderson, H. Barnum, J. Dixon, and J. Tan. 2001. *Economic Analysis of Investment Operations: Analytical Tools and Practical Applications*. Washington D.C.: World Bank Institute.

[9] Beltz, J and M. Frank, 1996, "*Risk and corporate holdings of highly liquid assets*", Hong Kong University of Science and Technology Working Paper.

[10] Blanchard, F. Lopez de Salinas, A. Shleifer, 1994, What do firms do with cash windfalls?, *Journal of Financial Economics* **36**, 337 - 360.

[11] Brealey, Richard A. and Stewart C. Myers, 1996, *Principles of Corporate Finance*, 5th ed. McGraw-Hill.

[12] Brealey, Richard A. and Stewart C. Myers, 2003, *Principles of Corporate Finance*, 7th ed. McGraw-Hill.

[13] Brealey, Richard A., Stewart C. Myers and Alan J. Marcus, 1995, *Fundamentals of Corporate Finance*, McGraw-Hill

[14] Bruner, Robert F., 1985. "*The Use of Excess Cash and Debt Capacity as Motive for Merger.*" Colgate Darden Graduate School of Business (December).

[15] Caglayan-Ozkan, N., Ozkan, A., 2002, *Corporate Cash Holdings: An Empirical Investigation of UK Companies, University of York* – Heslington, working paper.

[16] Canada, J.R. y White, Jr., J.A., 1996, *Capital Investment Decision Analysis for Engineering and Management*, Prentice Hall.

[17] Coello, Tim, Estache, Antonio, Perelman, Sergio and Lourdes Trujillo, 2003, *A Primer on Efficiency Measurement for Utilities and Transport Regulators*, The World Bank, Washington, D.C., February

[18] Cooley, P. L., Roenfeldt, R. L. & Chew, I. (1975), 'Capital budgeting procedures under inflation', *Financial Management Winter*, **18**—27.

[19] Copeland, Tom, Tim Koller and Jack Murrin, 2000, *Valuation. Measuring and Managing the Value of Companies*, 3rd ed. Wiley.

[20] Damodaran, A., *http://pages.stern.nyu.edu/~adamodar/*. Visited on April 19, 2004

[21] Damodaran, Aswath, 1996, *Investment Valuation. Tools and Techniques for Determining the Value of any Asset*, Wiley.

[22] Dittmar J., A. and Mahrt-Smith and H. Servaes, 2003, International corporate governance and corporate cash holdings, *Journal of Financial and Quantitative Analysis* **38**.

[23] Dixon, John A. and Hufschmidt, Maynard M. (Eds), 1986, *Economic Valuation Techniques for the Environment. A Case Study Workbook*, The John Hopkins University Press.

[24] Estache, A., Rodríguez Pardina, Martín, Rodríguez, Jose María, and Germán Sember, 2002, *An Introduction to Financial and Economic Modeling for Utility Regulators*, The World Bank.

[25] Ezzell, John R and William A Kelly Jr, An APV Analysis of Capital Budgeting Under Inflation, *Financial Management* (pre-1986); Autumn 1984; 13, 3; pg. 49-54.

[26] Faulkender and R. Wang, 2004, *Corporate financial policy and the value of cash*, Working paper, Washington University in St. Louis.

[27] Faulkender Michael and Mitchell A. Petersen, 2004, *Does the source of capital affect capital structure?*, working paper series, Washington University.

[28] Faulkender Michael, 2004, *Cash holdings among small businesses*, working paper series, Washington University.

[29] Fazzari, S. M., R. G. Hubbard, and B. Petersen, 1988. Financing constraints and corporate investment. *Brookings Papers on Economic Activity* 19, 141-195.

[30] Fazzari, S. M. and B. C. Petersen, 1993, "Working capital and fixed investments: New evidence on financing constraints", *Rand Journal of Economics* (Autumn), 328-342.

[31] Findlay III M Chapman, Capital Budgeting Procedures Under Inflation: Cooley Roenfeldt And Chew, *Financial Management* (pre-1986); Autumn 1976; 5, 3; pg. 83

[32] Goldschmidt, Yaaqov and Jacob Yaron, 1991, Inflation adjustments of financial statements: application of international accounting standard 29: financial reporting in

hyperinflationary economies, *Working Papers*, Agricultural Policies Agriculture and Rural Development Department. The World Bank, May, WPS 670

[33] Grinblatt, M and S. Titman, 2002, *Financial Markets and Corporate Strategy*, Irwin-McGraw-Hill.

[34] Hoshi, T., A. Kashyap and D. Scharfstein, 1991. Corporate structure, liquidity, and investment: Evidence from Japanese panel data. *Quarterly Journal of Economics* **106**, 33-60.

[35] Howe, K. M. (1992), 'Capital budgeting discount rates under inflation: A caveat', *Financial Practice and Education* Spring/Summer, 31—35.

[36] Huberman, G., 1984, "External financing and liquidity", *Journal of Finance* (July), 895-908.

[37] Ingersoll, J. and S. Ross, 1992. Waiting to invest: Investment and uncertainty. *Journal of Business* **65**, 1-29.

[38] International Bank for Reconstruction and Development – The World Bank, 2002, *Financial Modeling of Regulatory Policy*, **2** CD set.

[39] Jensen, M. and W. H. Meckling, 1976, "Theory of the Firm: Managerial Behavior, Agency Costs and Ownership Structure," *Journal of Financial Economics*, **3**, 305-360.

[40] Jensen, M. C., 1986, "Agency costs of free cash flow, corporate finance and takeovers", *American Economic Review* (May), 323-329.

[41] Kim Chang-Soo, David C. Mauer, and Ann E. Sherman, 1998, The determinants of corporate liquidity: Theory and evidence, *Journal of Financial and Quantitative Analysis* **33**, 335{359.

[42] La Porta, R., Lopez-de-Silanes, F., Shleifer, A., and R. W. Vishny, 2000. "Agency Problems and Dividend Policies around the World." *Journal of Finance,* **55** (), 1-33.

[43] Levy, Haim and Marshall Sarnat, 1982, *Capital Investment and Financial Decisions*, 2nd ed. Prentice Hall.

[44] Levy, Haim and Marshall Sarnat, 1995, *Capital Investment and Financial Decisions*, 5th ed. Prentice Hall.

[45] Lucas, Robert E., Jr., 1988, "Money Demand in the United States: A Quantitative Review," in Karl Brunner and Bennett McCallum (eds.) *Money, Business Cycles, and Exchange Rates: Essays in Honor of Allan H. Meltzer, Carnegie-Rochester Series on Public Policy*, **29**, 137-168.

[46] McDonald, R. and D. Siegel, 1986. The value of waiting to invest. *Quarterly Journal of Economics* **101**, 707-727.

[47] Mehta, Dileep R, Michael D Curley and Hung-Gay Fung, Inflation, Cost of Capital, and Capital Budgeting Procedures, *Financial Management* (pre-1986); Winter 1984; 13, 4; pg. 48

[48] Meltzer, A. H. 1993, "The Demand for Money: A Cross-Section Study of Business Firms." *Quarterly Journal of Economics,* **77**, 405-422.

[49] Mikkelson, W. H. and M. Partch, 2003, Do persistent large cash reserves hinder performance, *Journal of Financial and Quantitative Analysis* **38**, 275-294.

[50] Mills, Geofrey T., 1996, The Impact Of Inflation on Capital Budgeting and Working Capital, *Journal of Financial and Strategic Decisions*, Volume 9 Number 1 Spring, pp 79-87.

[51] Miller, M. H., and D. Orr. 1966, "A Model of the Demand for Money by Firms." *Quarterly Journal of Economics*, **80**, 413-435.

[52] Minton, B. A. and C. Schrand, 1999, "The Impact of Cash Flow Volatility on Discretionary Investment and the Costs of Debt and Equity Financing", *Journal of Financial Economics* **54**, 423-460.

[53] Modigliani, Franco y Merton H. Miller, 1958, The Cost of Capital, Corporation Taxes and the Theory of Investment, *The American Economic Review.* Vol XLVIII, pp 261-297

[54] Modigliani, Franco y Merton H. Miller, 1959, The Cost of Capital, Corporation Finance, and the Theory of Investment: Reply, *The American Economic Review*, XLIX, pp. 524-527.

[55] Modigliani, Franco y Merton H. Miller, 1963, Corporate Income Taxes and the Cost of Capital: A Correction, *The American Economic Review.* Vol LIII, pp 433-443.

[56] Mulligan, Casey B., 1997, "Scale Economies, the Value of Time, and the Demand for Money: Longitudinal Evidence from Firms." *Journal of Political Economy*, **105**, 1061-1079.

[57] Mulligan, Casey B., and Xavier Sala-i-Martin, 1992, "U.S. Money Demand: Surprising Cross- Sectional Estimates," *Brookings Papers on Economic Activity*, **2**, 285-329.

[58] Myers, Stewart C. and Raghuram G. Rajan, 1998, The paradox of liquidity, *Quarterly Journal of Economics* August, 733-771.

[59] Nelson, C. R. (1976), 'Inflation and capital budgeting', *Journal of Finance* **31**, 923—931.

[60] Opler, T., L. Pinkowitz, R. Stulz, and R. Williamson, 1999, "The Determinants and Implications of Corporate Cash Holdings", *Journal of Financial Economics* **52**, 3-46.

[61] Ozkan Aydin and Neslihan Ozkan, 2002, *Corporate cash holdings: An empirical investigation of UK companies*, working paper,. *http://papers.ssrn.com*

[62] Pinkowitz Lee and Rohan Williamson, 2001, Bank power and cash holdings: Evidence from Japan, *Review of Financial Studies* **14**, 1059-1082.

[63] Pinkowitz Lee and Rohan Williamson, 2004, *What is a dollar worth? the market value of cash holdings*, working paper series, Georgetown University.

[64] Pinkowitz Lee, Rene Stulz, and Rohan Williamson, 2004, Investor right and the value of cash holdings to minority shareholders, *Working paper, NBER* No. **10188**.

[65] Pinkowitz Lee, Rene Stulz, and Rohan Williamson, 2003, *Why do firms in countries with poor protection of investor rights hold more cash, working paper,* NBER No.**10188**.

[66] Rappaport, A. & Taggart, R. A. (1982), 'Evaluation of capital expenditure proposals under inflation', *Financial Management Spring*, 5—13.

[67] Ross, S. A., R. W. Westerfield and J. Jaffe, 1999, *Corporate Finance,* Irwin-McGraw-Hill.

[68] Ruback, Richard S., 2000, *Capital Cash Flows: A Simple Approach to Valuing Risky Cash Flows*, Working Paper, Social Science Research Network. Also published at *Financial Management,* Vol. 31, No. 2, Summer 2002

[69] Schnure, C., 1998, "Who holds cash? And why?", Federal Reserve Board *Working Paper* **98**-13 (January).

[70] Tham, Joseph and Ignacio Vélez-Pareja, 2002, Modeling the Impacts of Inflation in Investment Appraisal, *Working Paper*. Available through the Social Science Research Network (SSRN).

[71] Tham, Joseph and Vélez-Pareja, Ignacio, 2004a, *Principles of Cash Flow Valuation. An Integrated Market Approach*. Academic Press

[72] Tham, Joseph and Vélez-Pareja, Ignacio, 2004b, "Top 9 (Unnecessary and Avoidable) Mistakes in Cash Flow Valuation" (January 29). Social Science Research Network (SSRN) *http://ssrn.com/abstract=496083*

[73] Van Horne, J. C. (1971), 'A note on biases in capital budgeting introduced by inflation', *Journal of Financial and Quantitative Analysis* **6**, 653—658.

[74] Van Horne, J.C., 1997, *Financial Management and Policy*, 11th Ed., Prentice Hall.

[75] Vélez-Pareja, Ignacio and Burbano-Pérez, Antonio, 2003, "A Practical Guide for Consistency in Valuation: Cash Flows, Terminal Value and Cost of Capital" (November 9, 2003). Social Science Research Network (SSRN) *http://ssrn.com/abstract=466721*

[76] Velez-Pareja, Ignacio and Tham, Joseph, 2004, "Timanco S.A.: Unpaid Taxes, Losses Carried Forward, Foreign Debt, Presumptive Income and Adjustment for Inflation. The Treatment with DCF and EVA(c)" (March 10, 2004). Social Science Research Network (SSRN) *http://ssrn.com/abstract=438242*

[77] Vélez-Pareja, Ignacio and Tham, Joseph, 2002, "Valuation in an Inflationary Environment" (May 31, 2002). *http://ssrn.com/abstract=329020.* Paper at Conference "Valuation in Emerging Markets" Darden School of Business Administration, University of Virginia, May 29-31, 2002, Charlottesville, Virginia.

[78] Vélez-Pareja, Ignacio, 1987, *Decisiones de inversión*, Facultad de Administración, Universidad de los Andes, (mimeo) May 1987, pp. 459.

[79] Vélez-Pareja, Ignacio, 1998, *Decisiones de inversión, Una aproximación al análisis de alternativas*, CEJA, 1998.

[80] Vélez-Pareja, Ignacio, 2004a, "Modeling the Financial Impact of Regulatory Policy: Practical Recommendations and Suggestions. The Case of World Bank" (August 20, 2004). Social Science Research Network (SSRN) *http://ssrn.com/abstract=580042*

[81] Vélez-Pareja, Ignacio, 1983, Note: *"Replacement models: Technology inappropriate to non industrialized countries"*, *Interfaces*, Vol. 13, No. 5, October 1983, pp. 122- 123.

[82] Vélez-Pareja, Ignacio, 2005, "Once More, the Correct Definition for the Cash Flows to Value a Firm (Free Cash Flow and Cash Flow to Equity)" (January 3, 2005). Social Science Research Network (SSRN) *http://ssrn.com/abstract=642763*

[83] Vélez-Pareja, Ignacio, 1999, "Project Evaluation in an Inflationary Environment" (February 11, 1999). *Working Paper* No. **2**. Social Science Research Network (SSRN) http://ssrn.com/abstract=148410

[84] Vélez-Pareja, Ignacio, 2004b, "The Correct Definition for the Cash Flows to Value a Firm (Free Cash Flow and Cash Flow to Equity)" (September 29, 2004). Social Science Research Network (SSRN) *http://ssrn.com/abstract=597681*

[85] Weston, J. Fred and Copeland, T.E., 1992, *Managerial Finance*, 9th ed. The Dryden Press.

[86] Whalen, Edward L., 1965, "A Cross-Section Study of Business Demand for Cash," *Journal of Finance*, **20**, 423-443.

Chapter 3

Chapter Three:Structural Core Inflation Estimation
can be found in
Offprints in Holloway Road Library
Ask for Offprint by Claudio Morana

In: Trends in Inflation Research
Editor: Barbara T. Credan, pp. 187-205
ISBN: 1-59454-825-0
© 2006 Nova Science Publishers, Inc.

Chapter 4

INFLATION CONVERGENCE AFTER THE INTRODUCTION OF THE EURO

Markus F. Mentz [a] ***and Steffen P. Sebastian*** [b*]

[a] Department of Finance, European Business School, 65375 Oestrich-Winkel, Germany
[b] Department of Finance, Goethe-University, 60054 Frankfurt/Main, Germany

ABSTRACT

Using the *Johansen* test for cointegration, we examine to which extent inflation rates in the Euro area have converged after the introduction of a single currency. Since the assumption of non-stationary variables represents the pivotal point in cointegration analyses we pay special attention to the appropriate identification of non-stationary inflation rates by the application of six different unit root tests. We compare two periods, the first ranging from 1993 to 1998 and the second from 1993 to 2003 with monthly observations. The *Johansen* test only finds partial convergence for the former period and no convergence for the latter.

JEL classification: C32 ; E31 ; F15
Keywords: Unit root; Cointegration; Inflation convergence

We are grateful to Martin Bohl and Uwe Hassler for helpful comments.

1 INTRODUCTION

Prior to the introduction of a single currency within the European Union economists considered it a necessity that monetary decisions of the member states be synchronized. This gave way to a regulatory framework which ranges from the European Monetary System (EMS) of 1979 (limitation of exchange rate divergence) to the Maastricht Treaty of 1992. Among other convergence criteria the Maastricht Treaty defined explicit convergence goals for inflation rates. Inflation rates were to stay within certain borders, interdependent of the

* E-mail address: sebastian@wiwi.uni-frankfurt.de, Corresponding author. Tel.: +49-69-798-22665; fax: +49-69-798-25210

development in the fellow member states. Since the beginning of the eighties until the introduction of the Euro, inflation rates declined within the Euro area. In recent years, however, a proliferating inflation divergence has been noticeable and it remains questionable if this divergence is only short-natured or if inflation rates in the Euro area have been drifting apart systematically after the introduction of the Euro.

The question whether inflation gaps develop in a systematic manner arises against the background that temporary inflation differences within closed economies are considered as adaptations to differences in demand preferences as well as regional circumstances (*Remsberger* 2002: 2). They have been documented for large economies such as the US-economy (see, for example, *Engel/Rogers* 1996: 1113-1120). Within the European Monetary Union on the other hand, where member economies are rather a confederation than a federal state with governments that still have taxation and debt autonomy, and where convergence towards an economic union remains a political objective, the systematic price divergence should be avoided and hence closely monitored.

In this paper, the *Johansen* test is used to measure the actual degree of inflation convergence after the introduction of the Euro. The assumption of non-stationary inflation rates plays an important role in cointegration tests for the convergence of economic variables. Whether inflation rates are stationary or not is a controversially debated issue (see, for example, *Culver/Papell* 1997: 453; *Lee/Wu* 2001: 480). Thus, before applying the *Johansen* procedure in the Euro area we pay special attention to the appropriate identification of non-stationary inflation rates. Six different unit root tests are applied to test the stationarity of the inflation rates.

The second part of this paper explains the econometric strategy and outlines the unit root tests as well as the *Johansen* test. Thereafter, five inflation rate time series are analysed by a cointegration approach based on the results of the unit root tests. The last part of the paper sums up the findings.

2 ECONOMETRIC STRATEGY

2.1 *Johansen* Test for Cointegration

If the synchronization of two variables X_{1t} and X_{2t} (e.g. inflation rates in two countries) is measured by linear regression models, results can be spurred in case non-stationary endogenous and exogenous variables are used (see, for example, *Granger/Newbold* (1974: 117). On the other hand, the fact that two time series are non-stationary does not always have to indicate spurred regression results. If the residuals of a regression are stationary two variables are said to be cointegrated. The concept of cointegration thus indicates that, while both variables have stochastic trends and short-run random divergences associated therewith, they develop in a coherent way in the long-run.[1]

---

[1]Formally, this condition can be expressed as follows: Two processes x_{1t} and x_{2t} are said to be cointegrated, if they obey to the conditions:

x_{1t}, x_{2t} are $I(d)$; (2.1)

$b_1 x_{1t} + b_2 x_{2t} = \varepsilon_t$; (2.2)

$\varepsilon_t \sim I(d-b)$, with $b > 0$. (2.3)

The *Johansen* test (*Johansen* 1991: 1555) examines several non-stationary variables for cointegration. It enables an analysis of the convergence of k economic variables by starting with a vector error correction model of the form:

$$\Delta X_t = A_1^* \Delta X_{t-1} + A_2^* \Delta X_{t-2} + \ldots + A_{p-1}^* \Delta X_{t-p+1} + \Pi X_{t-1} + \varepsilon_t \qquad (2.4)$$

The vector error correction model can be interpreted as a vector autoregressive model in first differences whereas the penultimate addend "corrects" short run fluctuations of the variables and describes its long-run relationship (cointegration relationship). In order to determine the number of cointegration relationships between the k variables the rank h of matrix Π is examined, assuming that not all variables are stationary.[2]

The rank h of Π is equivalent to the number of cointegration relationships among the k variables under examination. The *Johansen* test relies on two test statistics for the identification of the cointegration rank h under the assumption that the residuals are white noise. The null and alternative hypotheses of these statistics, i.e. the maximum eigenvalue test (λ_{max} test) and the trace test, can be written as follows:

$$\begin{array}{ll} \lambda_{max} & - H_0 : h = j \;\; against \;\; H_1 : h = j+1 \;\; , j = 0,\ldots,k-1 \\ trace & - H_0 : h \leq j \;\; against \;\; H_1 : h > j \qquad , j = 0,\ldots,k-1 \end{array} \qquad (2.5)$$

In the course of *Johansen's* test procedure, deterministic components can be added to the vector error correction model in (2.4). Firstly, deterministic components can be added to the cointegration term (long-run relationships) secondly, they can be added to the remaining terms of the model (short-run relationships). Before applying the *Johansen* procedure, one has to determine how many lagged variables p should be taken into account. The *Johansen* test presupposes that the residuals of the vector ε_t are independently distributed, which suggests a rather high value for p. On the other hand, the value of p determines the length of deviations from the long-run cointegration relationship, which would put forward a small value for p. Thus, in small samples the choice of p is a trade-off between distortions of the test results on the one hand and the statistic requirements on the other. In general, the robustness of the test results should be confirmed by a variation of the lag length p.

2.2 Unit Root Tests

2.2.1 Augmented Dickey-Fuller and Phillips-Perron Tests

The standard Augmented *Dickey-Fuller* and *Phillips-Perron* tests are applied as benchmarks and starting points for the identification of non-stationary inflation rates. The

---

(b_1, b_2) stands for the cointegration vector. If more than two, namely k processes are considered, a maximum of $h < k$ cointegration relationships among the variables is possible (h denoting the cointegration rank).

[2]The vector error correction model in (2.4) can only be consistently set up if the rank h of the matrix Π is not full. This is due to the fact that all variables on the left side of the equation are stationary since they are first differenced. The same applies for the variables on the right side of the equation except for X_{t-1}. If the rank of the matrix Π is full then all variables in X_{t-1} should be stationary.

former test, first described in *Fuller* (1976: 333), assumes an autoregressive model of order p with white noise residuals and computes the t-statistics for the null that $\phi = 0$:

$$\Delta x_t = \phi x_{t-1} + \sum_{j=1}^{p-1} \varphi_j (x_{t-j} - x_{t-j-1}) + \varepsilon_t \tag{2.6}$$

Within the scope of the Augmented *Dickey-Fuller*-Test we determine the number of lags by the minimum in the *Schwarz* information criterion. Additionally, we choose a value for p that is high enough to obtain residuals free from autocorrelation. We assume an absence of autocorrelation in the residuals up to ten lags if the *Ljung-Box* statistic indicates white noise with a significance of over 95%.

The *Phillips-Perron* test defines the underlying process of the time series under examination as an AR(1)-process and adjusts the *Dickey-Fuller* test statistics to account for the presence of autocorrelated residuals. The adjusted test statistic, first described in *Phillips* (1987: 287), under the null of non-stationarity is calculated as:

$$Z_t = \left(\sum_{t=1}^{T} y_{t-1}^2 \right)^{1/2} \frac{(\hat{\phi})}{\hat{\lambda}^2(q)} - \frac{1}{2} \frac{(\lambda^2 - \gamma_0)}{\hat{\lambda}^2(q) \left(T^{-2} \sum_{t=1}^{T} y_{t-1}^2 \right)^{1/2}}, \tag{2.7}$$

while λ^2 denotes the *Newey-West* density estimator at frequency zero (see *Newey/West* 1987: 705).

2.2.2 Elliott-Rothenberg-Stock and Ng-Perron Tests

In addition to the analysis with the standard Augmented *Dickey-Fuller*- and *Phillips-Perron* tests two more unit root tests with better power and size characteristics are used in a comparative testing procedure. We make use of the point optimal test and the GLS-detrending of *Elliott/Rothenberg/Stock* (1996: 814-818) that have improved power characteristics compared to the Augmented *Dickey-Fuller* test and the *Ng-Perron* procedure (*Ng/ Perron* 2001: 1523-1527) which exhibits less size distortions compared to the *Phillips-Perron* test.[3]

Elliott/Rothenberg/Stock (1996) derive the power envelope and maximize the power for a given alternative hypothesis (point optimal test) against the background that no uniformly most powerful unit root test exists. The test statistic that consistently asymptotically satisfies this condition is:

$$P_T = \left[S(\overline{a}) - \overline{a} S(1) \right] / \hat{\omega}^2 \tag{2.8}$$

where ω^2 denotes the autoregressive spectral density estimator at frequency zero, $S(\overline{a})$ the sum of the squared residuals of a quasi-differenced OLS-regression given the alternative hypothesis $\overline{a}$. Here, the lag length in ω^2 is determined using the modified *Akaike* criterion,

[3] The *Phillips-Perron*-test has shown to exhibit size distortions in case the examined time series has negative Moving-Average terms (see, for example, *Schwert* 1989: 6-9).

which accounts for the effects due to distortions in the autoregressive calculation of ω^2 (see *Perron/Ng* 2001).

In addition to the point optimal test, *Elliott/Rothenberg/Stock* (1996) compute a second statistic. Given the alternative hypotheses $\overline{a}$, deterministic components are estimated and subtracted which yields GLS-detrended data. As a second step, *Elliott/Rothenberg/Stock* (1996) apply the Augmented *Dickey-Fuller* test to the GLS-detrended time series y_t^{dt} :

$$\Delta y_t^{dt} = \phi y_{t-1}^{dt} + \sum_{i=1}^{p} \varphi_i (y_{t-i}^{dt} - y_{t-i-1}^{dt}) + \varepsilon_t \tag{2.9}$$

Here, the number of lags p is again determined by the minimum in the modified *Akaike* criterion.

The *Ng-Perron* (2001) procedure applies four test statistics. The first calculates the ERS point optimal statistics for GLS-detrended data:

$$MP_T^{GLS} = \begin{cases} (\overline{c}^2 T^{-2} \sum_{t=1}^{T} (y_{t-1}^{dt})^2 - \overline{c} T^{-1} (y_T^{dt})^2) / \hat{\omega}_2 & \text{Constant} \\ (\overline{c}^2 T^{-2} \sum_{t=1}^{T} (y_{t-1}^{dt})^2 + (1-\overline{c}) T^{-1} (y_N^{dt})^2) / \hat{\omega}_2 & \text{Constant and Trend} \end{cases} \tag{2.10}$$

The remaining three test statistics MZ_α^{GLS}, MZ_t^{GLS} and MSB^{GLS} represent enhancements of the *Phillips-Perron* statistics which correct for size distortions in case of negatively correlated residuals (appendix 2). *Ng/Perron* (2001) subtract deterministic components from the initial time series first and apply the modified *Phillips-Perron* statistics afterwards. For the calculation of MZ_α^{GLS}, MZ_t^{GLS} and MSB^{GLS}, *Ng/Perron* (2001) also make use of the GLS detrending technique to calculate $\hat{\omega}^2$. In this context, *Ng/Perron* (2001) use the modified *Akaike* criterion to choose the lag length.

2.2.3 KPSS Test

Finally, the KPSS test is used for confirmation analysis since it formulates stationarity as the null hypothesis. Under the null of stationarity *Kwiatkowski et al.* (1992: 162) regress the series x_t under examination on a constant r_0 and compute the sum of the residuals S_t:

$$x_t = r_0 + \varepsilon_t, \tag{2.12}$$

$$S_t = \sum_{i=1}^{t} \hat{\varepsilon}_i = \sum_{i=1}^{t} (x_i - \hat{r}_0) = \sum_{i=1}^{t} (x_i - \overline{x}), \text{with } t = 1,2,...,T. \tag{2.13}$$

The KPSS test statistic is then calculated as:

$$\hat{\eta}_{\mu} = \frac{T^{-2}\sum_{t=1}^{T} S_t^2}{\hat{\lambda}^2(q)}. \tag{2.14}$$

3 Measuring Inflation Convergence

3.1 Motivation and Past Results

Since the introduction of the European Monetary System (EMS) inflation in most of the European countries has gone down drastically as figure 1 illustrates.

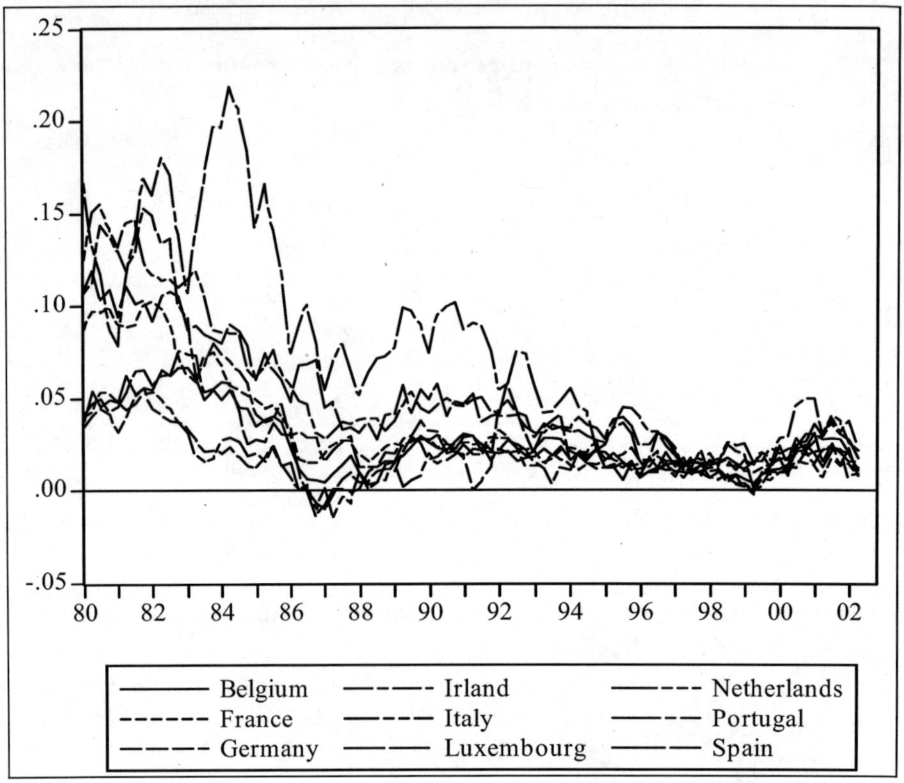

Fig. 1. Inflation convergence in the European Union. Continuously calculated quarterly inflation rates (1980:1-2002:4), Source: *International Financial Statistics.*

Empirical studies about the actual degree of inflation convergence in the EMS draw different conclusions.

Montuengea Gómez (2002: 124) measures inflation convergence based on a regression analysis of inflation differences (β-convergence). He confirms a general inflation convergence in eight EMS countries between 1983 and 1993. *Hafer/Kutan* (1994: 687) employ a sophisticated monetary convergence measure and distinguish between total and partial convergence. Full monetary convergence is assumed, if for a given number of k examined inflation rates k-1 cointegration relationships exist. In this case, full convergence corresponds to the association to one common stochastic trend within the time series under examination. Less than k-1 cointegration relationships are defined as partial convergence.

Caporale/Pittis (1993: 212) discover partial convergence of inflation differences in a sample of seven countries for the period between 1986 and 1990 but they do not find it between 1979 and 1990. On the other hand, *Thom* (1995: 585) finds a partial convergence of inflation rates between 1983 and 1992 as well as between 1986 and 1990 for the same countries that *Caporale/Pittis* (1993) examined. Based on monthly observations, *Siklos/Wohar* (1997: 138) discover partial convergence for five European countries. *Westbrook* (1998: 140-143) analyses the rate of price increase in five countries between 1979 and 1992. Calculating inflation rates based on a consumer price index, she finds complete convergence; if inflation rates are calculated based on a producer price index she finds partial convergence.

Conversely, *Holmes* (2002: 157) finds a lower degree of convergence after the Maastricht Treaty between 1993 and 1999 than before using a panel-cointegration approach. *Remsberger* (2002: 2) states that although the inflation gap within the EMS has decreased from 10% on average in the beginning of the eighties to 2% in 1998, inflation rates have been diverging since 1998. In 2001, the largest gap between two member states amounted to 4.2%. In addition, the standard deviation climbed from an average between 0.8% and 1% in 2000 to 1.2% between January and July 2002.

These findings spur a further investigation of inflation convergence in the EU beyond the introduction of the Euro. In the following, the cointegration behavior of yearly inflation rates in eight European countries is examined using the *Johansen* test. The time period ranges from January 1993 to June 2002. The analysis is twofold. As a first step, special weight is put on the correct identification of non-stationary variables. This happens against the background that all convergence examinations mentioned above that employed a cointegration approach solely relied on standard unit root tests such as the *Dickey-Fuller* test and the *Phillips-Perron* test. As the results in the following paragraph will show, a selection of non-stationary time series may have to be based on differing unit root test results for the country under examination.

3.2 Empirical Analysis – Data and Results

From the 12 member countries of the European currency unit, four countries had been excluded from the sample: Finland and Austria joined only in 1995. Greece did not meet the economic convergence conditions in March 1998 and joined a year later in January 2000 under the exemption rule. For Ireland, monthly inflation rates are not available for the period 1993:01-1997:01 are not available. Therefore, the initial sample consists of inflation rates from the eight Euro countries Belgium, France, Germany, Italy, Luxembourg, the Netherlands, Portugal, and Spain. As a starting point for the analysis we select January 1993, which lies after the ratification of the Maastricht Treaty in 1992. At that point in time, all of the eight countries had already been members of the European Monetary System. Annual inflation rates are computed as the differences of the natural logarithm of consumer price indices with a monthly rolling window. The data is obtained from the *International Financial Statistics* (*IFS*) database of the International Monetary Fund. Two periods are considered in the course of the analysis; the first being the time span until the fixation of exchange rates in

January 1999, the second being an extended period that ranges until June 2002. In order to examine cointegration relationships among economic variables, the variables should be integrated of degree one. In contrast to previous articles regarding inflation convergence, which usually only employed the Augmented *Dickey-Fuller* and the *Phillips-Perron* tests, additional unit root tests used in this paper indicate stationarity of inflation rates for several countries.

Based on the application of the unit root tests Luxembourg, the Netherlands, and Belgium are excluded from the sample due to ambiguous results. For the longer period ranging from January 1993 to June 2002 the *Ng-Perron* test as well as the ERS Point Optimal test reject the null for Belgium and the Netherlands at the 5% level (see table 1); the ERS Point Optimal test for Belgium is even significant at the 1% level. The Augmented *Dickey-Fuller* test cannot reject the unit root null for Luxembourg at the 5% level. Moreover, the test statistics of the KPSS test are neither significant for Luxembourg nor for Belgium at the 10% critical values.

However, the unit root analysis yields less evidence for stationary inflation rates of these countries regarding the shorter sample period. The *Ng-Perron* test rejects the unit root null for Belgium at the 5% level, the ERS Point Optimal test for the Netherlands at the 10% level. None of the employed tests is able to indicate stationarity for the inflation rates of Luxembourg. In order to use a consistent sample we exclude Luxemburg from the further analysis.

Included in the sample are inflation rates of Spain, Italy, Portugal, Germany, and France. While all unit root tests show non-stationary processes for Spain and Italy, unit root processes are assumed for all other countries. However, the *Phillips-Perron* test as well as the Augmented *Dickey-Fuller* test reject the null for Portugal significantly at the 5% level. Yet, the Augmented *Dickey-Fuller* test probably exhibits bad size characteristics since we find a high degree of autocorrelation in the residuals (*Ljung-Box* statistic of 15.368 for sample period 1; 6.922 for sample period 2). Furthermore, ARMA(1,1) estimations in first-differences for Portugal's inflation rates show negative polynomials (Appendix 3). The *Phillips-Perron* test results are thus seemingly distorted such that Portugal is included into the sample. Table 1 sums up the stationarity profile.[4]

In order to apply the *Johansen* test for cointegration the number of lags p in (2.1) has to be predetermined. *Hatanaka* (1996: 227) suggests a selection based on information criteria such as the *Schwarz* criterion. *Sawa* (1978: 1280) explains that the *Akaike* criterion more likely leads to overfitting of the model than the *Schwarz* criterion. Due to this fact and in accordance with previous articles, the *Schwarz* criterion is used here (see, for example, *Holmes* 1998: 11; *Morales Zumaquero* 2001: 7). Vector autoregressive models are estimated with and without deterministic components and values for the *Schwarz criterion* are computed (Appendix 1). The maximum number of lags, which was restricted by the size of the smaller sample, was set to ten. According to the *Schwarz criterion* the optimal number of lags for sample groups 1 and 2 was $p = 1$ (appendix 4).

[4] More detailed unit root test results can be obtained from the authors upon request.

Table 1. Stationarity of yearly inflation rates in EMS countries between 1993 and 2002.

	Sample Period 1: 1993 - 1998					Sample Period 2: 1993 - 2002				
	ADF¹	**ADF²**	**PP**	**KPSS**	**Ng-Perron (MZa)**	**ADF¹**	**ADF²**	**PP**	**KPSS**	**Ng-Perron (MZa)**
Belgium	-1.410	-1.122	-1.154	0.839 ***	-8.546 **	-2.623 *	-2.623 *	-2.201	0.240	-12.775 **
France	-0.771	0.524	-0.316	0.781 ***	-1.840	-1.831	-1.831	-2.328	0.366 *	-4.408
Germany	-1.317	-1.598	-1.308	0.893 ***	0.982	-2.127	-2.310	-1.464	0.498 **	0.064
Italy	-0.669	-1.278	-0.663	0.736 **	-1.524	-1.229	-1.900	-2.178	0.743 ***	-0.643
Luxembourg	-1.072	-1.568	-1.004	0.985 ***	0.235	-2.183	-2.920 **	-2.272	0.241	-4.296
Netherlands	-2.184	-1.430	-2.047	0.536 **	-4.220	-1.514	-1.497	-1.670	0.448 *	-10.317 **
Portugal	-3.015 **	-1.698	-2.873 *	1.007 ***	0.129	-3.043 **	-2.083	-3.307 **	0.603 **	-0.556
Spain	-0.156	-0.036	-0.139	0.987 ***	1.062	-1.527	-1.401	-1.550	0.547 **	-2.096
	Ng-Perron (MZt)	**Ng-Perron (MSB)**	**Ng-Perron (MPT)**	**ERS Point Optimal**	**ERS GLS Detrending**	**Ng-Perron (MZt)**	**Ng-Perron (MSB)**	**Ng-Perron (MPT)**	**ERS Point Optimal**	**ERS GLS Detrending**
Belgium	-1.820 *	0.213 **	3.775 *	14.143	-0.602	-2.378 **	0.186 **	2.493 **	0.088 ***	-1.310
France	-0.555	0.301	9.047	13.614	-0.088	-1.450	0.329	5.621	3.908 *	-1.182
Germany	0.824	0.840	50.995	80.191	0.599	0.046	0.717	32.586	46.781	-0.033
Italy	-0.621	0.407	11.536	14.101	-0.470	-0.386	0.600	21.376	16.199	-0.416
Luxembourg	0.127	0.540	22.140	50.697	-0.046	-1.397	0.325	5.816	12.603	-1.058
Netherlands	-1.296	0.307	6.030	3.712 *	-1.272	-2.210 **	0.214 **	2.617 **	5.194 *	-1.320
Portugal	0.131	1.013	58.974	94.254	0.141	-0.382	0.686	26.387	45.394	-0.403
Spain	0.783	0.738	41.539	28.731	0.468	-0.963	0.460	11.145	10.391	-0.901

1) Augmented *Dickey-Fuller* test, lag selection based on *Schwarz* criterion.

2) Augmented *Dickey-Fuller* test, residuals free from autocorrelation, critical values by *MacKinnon* (1996); *, **, *** denote statistical significance at 10%-,5%- bzw. 1%. levels.

3) $q = 6$ (1993-1998 for KPSS and PP), $q = 8, 9$ (KPSS) and $q = 10$ (PP) (1993-2002) are chosen as truncation lags.

Hall (1991: 323) explains that the *Johansen* test statistics are very sensitive to the lag choice. A parameterization with one lag seems little against the background of previous works. In order to test the robustness of our analysis we additionally estimate models with 4 and 6 lags. The main findings in our analysis will prove to be independent of the lag choice. Furthermore, in order to map possible (weak) trends among the inflation rates, a constant is added to the cointegration relationship.

Test results of the *Johansen* test show that independently of the lag choice *p* only partial convergence has occurred in the sample period 1. The trace test and the maximum eigenvalue test statistics indicate just one cointegration relationship for the model specifications with one and four lags (table 2).

Table 2. *Johansen* test for European Inflation rates.

$H_0(h)$	trace statistics					maximum eigenvalue statistics				
	number of lags			*crit. values*		*number of lags*			*crit. values*	
	p=1	*p=4*	*p=6*	*95%*	*99%*	*p=1*	*p=4*	*p=6*	*95%*	*99%*
					sample period 1 (1993 - 1998)					
$h \leq 0$	**88.834**	**101.120**	**129.693**	76.070	84.450	**45.955**	**52.640**	**54.018**	34.400	39.790
$h \leq 1$	42.878	48.480	**75.675**	53.120	60.160	19.840	20.060	40.185	28.140	33.240
$h \leq 2$	23.039	28.420	**35.491**	34.910	41.070	10.002	12.534	16.277	22.000	26.810
$h \leq 3$	13.037	15.886	19.214	19.960	24.600	9.039	9.675	11.488	15.670	20.200
$h \leq 4$	3.998	6.211	7.726	9.240	12.970	3.998	6.211	7.726	9.240	12.970
					sample period 2 (1993 - 2002)					
$h \leq 0$	**85.591**	64.044	74.402	76.070	84.450	**46.089**	27.338	33.743	34.400	39.790
$h \leq 1$	39.502	36.706	40.659	53.120	60.160	17.655	16.390	20.935	28.140	33.240
$h \leq 2$	21.847	20.316	19.724	34.910	41.070	10.075	12.170	13.412	22.000	26.810
$h \leq 3$	11.772	8.147	6.312	19.960	24.600	6.568	4.775	4.680	15.670	20.200
$h \leq 4$	5.203	3.372	1.633	9.240	12.970	5.203	3.372	1.633	9.240	12.970

This result corresponds to the existence of four common stochastic trends and can be interpreted as a low degree of convergence (*Holmes* 1998: 12). As for the model specification with six lags, both the trace test and the maximum eigenvalue test reject the null level that the cointegration rank is $h \leq 1$ at the 1% level. Thus we can only assume the existence of a maximum of two cointegrated relationships. At the critical level for 5% the trace statistic's test value without constant is additionally significant for a null that $h \leq 2$, which indicates three cointegrated vectors. To sum up, the *Johansen* test shows that partial convergence of inflation rates in the countries under examination has occurred in the period between 1993 and 1998.

The results of sample period 2 indicate four common stochastic trends and thus partial convergence under the parameterization of one lag. However, a drastic difference to the first sample comes up if the model accounts for more lags. No cointegration vectors are found, neither at the critical values for 1% nor at those for 5%. These results bring forth two conclusions. First, full convergence and hence the existence of one common stochastic trend cannot be observed for neither of the two sample periods. Thus, the results of the *Johansen* test indicate a lower degree of convergence after the ratification of the Maastricht Treaty than before considering the findings of *Westbrook* (1998: 142) who observes full convergence between 1979 and 1990. The results are in line with those of *Holmes* (2002: 157) mentioned above. Second, no cointegration relationship among inflation rates can be found for the time after 1999 (sample period 2). This can be interpreted as a decrease in inflation convergence despite the introduction of the Euro.

Less convergence in inflation rates could be due to the fact that price indices in the five countries consist of different goods, which lets inflation rates in some countries react stronger to shifts in relative prices than in others (composition effects). Calculating inflation rates based on the Harmonized Consumer Price Index (HCPI) which is promoted by the European Central Bank could reduce such composition effects. Unfortunately, the HCPI is only available since 1997 from official sources, and the soonest date for which it can be recalculated is 1996. Against this background, a further investigation of inflation convergence based on the measure of the HCPI appears sensible. Furthermore desirable would be an investigation of inflation convergence for the period from 1999 until today. However, a time span of four years does not suffice for the description of any long-run relationship between economic variables.

Referring to the conclusions stated above, two circumstances could hint to a flawed interpretation of the test results. First, the *Jarque-Bera* test shows that the assumption of normally distributed residuals in the vector autoregressive models does not hold in every case (appendix 5). However, *Cheung/Lai* (1993: 324) show in simulation studies that the test statistics of the *Johansen* test are relatively robust with regard to deviations from the normality assumption. Second, a low number of lags ($p = 1$, $p = 4$) results in high values of the *Ljung-Box* statistic and thus indicates autocorrelation in the residuals. Increasing the lag number to 6 could not solve the problem of autocorrelation entirely. As opposed to further increasing the lag number which makes an overfitting of the model likely, *Johansen* (1995: 21) recommends the redefinition of the test sample in the case of autocorrelated residuals. Future examinations of inflation convergence in the European Union should take advantage of a broader data sample in the course of an integration of new member states.

Cointegration analysis of inflation rates in Germany, France, Italy, Spain, Portugal. Critical values or obtained from *Osterwald-Lenum* (1992), results above critical values are marked in bold. *Schwarz* information criterion has a minimum for lag number $p = 1$. Test statistics are calculated with a constant in the cointegration relationship.[1]

4 Conclusion

The objective of this paper was the measurement of the inflation convergence among EU-Member States and especially to find out whether it has been weaker since the implementation of the Euro. For that purpose, inflation rates in the European currency area

[1] To test the robustness of the results, a vector autoregressive model with constant was applied as well. The result did not show further convergence among the inflation rates, see appendix 6. Furthermore, as the introduction of the Euro in January 1999 may represent a structural break, the cointegration test proposed by *Hansen/Johansen* 1993 was used. The results do not indicate the existence of a structural break in 1999.

are studied by means of current and recent unit root tests. The results are correlated with the cointegration analysis of the *Johansen* test.

Building up on the differentiated picture created by the stationary analysis of the inflation rates a study of the inflation convergence in Europe based on the *Johansen* test shows that even after the establishment of the European Central Bank and the introduction of an uniform currency as a consequence thereof, no complete convergence of the inflation rates is noticeable. Especially for the time period from 1993 until 2002 a single cointegration vector for more than two out of the three considered model specifications cannot be found. This fact can be interpreted as a decrease in inflation convergence after the introduction of the Euro.

Appendix 1. Regression of Elliott-Rothenberg-Stock

The deterministic component d_t is defined as the function of the deterministic variable z_t. For the derivation of an asymptotic power function *Elliott/Rothenberg/Stock* (ERS) present d_t more generally as it follows:

$$d_t = \beta' z_t \tag{A1}$$

whereas β' represents a q-dimensional parameter vector and z_t a q-dimensional data vector. ERS accomplished a regression of

$$Y_t = d_t + u_t \tag{A2}$$

$$u_t = a_1 u_{t-1} + v_t \tag{A3}$$

by defining the vectors as quasi-differenced variables as they follow:

$$Y_a = (Y_1, Y_2 - a_1 Y_1, \ldots, Y_T - a_1 Y_{T-1})' \tag{A4}$$

$$Z_a = (Z_1, Z_2 - a_1 Z_1, \ldots, Z_T - a_1 Z_{T-1})' \tag{A5}$$

The sum of the squared residues $\sum_{i=1}^{T} \hat{u}_i^2$ refers to an OLS-regression from Z_a to Y_a.

Appendix 2. *Ng/Perron* Test Statistics

The test statistics of *Ng/Perron* (2001) aim at the fact that the velocity of the convergence of a time series is supposed to be different for null hypotheses and alternative hypotheses

(*Perron/Ng* 1996). The *Ng-Perron* test statistics use this feature and concretize the *Phillips-Perron* test statistics Z_a and Z_t:[2]

$$MZ_a = Z_a + (T/2)(\hat{a}_1 - 1)^2 \tag{A6}$$

$$MZ_t = Z_t + (1/2)\left(\sum_{t=1}^{T} y_{t-1}^2 / \lambda^2\right)^{1/2} (\hat{a}_1 - 1)^2 \tag{A7}$$

$$MSB = \frac{Z_t}{Z_a} = T^{-2} \frac{\sum_{t=1}^{T} y_{t-1}^2}{s^2}, \quad \text{with} \quad s^2 = T^{-1}\sum_{t=1}^{T}(y_t - \bar{y})^2 \tag{A8}$$

Appendix 3. ARMA(1,1) Models for Yearly Inflation Rates (First Differences)

Sample Period 2: 1993 - 2002

France	process	$\Delta\pi_t = 0{,}708\Delta\pi_{t-1} + \varepsilon_t - 0{,}813\varepsilon_{t-1}$	
	standard error	(0,264303)	(0,217114)
Germany	process	$\Delta\pi_t = -0.877\Delta\pi_{t-1} + \varepsilon_t + 0{,}977\varepsilon_{t-1}$	
	standard error	(0,049438)	(0,015190)
Italy	process	$\Delta\pi_t = -0.709\Delta\pi_{t-1} + \varepsilon_t + 0{,}631\varepsilon_{t-1}$	
	standard error	(0,346763)	(0,381197)
Portugal	process	$\Delta\pi_t = 0{,}664\Delta\pi_{t-1} + \varepsilon_t - 0{,}502\varepsilon_{t-1}$	
	standard error	(0,157308)	(0,189681)
Spain	process	$\Delta\pi_t = 0{,}068\Delta\pi_{t-1} + \varepsilon_t + 0{,}353\varepsilon_{t-1}$	
	standard error	(0,214630)	(0,205267)

[2] The test statistic MSB represents a modification of the test statistic from *Sargan/Bhargava* (1983), see as well *Stock* (1999).

Sample Period 1: 1993 - 1998

France	process	$\Delta\pi_t = 0{,}686\Delta\pi_{t-1} + \varepsilon_t - 0{,}761\varepsilon_{t-1}$
	standard error	(0,567339) (0,511729)
Germany	process	$\Delta\pi_t = 0{,}965\Delta\pi_{t-1} + \varepsilon_t - 0{,}982\varepsilon_{t-1}$
	standard error	(0,024822) (0,013349)
Italy	process	$\Delta\pi_t = 0{,}858\Delta\pi_{t-1} + \varepsilon_t - 0{,}728\varepsilon_{t-1}$
	standard error	(0,179787) (0,239684)
Portugal	process	$\Delta\pi_t = 0{,}428\Delta\pi_{t-1} + \varepsilon_t - 0{,}052\varepsilon_{t-1}$
	standard error	(0,256098) (0,287760)
Spain	process	$\Delta\pi_t = 0{,}184\Delta\pi_{t-1} + \varepsilon_t + 0{,}118\varepsilon_{t-1}$
	standard error	(0,253113) (0,273853)

Appendix 4. *Schwarz* Criterion for Vector Autoregressive Models

	1993 - 2002		**1993 - 1998**	
Lag	**SIC (no Constant)**	**SIC (Constant)**	**SIC (no Constant)**	**SIC (Constant)**
1	-45.94737*	-45.76555*	-46.17558*	-46.02021*
2	-45.35377	-45.18699	-45.40132	-45.22866
3	-44.65444	-44.50212	-44.57119	-44.43694
4	-43.85563	-43.71745	-43.92549	-43.84602
5	-43.17097	-43.02197	-42.92694	-42.80934
6	-42.53260	-42.39049	-42.56711	-42.44902
7	-41.71572	-41.59618	-41.76877	-41.64766
8	-40.86713	-40.74798	-41.22853	-41.21751
9	-40.51919	-40.44653	-43.07949	-43.88115
10	-40.14954	-40.12666	-44.52511	-45.24402

SIC: *Schwarz* information criterion; * minimal value

Appendix 5. Residuals Vector Autoregressive Models

Sample Period 1 (1993 - 1998)

	Germany	France	Italy	Portugal	Spain
			a.) constant in VAR		
			p=1		
Jarque-Bera	55.603	1.764	53.326	5.316	3.159
Significance	0.000	0.414	0.000	0.070	0.206
Ljung-Box	6.140	32.646	23.882	16.600	11.660
Significance	0.803	0.000	0.008	0.084	0.308
			p=4		
Jarque-Bera	11.865	2.399	0.925	0.975	0.256
Significance	0.003	0.301	0.630	0.614	0.880
Ljung-Box	11.223	18.846	9.139	5.256	6.308
Significance	0.340	0.042	0.519	0.873	0.789
			p=6		
Jarque-Bera	2.470	4.682	1.273	0.078	1.305
Significance	0.291	0.096	0.529	0.962	0.521
Ljung-Box	7.257	11.308	9.454	4.094	8.350
Significance	0.701	0.334	0.490	0.943	0.595
			b.) no constant in VAR		
			p=1		
Jarque-Bera	54.626	1.775	53.228	5.815	1.755
Significance	0.000	0.412	0.000	0.055	0.416
Ljung-Box	6.068	32.556	23.713	15.223	12.155
Significance	0.809	0.000	0.008	0.124	0.275
			p=4		
Jarque-Bera	12.085	2.893	0.857	1.438	0.248
Significance	0.002	0.235	0.652	0.487	0.883
Ljung-Box	11.555	19.506	8.520	3.101	6.304
Significance	0.316	0.034	0.578	0.979	0.789
			p=6		
Jarque-Bera	1.668	3.184	0.127	0.106	1.319
Significance	0.434	0.203	0.938	0.948	0.517
Ljung-Box	5.923	9.387	9.928	4.251	8.303
Significance	0.822	0.496	0.447	0.935	0.599

Sample Period 2 (1993 - 2002)

	Germany	France	Italy	Portugal	Spain
			a.) constant in VAR		
			p=1		
Jarque-Bera	12.260	25.985	79.594	5.203	2.734
Significance	0.002	0.000	0.000	0.074	0.255
Ljung-Box	7.360	38.405	16.281	16.854	17.400
Significance	0.691	0.000	0.092	0.078	0.066
			p=4		
Jarque-Bera	5.267	25.594	10.100	0.773	0.144
Significance	0.072	0.000	0.006	0.680	0.930
Ljung-Box	7.180	32.029	3.339	3.573	8.943
Significance	0.708	0.000	0.972	0.965	0.538
			p=6		
Jarque-Bera	2.241	16.482	11.124	0.158	0.160
Significance	0.326	0.000	0.004	0.924	0.923
Ljung-Box	2.471	7.186	4.667	4.636	6.929
Significance	0.991	0.708	0.912	0.914	0.732
			b.) no constant in VAR		
			p=1		
Jarque-Bera	13.280	25.818	81.608	4.780	2.491
Significance	0.001	0.000	0.000	0.092	0.288
Ljung-Box	7.773	38.043	16.114	16.173	16.763
Significance	0.651	0.000	0.096	0.095	0.080
			p=4		
Jarque-Bera	5.346	23.501	9.986	0.564	0.310
Significance	0.069	0.000	0.007	0.754	0.856
Ljung-Box	7.591	31.078	3.304	4.867	9.490
Significance	0.669	0.001	0.973	0.900	0.486
			p=6		
Jarque-Bera	2.674	14.869	10.811	0.017	0.002
Significance	0.263	0.001	0.004	0.992	0.999
Ljung-Box	2.393	6.132	4.332	4.842	6.858
Significance	0.992	0.804	0.931	0.901	0.739

Appendix 6. *Johansen* Test for European Inflation Rates

***H*₀(*h*)**	**trace statistics**					**maximum eigenvalue statistics**				
	number of lags			***crit. values***		***number of lags***			***crit. values***	
	p=1	*p=4*	*p=6*	*95%*	*99%*	*p=1*	*p=4*	*p=6*	*95%*	*99%*
	sample period 1 (1993 - 1998)									
$h \leq 0$	79.653	83.876	113.461	68.520	76.070	45.790	52.089	49.099	33.460	38.770
$h \leq 1$	33.863	31.787	64.362	47.210	54.460	17.404	12.923	39.302	27.070	32.240
$h \leq 2$	16.459	18.864	25.060	29.680	35.650	9.801	10.833	14.636	20.970	25.520
$h \leq 3$	6.658	8.031	10.424	15.410	20.040	6.072	7.796	9.918	14.070	18.630
$h \leq 4$	0.586	0.235	0.506	3.760	6.650	0.586	0.235	0.506	3.760	6.650
	sample period 2 (1993 - 2002)									
$h \leq 0$	81.573	62.417	72.320	68.520	76.070	44.403	27.166	32.985	33.460	38.770
$h \leq 1$	37.170	35.251	39.335	47.210	54.460	17.378	16.385	20.929	27.070	32.240
$h \leq 2$	19.792	18.866	18.406	29.680	35.650	9.205	11.597	13.267	20.970	25.520
$h \leq 3$	10.587	7.269	5.140	15.410	20.040	6.561	4.076	3.996	14.070	18.630
$h \leq 4$	4.027	3.194	1.144	3.760	6.650	4.027	3.194	1.144	3.760	6.650

Cointegration analysis of inflation rates in Germany, France, Italy, Spain, Portugal. Critical values or obtained from *Osterwald-Lenum* (1992), results above critical values are marked in bold. *Schwarz* information criterion has a minimum for lag number $p = 1$. Test statistics are calculated applying a vector autoregressive model with constant.

REFERENCES

[1] Caporale, G., and N. Pittis (1993). Common Stochastic Trends and Inflation Convergence in the EMS. *Review of International Economics* **129**(2): 207-214.

[2] Cheung Y., and K. Lai (1993). Finite Sample Sizes of Johansen's Likelihood Ratio Tests for Cointegration. *Oxford Bulletin of Economics and Statistics* **(55):** 313-328.

[3] Culver, S., and D. Papell (1997). Is there a unit root in the inflation rate? Evidence from sequential break and panel data models. *Journal of Applied Econometrics* **(12)**: 435-444.

[4] Elliott, G., T. Rothenberg, and J. Stock (1996). Efficient Tests for an Autoregressive Unit Root. *Econometrica* **(64)**: 813-836.

[5] Engel, C., and J. Rogers (1996). How Wide is the Border?. *American Economic Review* **(86)** :1112-1125.

[6] Fuller, W. (1976). Introduction to statistical time series. New York: Wiley.

[7] Granger, C., and P. Newbold (1974). Spurious Regressions in Econometrics. *Journal of Econometrics* **(2):** 111-120.

[8] Hafer, R., and A. Kutan (1994). A Long-Run View of German Dominance and the Degree of Policy Convergence in the EMS. *Economic Inquiry* **(10):** 684-695.

[9] Hall, S. (1991). The Effect of Varying Lenth VAR Models on the Maximum Likelihood Estimates of Cointegrating Vectors. *Scottish Journal of Political Economy* **(38):** 317-323.

[10] Hansen, H.; Johansen, S. (1999). Some Tests for Parameter Constancy in Cointegrated VAR-Models. *Econometrics Journal* **(2)**, 306-333.

[11] Hatanaka, M. (1996). *Time-Series-Based Econometrics – Unit Roots and Co-Integration*. Oxford: Oxford University Press.

[12] Holmes, M. (1998). Inflation Convergence in the ERM. Evidence for Manufacturing and Services. *International Economic Journal* **(12):** 1-16.

[13] Holmes, M. (2002). Panel data evidence on inflation convergence in the European Union. *Applied Economics Letters* **(9):** 155-158.

[14] Johansen, S. (1991). Estimation and Hypothesis Testing of Cointegration Vectors in Gaussian Vector Autoregressive Models. *Econometrica* **(59):** 1551-1580.

[15] Johansen, S. (1995). *Likelihood-Based Inference in Cointegrated Vector Autoregressive Models*. Oxford: Oxford University Press.

[16] Kwiatkowski, D., P. Phillips, P. Schmidt, and Y. Shin (1992). Testing the null hypothesis of stationarity against the alternative of a unit root. *Journal of Econometrics* **(54):** 159-178.

[17] Lee, H., and J. Wu (2001). Mean Reversion of Inflation Rates: Evidence from 13 OECD Countries. *Journal of Macroeconomics* **(3):** 477-487.

[18] MacKinnon, J. (1996). Numerical Distribution Functions for Unit Root and Cointegration Tests. *Journal of Applied Econometrics* **(11):** 601-618

[19] Montuenga Gómez, V.M. (2002). Did the EMS Encourage Inflation Convergence?. *International advances in economic research* **(8):** 119–128.

[20] Morales Zumaquero, A. (2001). Inflation Convergence by Sectors in the EU: Structural Breaks and Common Factors, unpublished document. Madrid. 2001.

[21] Ng, S., and P. Perron (2001). Lag Selection and the Construction of Unit Root Tests with Good Size and Power. *Econometrica* **(69):** 1519-1554.

[22] Osterwald-Lenum, M. (1992). A Note with Quantiles of the Asymptotic Distribution of the Maximum Likelihood Cointegration Rank Test Statistics. *Oxford Bulletin of Economics and Statistics* **(54):** 461-471.

[23] Perron, P., and S. Ng (1996). Useful Modifications to some Unit Root Tests with Dependent Errors and their Local Asymptotic Properties. *Review of Economic Studies* **(63):** 435-463.

[24] Phillips, P. (1987): Time Series Regression with a Unit Root. *Econometrica* **(55):** 277-301.

[25] Remsberger, H. (2002). Inflationsdifferenzen als Problem in der EWU sowie im Aufholprozess der Beitrittsländer?. *Tagung des Arbeitskreises Europäische Integration, Bonn, und des Hamburgischen Welt-Wirtschafts-Archivs* (*HWWA*), http://www.bundesbank.de/presse/download/reden/2002/07/20020704remsperger.pdf, (8.11.2002): 1-16

[26] Sargan, J.D., and A. Bhargava, (1983). Testing Residuals form Least Squares Regression for Being Generated by the Gaussian Random Walk. *Econometrica* **(51):** 153-174.

[27] Sawa, T. (1978). Information Criteria for Discriminating Among Alternative Regression Models. *Econometrica* **(46):** 1273-1291.

[28] Schwert, W. (1989): Tests for Unit Roots: A Monte Carlo Investigation. *Journal of Economic Statistics* **(7):** 5-16.

[29] Siklos, P., and M. Wohar (1997). Convergence in Interest Rates and Inflation Rates across Countries and over Time. *Review of International Economics* **105**(1): 129-141.

[30] Stock, J. (1999). A Class of Tests for Integration and Cointegration, in: Robert Engle and Halbert White (ed.): Cointegration, Causality and Forecasting: A Festschrift for Clive W.J. Granger, Oxford: Oxford University Press: 135-167.

[31] Thom, R. (1995). Inflation Convergence in the EMS: Some Additional Evidence. A Comment. *Review of International Economics* **(131):** 577-586.

[32] Westbrook, J. (1998). Monetary Integration, Inflation Convergence and Output Shocks in the European Monetary System. *Economic Inquiry* **(36):** 138-144.

In: Trends in Inflation Research
Editor: Barbara T. Credan, pp. 207-213

ISBN: 1-59454-825-0
© 2006 Nova Science Publishers, Inc.

Chapter 5

INFLATION AND GROWTH: AN EMPIRICAL STUDY FOR THE COMPARISON OF THE LEVEL AND THE VARIABILITY EFFECTS[‡]

***K. Peren Arin*[*] *and Tolga Omay*[**]**
Massey University, Department of Commerce, Auckland, New Zealand
Department of Economics Çankaya University, Turkey

ABSTRACT

This paper analyzes the interaction between the inflation and growth within the Mankiw-Romer-Weil (1992) framework. Our results indicate that the inflation level has a significant negative effect on output in advanced capitalist economies, whereas inflation variability has a negative and significant effect on output in the long-run for all sub-samples. Our results also show that the variability effects are larger in terms of significance.

Keywords: Inflation, Economic Growth

1 INTRODUCTION

One of the most interesting research areas in the macroeconomics is the relationship between inflation and growth. However, there is no single theory for inflation and economic growth in the literature, and the empirical evidence is scant and mixed.[1]

Two different views, namely structuralist and monetarist, dominate economic literature with respect to the relationship between inflation rate and economic growth. The monetarists

---

‡ We would like to thank Chris Papageorgiou, Faik Koray, Ayca Altintig and the 2001 Southwestern Economic Association Meeting participants for their valuable suggestions. The usual disclaimer applies.

* Corresponding Author, Massey University Department of Commerce, Massey University, Auckland, New Zealand and Centre for Applied Macroeconomic Analysis (CAMA), Canberra, Australia. E-Mail: k.p.arin@massey.ac.nz .

** Department of Economics, Cankaya University, Ankara Turkey.

1 Temple (2000) reviews the "stories- short and tall" that economists tell about the growth effects of inflation.

assert that price stability is a prerequisite for economic growth, claiming that inflation causes some distortions, and through these distortions, retards growth. In the structuralist view, on the other hand, wage adjustments lag behind price adjustments, changing the income distribution in favour of capitalists. Making the Kaldorian assumption that the capitalists have a higher propensity to save, this income redistribution will increase total savings, total investment, and consequently economic growth. Meanwhile, some economists remain sceptical, arguing that a nominal variable can not affect a real one.

Inflation may be considered a measure of relative price between present and future. Uncertainty about inflation creates inefficiency for allocation decisions of the current period. Uncertainty about inflation is often measured by the inflation variability. Unfortunately, to the authors' knowledge, no previous studies have attempted to compare the level and variability effects of inflation.

This paper aims to test the validity of the above stated hypotheses, by introducing three different inflation variables, to the Mankiw-Romer-Weil (1992) framework. By doing so, we aim to compare the level and variability effects of inflation on output growth. The following section reviews the related literature. Section 3 discusses the data and methodology used. Section 4 presents the empirical results. Section 5 concludes.

2 Previous Literature

Several channels have been suggested through which inflation variability can affect output. Friedman (1977) argues that increased inflation volatility makes it difficult to extract signals about relative prices from absolute prices; therefore creates economic inefficiency, which depresses future economic activity. He then conjectures that higher rates of inflation are generally associated with higher inflation variability. Engle (1983) claims that unpredictability of future inflation is the major component of welfare losses associated with inflation. When inflation is unpredictable, risk-averse economic agents will incur losses even if all prices and quantities are perfectly flexible as they cannot contract for unforeseen events.

The claim that the high and volatile inflation would affect growth negatively is supported by some empirical studies, and rejected by the others. If we begin with a single-country time series analysis, Grimes (1991) try to explain the effects of current and lagged inflation on output growth for 21 countries, and finds a significant and negative effect of inflation on growth for thirteen of them. Similarly, Stanners (1993) found only a weak (but negative) correlation between inflation and growth using time-series data for nine industrialized countries. However, the results of these studies may be unbiased First of all, in almost all countries there is a positive short-run relationship between growth and inflation, with the direction of causation running from higher growth to higher inflation. In addition, single-country time-series observations that exhibit a negative correlation may be picking up the results of the central banks' reactions: a period of high inflation (or inflationary pressures) is likely to provoke a tightening of monetary policy, which in turn and (in the short run) growth to decline. Some time-series studies have also assessed the importance of inflation variability. McTaggart (1992) contends that inflation variability had a positive effect on the growth rate, but Jansen (1989) argues that inflation has a significant negative relationship with output growth.

Some studies attempted to test the effect of inflation on growth by using cross-country data. One of the earliest cross-sectional studies was by Kormendi and Meguire (1985). Using data for 47 countries over the 1950–77 period and a wide set of explanatory variables— each averaged over six-year periods—they found that inflation has a significant negative correlation with output growth, due to the negative association between inflation and investment. Grier and Tullock (1989) use pooled time series (five-year averages) and cross-sectional data between 1951 and 1980 for 113 countries and argue that a single empirical model could not explain differences in growth among these countries and therefore present different results for different country groups. For OECD countries, they find strong negative correlations between growth and the share of government spending in national income, and between growth and the variability of inflation, but no significant relation between growth and inflation. Elsewhere, the only significant relation between inflation and growth was a negative association in the African countries; and inflation variability had a significant negative relation with growth in the Asian countries. De Gregorio (1992, 1993) uses cross-sectional data for 12 Latin American countries to test the implications of an endogenous growth model in which the level and efficiency of investment are related negatively to the rate of inflation. He concludes that both inflation and its variance were negatively correlated with growth; the effect appeared to arise mainly because of a reduction in the efficiency of investment. Barro (1996) concludes that the unexpected inflation would affect growth negatively by decreasing the performance of households and firms. by using a sample of 100 countries for the 1960-1990 period. Finally, there are also a number of panel data studies, including Bruno and Easterly (1998) and Gylfason and Herbertsson (1996) which report a negative effect of inflation on economic growth. To our knowledge, none of these studies attempted to compare the level and variability effects of inflation.

3 Data and Methodology

The Neo-classical growth model proposed by Mankiw, Romer and Weil (1992) remains to be one of the most influential (therefore, most commonly used) models in analyzing the differences in levels of economic performance. The model suggests the accumulation of physical and human capital as the main source of differences in output levels. However, the model suggests the differences in saving rates as the only explanation for the differences in levels of physical and human capital accumulation. As stated above, one can argue that inflation, being a measure of relative price between present and future can also affect physical capital accumulation. In addition, uncertainty about inflation, measured by inflation variability, creates inefficiency for allocation decisions of the current period—therefore retards physical/human capital accumulation.

This study augments the neoclassical growth model proposed by Mankiw Romer Weil (1992), by using their original data, but introducing three different measures of inflation to the model: total inflation, average inflation, and inflation variability. Total inflation is the total percentage change in the price level (CPI) from the first year to the last year, , average inflation is the average percentage change in the annual price level during the sample period, and inflation variability is the standard deviation of the annual change in the price level for the sample period. All empirical models are estimated by using OLS.

4 EMPIRICAL RESULTS

Table 1-Dependent variable: Log GDP per working age person in 1985

Sample: OECD	Regression 1.1	Regression 1.2	Regression 1.3	Regression 1.4
Constant	3.780686 (7.130)***	6.663897 (10.507)***	5.798625 (10.027)***	5.289195 (4.458)***
Ln(I/GDP)	0.621698 (2.471)***	0.270011 (0.130)	0.201236 (0.897)	0.856639 (2.219)**
Ln(school)	0.034017 (0.214)	0.350113 (2.504)***	0.221152 (1.609)*	0.114586 (0.239)
Ln(n+g+d)	-1.201374 (-4.271)***	-1.391434 (-6.994)***	-1.306004 (-5.503)***	-1.931092 (-4.774)***
Average Inflation	-	-0.021431 (-0.311)	-	-
Inflation variability	-	-	-0.001204 (-5.339)***	-
Total Inflation	-	-	-	-0.000528 (-3.985)***

R^2: 0.3664 R^2: 0.6973 R^2: 0.6482 R^2: 0.6482 $\overline{R}^2$: 0.3325 $\overline{R}^2$:
0.6715 $\overline{R}^2$: 0.6091 $\overline{R}^2$: 0.3325**

The values in the parentheses are t statistics
* : significant at 10%
** : significant at 5%
***: significant at 1%

The econometric results for the OECD countries are presented in Table 1. For OECD countries, inflation and the inflation variability have significant negative effects on output in the long-run. It is obvious that for the advanced capitalist economies, price stability is a pre-requisite for economic growth.

Table 2-Dependent variable: Log GDP per working age person in 1985

Sample: Intermediate	Regression 1.1	Regression 1.2	Regression 1.3	Regression 1.4
Constant	6.350345 (9.309)***	8.173361 (14.728)***	8.500437 (9.010)***	8.209541 (12.063)***
Ln(I/GDP)	0584849 (2.471)***	-0.123863 (-0.615)	-1.077290 (-2.312)**	-0.680526 (-2.431)***
Ln(school)	0.459652 (1.863)**	1.050604 (5.443)***	0.056889 (0.209)	1.514596 (4.321)***
Ln(n+g+d)	-0.999859 (-3.513)***	-1.101840 (-5.496)***	0.971299 (-1.857)**	-0.876060 (-4.046)***
Average Inflation	-	-0.074896 (-1.501)*	-	
Inflation variability	-	-	-0.816429 (-4.328)***	-
Total Inflation	-	-	-	-0.000312 (-1.499)*

R^2: 0.3664 R^2: 0.6973 R^2: 0.6482 R^2: 0.6482 $\overline{R}^2$: 0.3325 $\overline{R}^2$:
0.6715 $\overline{R}^2$: 0.6091 $\overline{R}^2$: 0.3325**

The values in the parentheses are t statistics
* : significant at 10%
** : significant at 5%
***: significant at 1%

The estimation results for the intermediate sample are presented in Table 2. The less significant results for inflation may be due to the fact that output is below the potential output in these countries, and low levels of inflation may have some positive effects on growth.

Table 3-Dependent variable: Log GDP per working age person in 1985

Sample: Non-oil	Regression 1.1	Regression 1.2	Regression 1.3	Regression 1.4
Constant	4.800196 (14.213)***	4.528793 (9.388)***	4.858776 (14.032)***	4.794478 (14.401)***
Ln(I/GDP)	1.127994 (7.865)***	1.175217 (7.550)***	1.115460 (7.716)***	1.046467 (7.099)***
Ln(school)	0.494755 (6.046)***	0.467996 (5.275)***	0.482967 (5.797)***	0.52069 (6.367)***
Ln(n+g+d)	-0.320808 (-1.684)**	-0.233675 (-1.060)	-0.307147 (-1.603)*	-0.198190 (-1.001)
Average Inflation	-	-0.029301 (0.789)	-	
Inflation variability	-	-	0.0064 (1.948)**	-
Total Inflation	-	-	-	-2.371418 (-0.798)

R^2: 0. 6904 R^2: 0. 6925 R^2: 0. 7025 R^2: 0. 8419 $\overline{R}^2$: 0. 6805 $\overline{R}^2$:
0. 6792 $\overline{R}^2$: 0. 6897 $\overline{R}^2$: 0. 8350**

The values in the parentheses are t statistics
* : significant at 10%
** : significant at 5%
***: significant at 1%

The regression results for the non-oil sample are presented in table 3. Although the total inflation and average inflation variables become insignificant, the inflation variability variable remains significant. This suggests that the negative effects of growth mostly come from inflation variability.

5 Conclusion

Although theoretical models suggest that there must be a significant negative effect of inflation on growth, it is hard to detect this influence in empirical studies. The best explanation for this observation comes from the Rational Expectations hypothesis. According to Rational Expectations theory, anticipated variables do not have any effect on the real variables, like output growth. However, separating anticipated inflation from the unanticipated one necessitates further research.

Our results show that price stability is very important for economic growth, especially for advanced capitalist economies. The results also reveal the fact that the negative effects of inflation come mostly from inflation variability.

REFERENCES

[1] Barro, R. J. (1996), 'Inflation and growth', *Federal Reserve Bank of St. Louis Review*, **78**(3), 153-169.

[2] Bruno, M. and Easterly, W. (1998), 'Inflation crises and long-run growth', *Journal of Monetary Economics*, **41**(1), February, 3-26.

[3] De Gregorio, J. (1992), 'The effects of inflation on economic growth', *European Economic Review*, **36**, 417-24.

[4] De Gregorio, J. (1993), 'Inflation, taxation and long-run growth', *Journal of Monetary Economics*, **31**, 271-98.

[5] Engle, R. F. (1983), 'Estimates of the variance of US inflation based on the ARCH model', *Journal of Money, Credit and Banking,* **15**, pages 286–301.

[6] Friedman, M. (1977), 'Nobel lecture: inflation and unemployment', *Journal of Political Economy*, **85**, pages 451–72.

[7] Grier, K. B. and Tullock, G. (1989), 'An Empirical analysis of cross-national economic growth', *Journal of Monetary Economics*, **24**, pages 259-279.

[8] Grimes, A. (1991), 'The effects of inflation on growth: some international evidence' *Weltwirtschaftliches Archiv*, **127**, pages 631-644.

[9] Gylfason, T. and Herbertsson, T. T. (1996), 'Does inflation matter for growth?' *CEPR discussion paper* no. **1503**.

[10] Jansen, D. W. (1989), 'Does inflation uncertainty affect output growth? Further evidence', *Federal Reserve Bank of St Louis Review*, July/August, pages 43–54.

[11] Kormendi, R. C. and Meguire, P. G. (1985), 'Macroeconomic determinants of growth: cross-country evidence', *Journal of Monetary Economics,* **16**,pages 141–63.

[12] Mankiw,G, Romer,D., and Weil, D. (1992), 'A contribution to the empirics of economic growth', *Quarterly Journal of Economics* **107**(2), , 407-437.

[13] McTaggart, D. (1992), 'The cost of inflation in Australia', in *Inflation,Disinflation and Monetary Policy*, Reserve Bank of Australia.

[14] Temple, J. (2000), 'Inflation and growth: stories short and tall.' *Journal of Economic Surveys*, **14**(4), September, 395-426.

In: Trends in Inflation Research
Editor: Barbara T. Credan, pp. 215-228
ISBN: 1-59454-825-0
© 2006 Nova Science Publishers, Inc.

Chapter 6

QUANTIFYING INFLATION CREDIBILITY

Jane Ihrig, Jaime Marquez and Kristian Rogers*

Division of International Finance
Federal Reserve Board

ABSTRACT

Domestic inflation appears to have declined since the mid-1980s in many countries, including those that switched to inflation-targeting regimes. In theory, when a central bank establishes a credible inflation-targeting regime, this anchors inflation expectations and helps ward off inflationary impetus. Here we ask whether this has been the case in 5 industrial countries: Australia, Canada, New Zealand, Sweden, and the United Kingdom.

We model inflation before the adoption of inflation targets with a modified Phillips curve, which incorporates multiple factors, such as capacity utilization, commodity prices and exchange rates. From this model we control for how much each of these standard variables affects inflation. In addition, we measure the effects of a credible inflation-targeting regime in two ways. First, we estimate the Phillips curve model pre-target adoption, and then forecast inflation in recent history, comparing the forecasts to actual values to see how much the pre-inflation target model over-predicts inflation in the targeting-regime. Second, we conduct rolling Phillips curve regressions in order to see whether: 1) the utilization coefficient shifts toward zero around the time of target adoption, signifying that central bank credibility has dampened the effects of capacity constraints on inflation; and/or 2) the model's intercept moves toward the inflation target range.

Keywords: Phillips Curve, Unemployment, Inflation Forecasts, Rolling Regression

1 INTRODUCTION

In the early 1990s several countries decided to make an explicit commitment to creating and maintaining a low-inflation environment.[1] The strategy they chose was to set pre-

---

* Division of International Finance of the Federal Reserve Board. The views in this paper are solely the responsibility of the authors and should not be interpreted as reflecting the views of the Board of Governors of the Federal Reserve System or of any other person associated with the Federal Reserve System.

announced ranges for inflation to fluctuate within over the medium term. These countries hoped that by keeping inflation in their target bands their central banks would gain credibility, and they would anchor market expectations for future inflation.

Figure 1 - Mean vs. Standard Deviation of Inflation, 1970Q1 to 1990Q4 and 1991Q1 to 2002Q4

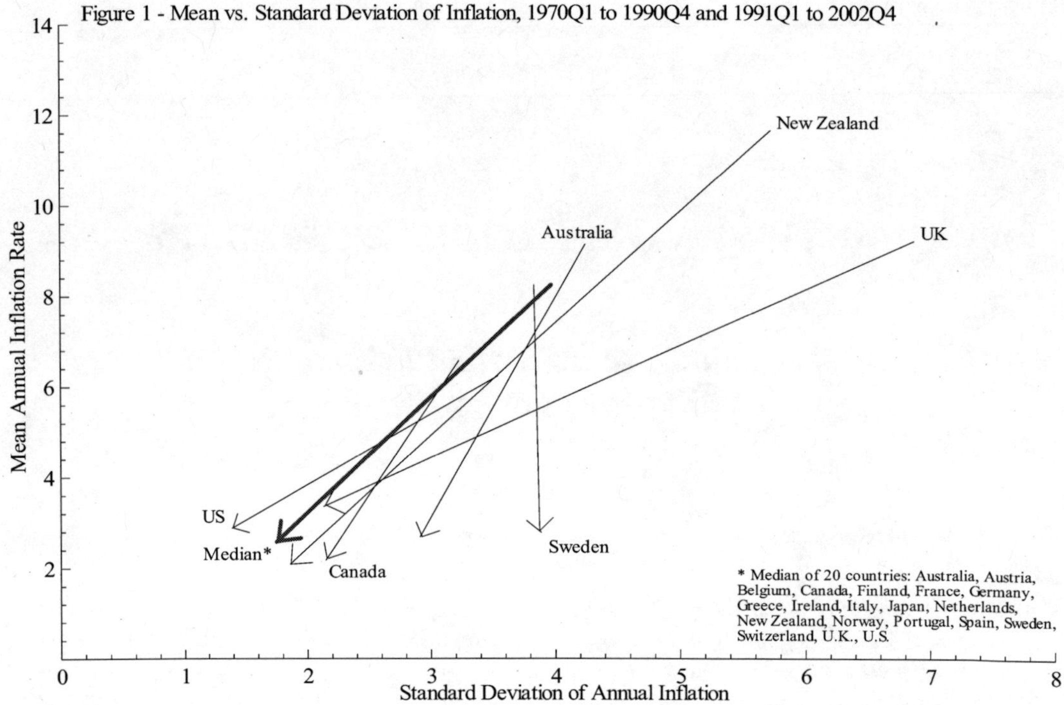

The question we ask here is: Has inflation targeting worked to anchor the rate of inflation at a relatively low level? A simplistic way to try to capture the effect of monetary policy credibility on inflation is to compare the mean and standard deviation of inflation before and after the implementation of the target. Figure 1 shows the means and standard deviations of inflation in six industrial countries over the period 1970Q1 (the first quarter of 1970) to 1990Q1 to the period 1991Q1 to 2002Q4. Five of the six countries—the United Kingdom, Sweden, New Zealand, Canada and Australia—have been explicitly targeting inflation since the early 1990s, while the United States, not an official targeter, is thought to target inflation implicitly over the second sample period.[2] Except for Sweden, both the mean and standard deviation of inflation decreased in each of these countries. Sweden's mean inflation also decreased, but its standard deviation remained roughly unchanged. On the surface, these results suggest that inflation targeting has successfully kept inflation low.[3]

One should note, however, that U.S. inflation declined in terms of both its mean and standard deviation over this time period. And, looking across 20 industrial countries, all of

[1] For in-depth discussion of inflation-targeting issues and the theory behind the practice see Truman (2003) and Bernanke and Woodford (2005).

[2] See, for example, Clarida et al. (1998), who argue there was a shift toward fighting inflation in the United States after the appointment of Paul Volcker to the Federal Reserve Board.

[3] In order to determine whether the differences in means before and after 1990 are significant, we conducted 2-sample t-tests (at a 5%-significance level), finding that inflation in each country is significantly different from pre- to post-1990.

which are not inflation targeters, the median mean and standard deviation of inflation also fell. This highlights that the reduction in inflation was not solely associated with targeting countries. It could be that the low-inflation environment is a result of other economic conditions experienced by all these 20 industrialized countries. So, to quantify the effect a credible targeting regime has on inflation, we must look for alternative tests.

Our analysis relies on a modified Phillips curve model to reveal the effects of monetary policy credibility. Independent variables in the model include capacity utilization, commodity prices and exchange rates. In general, the model suggests that capacity pressures, commodity price inflation and local currency depreciation can each lead to domestic inflation. However, when a country shifts to an inflation-targeting regime, the effect of capacity pressures on inflation should dampen, as agents believe the central bank is credible and will act to counter inflationary pressures. As a result, the linkage between inflation and capacity should diminish after the implementation of a targeting regime (which, in terms of the model, would be expressed as a decrease in the coefficient on capacity utilization after target adoption).

First, we estimate the model using a sample from the 1970s until the time of target adoption (the early 1990s, for most countries) for each of five targeting countries—the United Kingdom, Sweden, New Zealand, Canada and Australia—as well as the United States, the one non-targeter in our analysis. Then we use these models to predict inflation in recent history. Comparing the out-of-sample forecasts to actual inflation, we find that the models over-predict inflation, suggesting that the relationships that existed between inflation and its determinants before the adoption of targets became less significant after adoption.

Our second test with the Phillips curve looks for changes in the parameter estimates associated with structural changes in monetary policy. Credibility should show up as a reduction in the Phillips curve coefficient on capacity utilization and a shift in the value of the model's constant. By estimating rolling regressions, we find a noticeable shift in these parameters around the time of the inflation-targeting regime. The coefficient estimates move in a manner that coincides with agents shifting their beliefs to a credible inflation-targeting regime.

The remainder of the paper is organized as follows: Section 2 presents the Phillips curve model we use throughout the analysis. Section 3 discusses the estimation results, both the out-of-sample forecasts and the rolling regressions coefficients. Section 4 concludes.

2 Model

Our analysis relies on a standard Phillips curve model:

$$\pi_t = \alpha_0 + \sum_{i=1}^{4} \alpha_{1i}\pi_{t-i} + \sum_{i=1}^{4} \alpha_{2i} util_{t-i} + \sum_{i=1}^{4} \alpha_{3i} exch_{t-i} + \sum_{i=1}^{4} \alpha_{4i} comm_{t-i} + \varepsilon_t, \tag{1}$$

where π is the inflation rate, *util* is a utilization measure (either the unemployment rate or the output gap[4]), *exch* is the percent change in the nominal effective exchange rate, and *comm* is the percent change in a U.S. dollar-denominated commodities price index. Following Bernanke et al. (2001), the exchange rate and the commodities price index are included in the regression only if they improve its adjusted R^2.

We expect the lagged inflation coefficients to sum to between zero and one, indicating a stable autoregressive process. Second, Phillips (1958) theorized, and subsequent empirical studies have reinforced, the existence of an inverse association between output and inflation: above-capacity production or employment should put upward pressure on the price level. Therefore, we expect a negative sign on the unemployment gap coefficients and a positive sign on the output gap coefficients. Finally, higher prices for commodities and foreign currency should put upward pressure on the domestic price level, suggesting a positive sign on these coefficients.

3 Empirical Results

We collect data on the above variables for six countries: New Zealand, Canada, Australia, Sweden and the United Kingdom, all of which are inflation targeters, as well as the United States, a non-targeter that is used for comparison. All data are quarterly, and percent changes are reported at an annual rate. Table 1 presents means and standard deviations of the variables in the pre- and post-targeting regimes. As seen, both the means and standard deviations of inflation in all countries decrease substantially from pre- to post-target adoption, and the change in means is statistically significant. For the capacity measures, we have various movements across the two samples. In the case of New Zealand, its unemployment rate increased from an average of 3.29 pre-adoption to 7.13 post-adoption, which is consistent with the story that lower inflation is associated with a higher unemployment rate (assuming a constant natural rate of unemployment). However, for the United Kingdom, its mean unemployment rate decreased after target adoption. And, for Sweden, the output gap switches from negative to positive. These movements would suggest price pressures, unless these are examples of how inflation targeting helped to loosen the link between capacity pressures and inflation.[5] Turning to commodity price inflation and changes in the exchange rates, these series exhibited high variance relative to changes in their means, so they are not likely significant contributors to the deflationary episodes. To tease out the effect of credibility on inflation, we now move to the Phillips curve estimation.

---

[4] Utilization measure is the unemployment rate in all countries except Sweden, where it is the output gap. The unemployment rate is the percent of the civilian labor force that is unemployed. The output gap is measured as $100 * \left(\left(Y_t - Y_t^* \right) / Y_t^* \right)$, where Y_t is real GDP and Y_t^* is potential output, estimated with an H-P filter. Inflation for the United Kingdom is calculated from the RPI excluding mortgage payments; for the other countries we use a CPI excluding food and energy.

[5] It has been well documented that the United States experienced both deflation and a lower unemployment rate in the 1990s; this seemingly incongruous phenomenon has been explained by rising labor productivity during that decade (see, e.g., Ball and Moffitt (2001)). However, subsequent studies have shown that productivity did not significantly influence the deflation of the 1990s in the inflation-targeting countries in this study (Ihrig and Marquez, 2004a and 2004b).

Table 1. Descriptive Statistics: Means (Standard Deviations).

Country	Time Period	Inflation	Utilization	Commodities	Exchange Rates
New Zealand	76Q1-89Q4	12.56 (4.63)	3.29 (1.81)	---	-4.21 (7.23)
	90Q1-04Q1	2.20 (1.57)	7.13 (1.85)	---	.53 (8.13)
Canada	72Q2-90Q4	6.51 (2.61)	8.28 (1.90)	5.20 (17.95)	-1.29 (13.20)
	91Q1-04Q3	1.90 (1.95)	8.87 (1.53)	1.55 (17.312)	.39 (12.06)
Australia	75Q2-89Q4	8.83 (3.60)	6.91 (1.48)	3.29 (15.28)	-1.58 (16.77)
	90Q1-04Q2	2.63 (2.67)	7.88 (1.55)	1.04 (17.34)	.70 (13.49)
U.K.	75Q2-92Q3	8.51 (6.00)	7.03 (2.57)	---	---
	92Q4-04Q3	2.49 (.68)	5.36 (2.44)	---	---
Sweden	72Q2-92Q4	7.95 (3.91)	-.07 (1.61)	4.31 (17.79)	---
	93Q1-04Q3	1.49 (2.09)	.13 (.91)	2.50 (17.71)	---
U.S.	72Q2-90Q2	6.31 (3.50)	6.86 (1.43)	5.72 (17.79)	-.77 (12.99)
	90Q3-04Q2	2.71 (1.27)	5.59 (1.04)	1.00 (17.56)	-.24 (12.54)

Standard deviations computed using T-1 degrees of freedom.

Sources: Inflation data are from Haver G10 for the United Kingdom, Australia, New Zealand, Sweden and the United States, from the BIS for Canada. The unemployment rates are from the Department of Employment for the United Kingdom, from Statistics Canada for Canada, from the Reserve Bank of Australia for Australia, from the New Zealand Institute of Economic Research for New Zealand. GDP data are from the National Central Bureau of Statistics for Sweden. Commodity price inflation is calculated from a global commodity price index, excluding energy, in $U.S.; from the BIS. Exchange rates are the NEERs; from the IMF for New Zealand, Canada and the United States.

3.1 Pre-target Phillips Curve Estimation

For each country we run two regressions, both estimated using the method of ordinary least-squares. The first regression has the general, unrestricted form specified in equation (1), with four lags of each variable. The second is a more parsimonious version, whose lag structure is determined by a four-stage reduction algorithm. This algorithm first estimates the general unrestricted model and tests it for congruence (i.e., white-noise residuals, constant parameters). Second, it implements multiple reduction paths simultaneously. For example, one path might start by excluding the least significant variable while another might eliminate a whole block of statistically insignificant variables. Third, it tests whether each resulting specification is congruent and, if so, continues implementing reductions and testing for congruence until an incongruent specification is found. At this time, the immediately preceding specification is designated as *final model*. Finally, it assembles the final models from all of the different reduction paths and selects the one that encompasses all the others. In the absence of such a model, the algorithm creates a model including the variables from all of the final models and re-submits it to the whole reduction process. If even this fails, the algorithm selects the final model that minimizes the Akaike, Schwarz and Hannan-Quinn information criteria.[6]

The estimation samples, which do not depend on whether the model is general or specific, extend from 1971:Q2, or from the first quarter where all the necessary data become available, until the last quarter before the adoption of the inflation-targeting regime for each country. For the United States, the only non-targeter in this analysis, the sample ends at 1990:Q2 in order that our results might be comparable to Bernanke et al. (2001).

Table 2 presents both the general and parsimonious estimation results for the six countries. Each coefficient shown is the sum of the coefficients on the lags of each variable.[7] We measure coefficient significance with an F-statistic testing the exclusion of all lags of each variable at the .05 level. Looking across regressions, we find parameter estimates consistent with past literature.[8] The R^2's indicate a reasonably good fit for all regressions and countries except Australia and Sweden. In the general model all long-run inflation coefficients are significant and between 0 and 1, as expected. The utilization coefficient is significant in four of the six regressions. Specifically, four of the five unemployment coefficients are significant and all five are negative, and the output gap is positive but insignificant. The exchange rate is significant only for New Zealand, and commodity prices are not significant.[9]

3.2 Out-of-Sample Forecast Errors

Now we compare predicted inflation from the general Phillips curve models in the preceding section with actual inflation during the inflation-targeting regimes. The model's forecasts should estimate what inflation would have been like with economic variables at that time, but in an environment without the credible targeting regime. If the existence of a credible inflation target affected inflation and expectations thereof, beyond what real economic conditions alone would have predicted, then we would expect to see a disparity between actual and forecasted inflation. More specifically, we expect actual inflation to be less than forecasted, since a credible target should, *ceteris paribus*, push inflation down.

---

6 See Hendry and Krolzig (2001) for more details on the model-reduction process.

7 We do not impose the restriction that the long-run autoregressive coefficient sums to 1.

8 For example, see Bernanke et al. (2001). Signs on all our coefficients are consistent with his regression results, as are most of our significance results. The absolute values of our point estimates of utilization variables are consistently more negative than in Bernanke et al., while other variables are quite close.

9 The result that neither the exchange rate or commodity prices were significant is consistent with Bernanke et al.

Table 2. Forecasting Inflation from Phillips Curves

	New Zealand	Canada	Australia	U.K.	Sweden	U.S.
Utilization Measure	**Unemp Rate**	**Unemp Rate**	**Unemp Rate**	**Unemp Rate**	**Output Gap**	**Unemp Rate**
Sample	**77Q1-89Q4**	**73Q2-90Q4**	**71Q2-89Q4**	**76Q2-92Q3**	**73Q2-92Q4**	**73Q2-90Q2**
	A. Basic Specification, Four Lags of Each Variable Included					
Adj R Square	**.91**	**.65**	**.36**	**.77**	**.26**	**.77**
	Long-run coefficients (F-statistic from testing the exclusion) of all lags of variable:					
Inflation	.82 (43.37)*	.95 (15.30)*	.69 (6.33)*	.50 (5.83)*	.57 (5.56)*	.87 (25.63)*
Utilization Measure	-.22 (6.73)*	-.40 (3.29)*	-.40 (3.83)*	-.62 (3.35)*	.74 (1.22)	-.15 (1.61)
Exchange Rate	.06 (7.41)*	.03 (.98)				.00 (.61)
Commodity Prices		.03 (.89)			.05 (.82)	.07 (2.54)
	B. Parsimonious Specification					
Inflation	.85 (1, 212.96)*	.97 (3, 26.67)*	.48 (1, 23.06)*	.39 (1, 31.58)*	.48 (1, 21.46)*	1.00 (2, 96.34)*
Utilization Measure	-.17 (2, 18.26)*	-.42 (2, 8.45)*	-.53 (2, 8.61)*	-.70 (1, 19.78)*	.77 (1, 8.16)*	-.04 (2, 5.69)*
Exchange Rate	.04 (2, 23.38)*	.03 (1, 3.10)				
Commodity Prices		.03 (1, 5.36)*			.05 (1, 4.50)*	.05 (1, 11.67)*

Results from regressing quarterly inflation (annualized) on its own lags, a utilization measure and annualized rates of change in the nominal effective exchange rate and in commodity prices prior to the adoption of inflation targets (prior to 1990Q3 for the U.S. and 1990Q1 for Australia). In parentheses are F-statistics from testing the exclusion of all lags of each variable. Asterisk denotes significance at the 5% level.

We conduct both dynamic and 1-step-ahead forecasts. Dynamic forecasts use the pre-targeting sample as initial conditions for estimating a model (viz., the previous section), then forecast by extending the estimation sample into the future, using actual values for all regressors *except for* lagged inflation: all inflation values used beyond the initial sample are estimated from the model and fed back into the model. By contrast, the 1-step-ahead forecasts use actual values of all variables. Though we present both types of forecast errors, dynamic forecasts are more realistic for our purposes: Since we want to estimate what inflation would have been without targeting, it makes sense to use only information that would have been available to a non-targeting world.

Table 3. Forecast Results, Short Term.

	In-Sample	*Out-of-Sample*		*Horizon (Quarters)*	*Horizon (Dates)*
	Criterion: Adj R Square	**Criterion: Mean Forecast Error* (Standard Deviation of Error)**			
		1-Step Ahead	**Dynamic**		
New Zealand	.91	.59 (1.43)	.68 (2.50)	8	90Q1-91Q4
Canada	.65	-.64 (3.14)	-2.38 (2.29)	8	91Q1-92Q4
Australia	.36	1.92 (3.44)	3.88 (2.86)	8	90Q1-91Q4
U.K.	.77	.95 (.79)	1.52 (.97)	8	92Q4-94Q3
Sweden	.26	1.17 (4.09)	1.48 (4.44)	8	93Q1-94Q4
U.S.	.77	-.48 (1.57)	-1.38 (1.31)	8	90Q3-92Q2

*Forecast errors are predicted values minus actual, expressed in percentage points of inflation.

Table 4. Forecast Results, Long Term.

	In-Sample	*Out-of-Sample*		*Horizon (Quarters)*	*Horizon (Dates)*
	Criterion: Adj R Square	**Criterion: Mean Forecast Error* (Standard Deviation of Error)**			
		1-Step-Ahead	**Dynamic**		
New Zealand	.91	1.82 (1.74)	9.06 (6.61)	57	90Q1-04Q2
Canada	.65	.03 (2.02)	-1.50 (1.94)	55	91Q1-04Q3
Australia	.36	1.72 (2.66)	4.76 (2.94)	58	90Q1-04Q2
U.K.	.77	3.23 (1.81)	6.18 (3.35)	48	92Q4-04Q3
Sweden	.26	2.59 (2.44)	5.65 (3.21)	47	93Q1-04Q3
U.S.	.77	.37 (1.43)	1.91 (2.22)	57	90Q3-04Q3

*Forecast errors are predicted values minus actual, expressed in percentage points of inflation.

Tables 3 and 4 present the forecast results for two different horizons: 8 quarters ahead (short term) and until the last quarter of the available data (long term), respectively. The forecast errors are expressed in percentage points of inflation, predicted values of inflation minus actual. The mean errors from the dynamic forecasts are consistently larger than the 1-step-ahead ones, which makes sense because the dynamic forecasts use estimated inflation in their computations, whereas the 1-step-ahead forecasts use actual inflation. In addition, the long-term-horizon forecast errors are much larger than their short-term-horizon counterparts, which suggests that the forecast means tend to diverge from actual inflation over time. Except for Canada, all dynamic forecasts over-predict inflation on average. In fact, despite having in several cases fairly high adjusted R^2's (the chosen in-sample goodness-of-fit criterion), the models yield fairly large out-of-sample mean forecast errors.[10] As an extreme example, New Zealand has the highest adjusted-R^2 and yet the highest long-term-horizon dynamic mean forecast error at 9.06%, meaning the Phillips models that were estimated using the pre-targeting samples, even if they fit the within-sample data well, can do a poor job of modeling the post-targeting environment. Notice also that both kinds of forecast errors at both horizons exhibit large standard deviations relative to their means, suggesting that *on average* inflation forecasted by the Phillips curve is not significantly different from actual inflation for most countries.

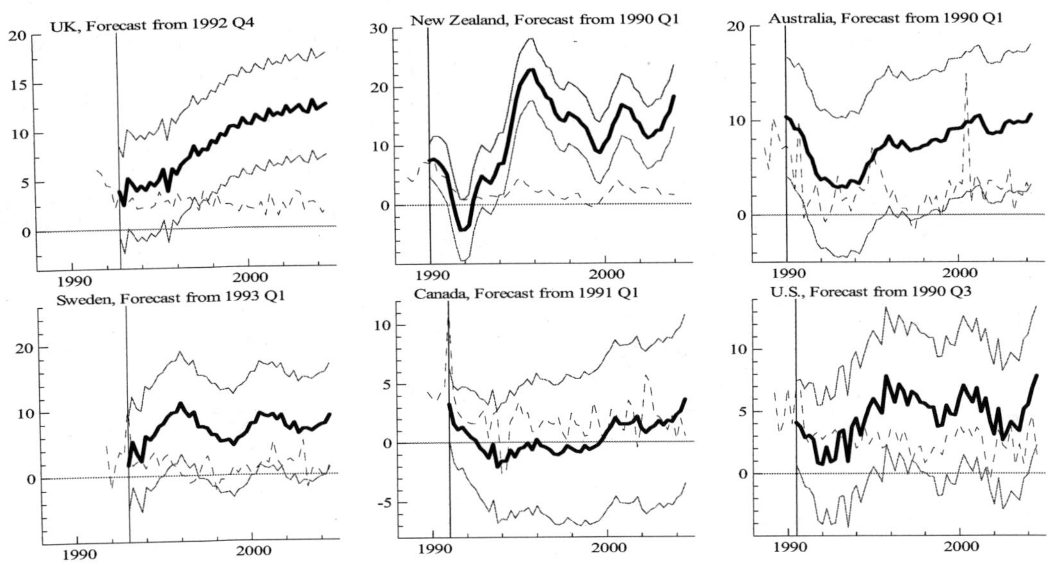

----- Actual

– Predicted +/- 2*SE

Fig. 2. Inflation Forecasts from Phillips Curves.

The means and standard deviations in Tables 3 and 4 are of course limited in their ability to describe patterns or movement over time. To that end we graph the forecasts versus actual inflation. Figure 2 shows the dynamic forecasts (solid line) and their confidence intervals (plus and minus two standard deviations) along with actual inflation (dashed line) across the whole post-adoption time period. The vertical bars mark the date of target adoption in each country. In four of the six cases the estimated inflation diverges from actual inflation. The most striking cases are New Zealand and the United Kingdom, whose forecasts become significantly different from actual inflation by the mid-1990s. Australia and Sweden also diverge, but the actual inflation rates remain close to the lower bound of the confidence bands. Canada is again the exception, with actual inflation rates above forecasted values more

10 Our 8-quarters-ahead forecast errors are sometimes several percentage points larger than in Bernanke et al., perhaps because we are drawing on some different and updated databases, because some of our sample sizes are shorter due to data availability, or because we might be using a slightly different method of annualizing our data. In any case, the signs of the errors are entirely consistent.

often than not, though the difference is not significant.[11] It is interesting to note that, while four of the five inflation targeters eventually exhibit either significant or suggestive differences between forecasted and actual inflation, the United States does not. Though its inflation forecasts lie above actual inflation for years, the two do not remain apart, let alone continue to diverge.

Figure 3 also shows each country's inflation forecast (solid line) and actual inflation (dashed line) but adds a shaded box representing its inflation target range (which is of course absent for the United States).[12] Except for Australia, whose inflation exhibits high variance, inflation rates in the targeting countries have for the most part been within the target range. Moreover, for all targeters actual inflation fluctuates within or around their target ranges, while predicted inflation lies well above the targets, suggesting that the credible targets successfully anchored inflation lower rate than would otherwise have prevailed.

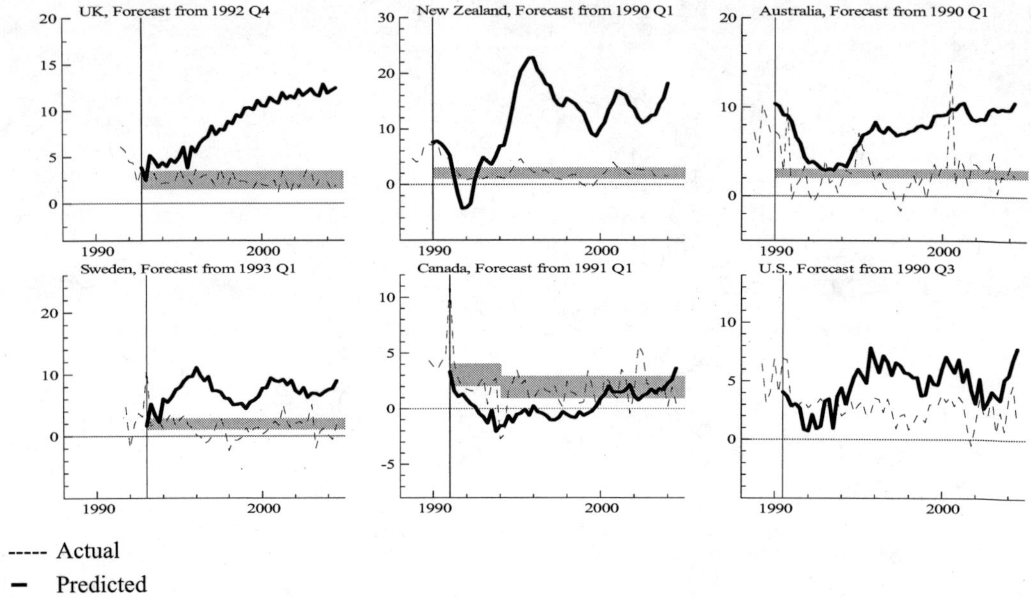

Fig 3. Inflation Forecast and Targets.

3.3 Rolling Regressions

The second method we use to examine how a credible targeting regime affects inflation is a rolling regression. This econometric technique repeatedly estimates the Phillips curve model for a given number of observations by starting with an initial sample and then moving the estimation window forward one quarter at a time, keeping the number of observations in the sample constant (Hendry and Krolzig, 2001).

[11] Our forecast results for Canada are consistent with Bernanke et al., whose Phillips curve model for that country, unlike those for the other inflation targeters, yields slightly lower inflation than actually occurred.

[12] Notice that Canada adjusted its target range downward from 3% to 2% with a 1-percentage-point allowance in December 1994.

Our estimation window is 40 quarters, giving us enough observations for a reliable estimation but not so many so as to hide the pattern of parameter movement over time. The window moves forward in increments of one quarter across both pre- and post-target adoption periods, and the coefficients are re-estimated at each increment. The model used is the general-form regression of equation (1). Our main interest is the evolution of two parameters—the coefficient on the utilization variable and the constant. Since capacity pressures should not affect a credible inflation targeter, as agents believe in their central bank's ability to counter inflationary pressure, we expect the utilization coefficients of targeting countries to move to zero. And, as the effects of the other inflation determinants diminish, the inflation target alone should prevail as the expected rate of inflation. That is, as the coefficients on the independent variables converge to zero, the constant should converge to the mean target value. For the United Kingdom, for example, the constant should move to 2.5 percent, the Bank of England's target (plus or minus 1 percentage point) for RPIX during our sample period.

The results of the rolling regressions for the utilization coefficient and the constant are graphed in Figures 4 and 5, respectively. The coefficient estimates are constant (forming the flat line in the figures) from the initial date (which varies by country, but is around the early to mid-1970s) to the initial date plus 40 quarters (somewhere early to mid-1980s), as that time-span constitutes the first estimation window. The coefficient begins to vary starting at the initial date plus 41 quarters, as the estimation window begins to move. The vertical bars in the graphs denote the onset of the targeting regimes in each country.

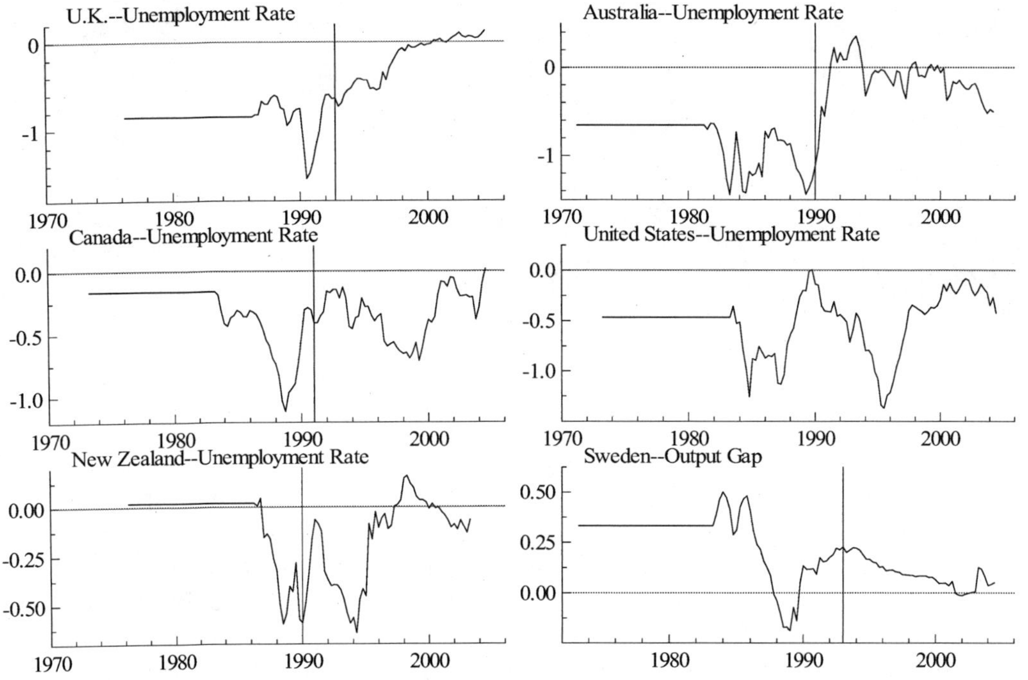

Fig. 4. Utilization Coefficient from Rolling Regressions.

Beginning with the capacity coefficient estimates, we see that three of the five inflation targeters—Australia, Sweden and the United Kingdom—show striking shifts in their utilization coefficients toward zero after adopting an inflation-targeting regime. Australia, whose coefficient varies consistently around -1 prior to inflation targeting, shows a sudden drop in value towards zero in the first few years after its target adoption. The United Kingdom and Sweden's capacity coefficients also converge to zero, just at a slower rate. New Zealand's coefficient exhibits large and rapid variance around a mean of about -.75, then seems to make a sustained shift toward zero around the mid-1990s. Strangely, New Zealand's coefficient is slightly above zero in the first few estimation samples. In order to investigate this oddity, we run the regression for just the first 40 quarters and find the long-run unemployment coefficient to be about .02, with a standard error of .221, making it not significantly different from zero in that time period. Canada's coefficient shows a very gradual upward trend, beginning just before 1990 and finally hitting zero around 2004.

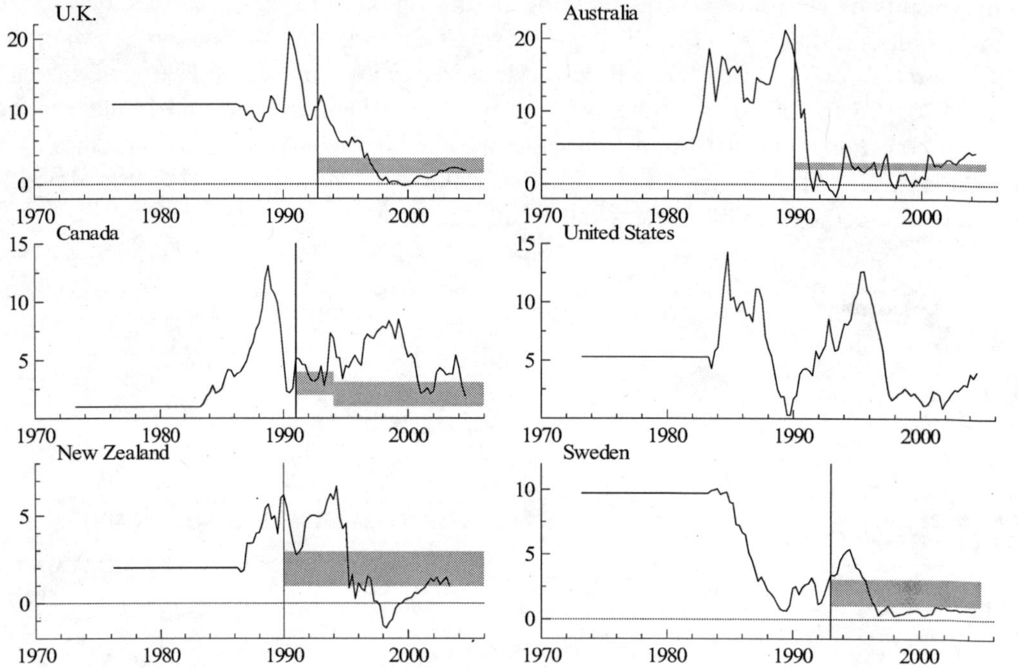

Fig. 5. Constant from Rolling Regressions.

The results for the constant, shown in Figure 5, lead us to similar conclusions. The United Kingdom, Australia and Sweden show clear shifts toward the inflation-target ranges after adoption, while New Zealand's is more gradual. Australia's intercept makes a sudden movement toward its target of 2-3%, while the United Kingdom's and Sweden's decline evenly and more gradually.[13] Interestingly, Sweden's constant starts decreasing steadily in the mid-1980s, well before their target adoption and almost as soon as the estimation window

[13] In December 2003 the Bank of England switched the price index on which it based its inflation targets from the RPI to the harmonized CPI. Since it used the RPI from adoption until 3 quarters before the end of our sample, we compare the forecasts with the RPI target.

starts moving forward. This is perhaps because the Phillips curve model could not adequately capture the overheating Swedish economy, operating under a fixed-exchange-rate regime at that time.[14] Canada is again showing only a very rough and gradual move toward its inflation target (which changed, as shown, in December 1994 from 3% to 2% with a 1-percentage-point allowance).

For comparison, the United States, which is not an official targeter, shows no sign of convergence to any value for its intercept or utilization coefficient. These coefficient estimates show just as much fluctuation after 1990 as before. It seems that capacity utilization, in the absence of an explicit inflation-target regime, has remained a significant determinant of U.S. inflation. These results are suggestive that monetary policy credibility of the inflation-targeting countries is being captured in the Phillips curve coefficients.

4 Conclusion

In this paper we attempted to quantify the effect of credible inflation-targeting regimes on the rate of inflation. We began by estimating Phillips curve models for six countries, five of which are targeters, based on economic relationships observed in the 1970s and 1980s, before any of them implemented a targeting regime. From these inflation models we were able to see how inflation might have behaved during the targeting regimes in the absence of credible targets. The results suggest that inflation under the non-targeting regime would have been larger than what was actually recorded (i.e., the inflation predicted by the model was larger than what prevailed in reality in the targeting regime). Rolling regressions illustrate that monetary policy credibility most likely reduced the impact utilization measures have on the rate of inflation. Not only did the coefficient estimates on capacity fall for targeters once they shifted to inflation-targeting regimes, but results for the United States, the one non-targeter in our analysis, shows no consistent pattern in either its forecast comparison or its rolling regressions.

These results imply that the relationship between inflation and the standard Phillips curve determinants changed for these inflation-targeting countries after the implementation of this monetary policy regime. Comparing these industrial countries to the United States, we see the changes were particular to inflation targeters. Though many argue that the United States is at least an implicit inflation targeter, the fact is that its Phillips-curve relationship has not been affected like the explicit targeters.

References

[1] Bäckström, Urban, 2000, "The Swedish Economy—Cyclical Upswing or a More Fundamental Improvement?" *BIS Review*, **41**.

[2] Ball, L. and R. Moffitt, 2001, "Productivity Growth and the Phillips Curve," *The Roaring Nineties: Can Full Employment Be Sustained?* Russel Sage Foundation.

[3] Bernanke, B. and M. Woodford, 2005, *The Inflation-Targeting Debate*, The University of Chicago Press, Chicago and London.

[14] See Bäckström [2000] for details on the Swedish economy in the late 1980s.

[4] Bernanke, B., T. Laubach, F. Mishkin, and A. Posen, 2001, *Inflation Targeting: Lessons from International Experience*, Princeton University Press, Princeton, N.J.

[5] Clarida R., J. Gali and M. Gertler, 1998, "Monetary Policy Rules in Practice: Some International Evidence," *European Economic Review*, **42**:6, 1033-1067.

[6] Hendry, D. and H. Krolzig, 2001, *Automatic Econometric Model Selection Using PcGets*, Timberlake Consultants, London.

[7] Huh, Chan, 1997, "Inflation Targeting," FRBSF Economic Letter. *http://www.frbsf.org /econrsrch/wklyltr/el97-04.html*

[8] Ihrig, J. and J. Marquez, 2004(a), "Productivity and Inflation in OECD Countries: an Econometric Investigation," forthcoming in *Economic Growth and Productivity*, Nova Science Publishers, Inc.

[9] Ihrig, J. and J. Marquez, 2004(b), "An Empirical Analysis of Inflation in OECD Countries," *International Finance*, **7**:1, 61-84.

[10] Phillips, A. W., 1958, "The relationship between unemployment and the rate of change of money wage rates in the United Kingdom, 1861-1957," *Economica*, **25**:100, 283-299.

[11] Truman, Edwin, 2003, *Inflation Targeting in the World Economy*, Institute for International economics, Washington, D.C.

In: Trends in Inflation Research
Editor: Barbara T. Credan, pp. 229-243
ISBN: 1-59454-825-0
© 2006 Nova Science Publishers, Inc.

Chapter 7

STRATEGIES FOR CONTROLLING INFLATION IN A MONETARY FRAMEWORK

Franz Seitz[a*] ***and Karl-Heinz Tödter***[b**]
[a] University of Applied Sciences, Amberg-Weiden, Hetzenrichter Weg 15, -92637 Weiden, Germany
[b] Deutsche Bundesbank, Economic Research Centre, Wilhelm-Epstein-Str. 14, D-60431 Frankfurt, Germany

ABSTRACT

Inflation is widely regarded as a monetary phenomenon. The long run relationship between money and prices has been confirmed by a large number of empirical studies across countries and across time. Nevertheless, the *"science of monetary policy"* (Clarida, Gali, Gertler 2001) largely neglects money. In the now popular New Keynesian type models money plays no active role. Analysing monetary policy without money is so widely accepted that it is now standard in macroeconomics textbooks. In contrast, some authors question the redundancy of money and argue that an independent role for money in the transmission mechanism should be taken seriously. The P-Star model offers a convenient framework of *"putting 'M' back in monetary policy."* In this model money plays an active role in the transmission process and monetary policy affects inflation through two channels, output and liquidity. It is shown that New Keynesian models are special cases of the P-Star-model. This paper analyses alternative monetary policy rules in the P-Star model. We find that inflation targeting is not a robust strategy for monetary policy. If the central bank does not solely care about inflation, a Taylor rule, monetary targeting or a two pillar strategy, combining monetary and inflation targeting, are clearly superior to inflation targeting. This holds if there is model uncertainty. Moreover, under asymmetric information, monetary targeting outperforms inflation targeting and a Taylor rule even if the central bank is geared to stabilising inflation and output.

Keywords: P-Star, monetary policy rules, Taylor rule, monetary targeting, inflation targeting
JEL: E41, E52, E58

---

[*] E-mail address: f.seitz@fh-amberg-weiden.de, Tel.: +(49)-961/382-172
[**] E-mail address: karlheinz.toedter@bundesbank.de, Tel.: +(49)-69/9566-2380

I Introduction

Although inflation is widely regarded as a monetary phenomenon in the long run, analyses of monetary policy are often based on New Keynesian (NK) models in which money plays no active role in the propagation of inflationary shocks and the transmission process in general.[1] In contrast, in the P-Star model money plays an active role in the transmission of monetary policy impulses and monetary policy has an impact on inflation through both the goods market and the money market.

This study investigates monetary policy rules on the basis of the P-Star model and the NK model. The basics of the models are outlined in section II. Applying euro area parameters, section III analyses alternative monetary policy strategies: a Taylor rule, monetary targeting, inflation targeting and a combination of monetary and inflation targeting. Section IV investigates the robustness of these rules with respect to model uncertainty. Section V considers asymmetric information in the sense that the central bank has an informational advantage on monetary growth. Finally, section VI concludes.

II The Models

The P-Star model may be summarised by the following equations (1) – (5):

$$y_t = y_t^* - \alpha(i_t - \Delta p_t - r_t^*) + \varepsilon_t \tag{1}$$

$$\Delta p_t = \Delta p_{t-1} + \eta(p_t^* - p_t) + \upsilon_t \tag{2}$$

$$m_t = p_t + \beta y_t - \gamma i_t + u_t \tag{3}$$

$$p_t^* = m_t - \beta y_t^* + \gamma i_t^* \tag{4}$$

$$i_t = i_t^* + g(\Delta p_{t-1} - \pi^T) \tag{5}$$

Except interest rates, all variables are in logarithms. Δ denotes differences and all the parameters *(α, β, γ, η, g)* are non-negative.[2] Equations (1) and (2) describe the goods market, equations (3) and (4) the money market and equation (5) is a monetary policy reaction function. (1) is a standard aggregate demand or IS function postulating that output y_t is above potential y_t^* if the real interest rate i_t - Δp_t is below its equilibrium or natural level r_t*, and vice versa. (2) is a Phillips-type relationship according to which inflation Δp_t accelerates if

[1] For prototype models in this spirit see McCallum (2001). Textbook versions may be found in Romer (2000) and Woodford (2003).

[2] A critical discussion of the P-Star model may be found in Svensson (2000, 2001) and Seitz and Tödter (2001).

there is a positive price gap (p_t* - p_t).[3] The long-run demand for real balances m_t - p_t in (3) depends on a transactions variable and opportunity costs of money holdings, approximated by real output y_t and the nominal interest rate i_t, respectively. The monetary overhang u_t captures deviations between current money holdings and long-run money demand. Equation (4) defines the equilibrium price level p_t^* (P-Star) as the price level that would emerge, given current money holdings, if output and the nominal interest rate are at their equilibrium levels y_t^* and i*, respectively. The equilibrium nominal interest rate i_t* in turn is made up of the equilibrium real interest rate r_t* and the inflation target of the central bank π^T. Combining (3) and (4) yields an expression for the price gap:

$$p_t^* - p_t = \beta(y_t - y_t^*) - \gamma(i_t - i_t^*) + u_t \tag{6}$$

Hence, upward pressure on prices results from the combination of three factors: a positive output gap (y>y*), an interest-rate below equilibrium (i<i*) and/or a monetary overhang (u>0).[4] Using the equation of exchange ($m + v \equiv p + y$) and ($m + v^* \equiv p^* + y^*$), where v is the velocity of circulation, the price gap may alternatively be written as the sum of the output gap and the liquidity gap,

$$p_t^* - p_t = (y_t - y_t^*) + (v_t^* - v_t) \tag{6'}$$

where the liquidity gap is $v_t^* - v_t = (\beta - 1)(y_t - y_t^*) - \gamma(i_t - i_t^*) + u_t$. Finally, the monetary policy reaction function (5) represents a strict form of direct inflation targeting. It states that the nominal interest rate reacts with a lag of one period to observed deviations of inflation from the inflation target π^T. For simplicity, all three types of shocks (demand shocks ε, price shocks υ and monetary shocks u) are assumed *iid* with zero means and constant variances.

In the long run equilibrium (if it exists) $y = y^*$, $\Delta p = \pi^T$ and $i = r^* + \pi^T$. The reduced form for the inflation process is

$$\Delta p_t = \pi^T + \theta(1 - \eta(\alpha\beta + \gamma)g)(\Delta p_{t-1} - \pi^T) + \theta\omega_t \tag{7}$$

where $\theta = 1/(1 - \eta\alpha\beta)$ and $\omega_t = \eta\beta\varepsilon_t + \eta u_t + \upsilon_t$ is a linear combination of all three types of shocks. In the P-Star model money plays an active role in determining inflation. Consequently, monetary policy acts through two transmission channels. The first runs from interest rates via the real demand for goods and the output gap to the inflation rate. In the second channel, interest rates have an influence on inflation dynamics via money demand and the liquidity gap. Consequently, not only excess demand for goods but low interest rates and

---

[3] Tödter (2002) provides a microeconomic foundation for such a relation along the lines of Rotemberg (1982).

[4] Alternatively, one could define an equilibrium money stock as money demand that would emerge, given current prices, if output and the nominal interest rate are at their equilibrium levels: $m^* = p + \beta y^* - \gamma i^*$. However, the resulting "money gap" is identical to the price gap: m - m* = p* - p.

excess money holdings as well exert an upward pressure on inflation. Note that an active role of money does not require money to appear in the IS equation nor in the policy reaction function.

With a passive monetary policy (*g = 0*), the coefficient of the lagged inflation rate in (7) is greater than one, rendering the system unstable. Stability requires an active monetary policy: $g > \alpha\beta/(\alpha\beta + \gamma)$. However, a strong response in line with the Taylor principle (*g > 1*) is not needed as long as money demand is interest elastic ($\gamma > 0$).[5] To illustrate, assume that $\alpha = 0.5$, $\beta = 1.3$, $\gamma = 0.7$ and $\eta = 0.2$. This yields the stability condition: $g > 0.48$.

The foregoing calibration is broadly consistent with empirical results obtained for the euro area.[6] Estimated interest elasticities of aggregate demand (α) range from values insignificantly different from zero (Goodhart and Hofmann 2000) to values close to one (Scharnagl 2002). The long run income elasticity and the interest elasticity of broad money demand (β, γ) are in line with estimates of EMU wide money demand (see Deutsche Bundesbank 2000 and Carstensen 2003 for results with different specifications). The response of the rate of inflation to changes in the output gap and the price gap (η), respectively, is consistent with estimates of Goodhart and Hofmann (2000), Smets (2003), Gerlach and Svensson (2003) and Scharnagl (2002).

NK - type models (see e.g. Taylor 1999, Clarida et al. 1998, 1999) are special cases of the P-Star model. Formally, the NK model is obtained if the price gap in (2) is replaced by the output gap. Dropping the effect of the liquidity gap on inflation de-activates the role of money, i.e. money becomes a recursive, passive variable. The usual LM relation in such a framework serves the sole purpose of determining the quantity of money the central bank needs to supply to clear the money market. In the NK model inflation only responds to the output gap.[7] Consequently, inflation can only be stabilised if the central bank reacts disproportionately $(g > 1)$ to deviations from the inflation target. As the real interest rate is the sole transmission channel of monetary policy, the Taylor restriction is necessary in order for an increase in the nominal rate to bring about a rise in the real rate. Interest-rate policy has little impact if the interest elasticity of the demand for goods is low and/or if the inflation rate reacts weakly to changes in the output gap. The NK system is dynamically unstable if only one of the following three conditions is violated: $g > 1, \alpha > 0, \eta > 0$.[8]

Given the calibration above and for any admissible value of *g*, monetary policy in the P-Star model is more efficient in terms of stabilising inflation than in the NK model. Higher

---

[5] The existence of a second transmission channel may explain why estimated reaction coefficients of monetary policy are often smaller than might be expected for monetary policy rules in the Taylor model; see Clarida et al. (1999). Benhabib et al. (2001) show theoretically that whether a particular system is stable or not depends crucially on the way money is assumed to enter preferences and technology.

[6] For the following calculations we also need numerical values for the variance of the three types of shocks. We normalise the variance of demand shocks to 1 and, in line with empirical evidence, set the variance of price shocks to 0.5 and the variance of monetary shocks to 2.

[7] This also means that these models are heavily influenced by the mismeasurement of the output gap and its effects on inflation and monetary policy, see e.g. Orphanides and van Norden (2003) and Gerberding et al. (2004). In this direction money might be helpful, too (Coenen et al. 2004).

[8] Christiano and Rostagno (2001) review various ways in which a monetary policy characterised by a Taylor rule can inject volatility into the economy. In their examples, a particular modification to the Taylor rule can reduce or even entirely eliminate the problems. Under their modified rule, the central bank monitors the money growth rate and commits to abandoning the Taylor rule in favour of a money growth rule in case money growth passes outside a particular monitoring range.

efficiency does not come at the cost of larger output fluctuations (see Table 1). Moreover, in the P-Star model, a policy of disinflation is associated with smaller output losses than in the NK model. The sacrifice ratio, i.e. the cumulative loss in output given a sustained decline in the inflation rate by 1 percentage point, in the P-Star model is markedly smaller than in its NK counterpart. [9] These results hold even for the assumed case of a high monetary volatility σ_u^2.

Table 1. Comparison of the P-Star-model and the NK-model.

		P-Star model	NK model
Dynamic stability	$g>$	0.48	1.00
Variance of inflation		1.61	6.17
Variance of output		1.78	1.87
Sacrifice ratio		0.91	5.00

$\alpha = 0.5, \beta = 1.3, \gamma = 0.7, \eta = 0.2, g = 1.5; \ \sigma_\varepsilon^2 = 1, \ \sigma_\upsilon^2 = 0.5, \ \sigma_u^2 = 2$.

In an empirical study for 17 industrial countries, Goodhart and Hofmann (2000) estimate aggregate demand equations (IS curves) and price equations (Phillips curves). Their results reveal that, although inflation dynamics in most countries depend on the output gap, interest-rate policy impulses do not even overcome the first hurdle of the transmission channel *"since it was not possible in almost all cases to detect any significant effect of the short-term real interest rate on the output gap"* (p 16). This evidence, denoted as the IS puzzle by Nelson (2001), calls into questions the suitability of the NK model as a standard tool for analysing monetary policy. In contrast, Favara and Giordani (2002) provide evidence that money demand shocks have substantial and persistent effects on output and prices.

The P-Star model has empirical relevance if the long-term money demand function is stable and if inflation is driven by the price gap. This requires stationarity of both, the monetary overhang (u) and the price gap (p^* - p). Since its origins (see Hallman et al. 1991), the P-Star approach has been investigated in numerous empirical analyses (Tatom 1992, Hoeller and Poret 1991, Kole and Leahy 1991, Deutsche Bundesbank 1992, Issing 1992, Reimers and Tödter 1994, Issing and Tödter 1995, Kimura 2001 and Orphanides and Porter 2001). Recently, Herwartz and Reimers (2001) tested the P-Star model with a comprehensive database for 110 countries for the period from 1960 to 1999. Their panel cointegration approach provides evidence for the existence of cointegration relationships between p and p^*, both for the entire sample and separately for the OECD countries and the countries of Latin America. Moreover, empirical evidence also supports the hypothesis of a stable long-term money demand relationship in the euro area (see for a recent overview of the arguments Calza and Sousa 2003).The P-Star concept has also been successfully applied to explaining inflation dynamics in the euro area (Scheide and Trabandt 2000, Gottschalk and Bröck 2000, Gerlach and Svensson 2003, Trecroci and Vega 2002, Calza et al. 2001, Fase 2001, Nicoletti-Altimari 2001, Scharnagl 2002). Hence, empirically, both conditions of the P-Star model seem to be supported by the available evidence for the euro area.

[9] Analytically, the sacrifice ratio is: $\alpha(g-1)/\eta(\alpha\beta(g-1)+\gamma g)$, collapsing to $1/\eta$ in the NK model.

Allowing for two transmission channels in the P-Star model, the output gap and the liquidity gap, has important consequences. Compared to a standard NK model, the P-Star model is stable under weaker conditions, monetary policy is more efficient in stabilising inflation and output, disinflation is less costly, and, conversely, inflating the economy is less beneficial.

III Alternative Policy Rules

So far, only one target, the inflation target, has been considered. In what follows, let us assume the following general loss function which the central bank seeks to minimise

$$L = E(\Phi_\pi \pi^2 + \Phi_y y^2 + \Phi_\mu \mu^2 + \Phi_i (i - i^*)^2), \tag{8}$$

where time indices are omitted to simplify notation and potential output y^* is normalised to zero. The variables $\pi = \Delta p - \pi^T$ and $\mu = \Delta m - \mu^T$ denote deviations of inflation (Δp) from the inflation target (π^T) and money growth (Δm) from the monetary target (μ^T), respectively. The first two terms take into account deviations from the inflation target and fluctuations of the output gap. The third term captures deviations from a target for monetary growth. Usually, rates of monetary growth are regarded as an intermediate objective or as an indicator variable and not as a final goal of monetary policy. Yet, the incorporation of this term into the loss function may be justified by the fact that inflation, in the long run, is caused by excess money growth or that money serves other useful purposes, e.g. as an information variable or as a 'summary statistic' for the transmission of monetary policy (see e.g. Nelson 2002, 2003 and Brand et al. 2003).[10] Therefore, the central bank should not be indifferent to money growth volatility. The final term penalises interest-rate fluctuations. Empirical evidence suggests that central banks tend to change interest rates gradually, i.e. they smooth interest rates (see e.g. Clarida et al. 1998). The optimum rule which follows from loss function (8) is complex - even in our stylised model - and difficult to communicate to the general public. In practice, therefore, preference is often given to simpler and more transparent rules. However, as a benchmark we calculate the optimal meta-strategy that follows from (8) using the weights

$$\Phi_\pi = 0.5,\ \Phi_y = 0.25,\ \Phi_\mu = \Phi_i = 0.125 \tag{8'}$$

The highest priority is assigned to the inflation target, followed by the output target. Both, the monetary target and the objective of smoothing interest rates receive modest yet not negligible weights. In addition to inflation targeting, a Taylor rule, monetary targeting and a combination of monetary and inflation targeting (*MIT*) are analysed.

---

[10] Other reasons why money might not be redundant are summarised by Leeper and Roush (2003), 10f. Clausen (2003) discusses the drawbacks of not incorporating the role of money adequately in the inflation forecast targeting framework.

In the following we analyse these monetary policy strategies within the P-Star model. For this purpose we use a slightly generalised version of the model (1) - (5) in which q denotes the price gap:[11]

$$y = -\alpha(i - \pi - r^*) + \varepsilon \tag{9}$$

$$\pi = \lambda \pi_{-1} + \eta q + \upsilon \tag{10}$$

$$q = \beta y - \gamma(i - i^*) + u \tag{11}$$

$$\mu = \pi + \Delta q \tag{12}$$

The demand equation (9) is the same as in (1). The inflation equation (10) originates from $\Delta p = E(\Delta p) + \eta q + \upsilon$, with expectations $E(.)$ being formed at the end of period $t\text{-}1$. Inflation expectations are assumed to depend on the most recently observed inflation rate and the central bank's inflation target: $E(\Delta p) = \lambda \Delta p_{-1} + (1\text{-}\lambda)\pi^T$. For $\lambda = 1$, inflation expectations are purely backward looking, for $\lambda = 0$, they are geared to the central bank's inflation target.[12] Combining both hypotheses yields (10). (11) defines the price gap on the basis of the long-run money demand function as in (6). From (3), the rate of growth of the money stock is $\Delta m = \Delta p + \Delta(\beta y - \gamma i + u)$. Accordingly, the monetary target is defined as $\mu^T = \pi^T + \Delta(\beta y^* - \gamma i^*)$. The deviations from the monetary target ($\mu = \Delta m - \mu^T$) may therefore be written like in (12) as the sum of the deviations from the inflation target plus changes in the price gap. From this point of view, monetary targeting extends inflation targeting by taking into account changes of the price gap, which, in turn, drives inflation. Also note that the variable μ is recursive, unless it appears in the reaction function of monetary policy. The latter has been omitted for the time being. It is replaced below by alternative loss functions for monetary policy.

From (9) - (12), the reduced form of the inflation process is

$$\pi = \lambda \theta \pi_{-1} + \theta \omega - \theta \psi (i - i^*) , \tag{13}$$

where $\psi = \eta(\alpha\beta + \gamma)$, $\theta = 1/(1 - \eta\alpha\beta)$ and $\omega_t = \eta\beta\varepsilon_t + \eta u_t + \upsilon_t$. Hence, inflation is driven by three factors: its own dynamics (inflation persistence), innovations (demand shocks, supply shocks and monetary shocks), and the stance of monetary policy.

---

[11] Clarida et al. (1999) discuss a similar model with forward-looking expectations. Estrella and Fuhrer (2003) provide evidence that the backward looking Phillips curve is more stable and fits US data better than its forward-looking counterpart. Similar evidence for the euro area is provided by Bardsen et al. (2004). Furthermore, Woodford (2003) shows how optimal monetary policy (and thus optimal inflation expectations) will be characterised by history-dependency. In such a situation, both central bank actions and expectations of the private sector depend on past economic conditions.

[12] Owing to the introduction of the persistence parameter λ, the P-Star model is stable even with a passive monetary policy ($g = 0$), provided $\lambda < 1\text{-}\eta\alpha\beta$.

Strict inflation targeting may be captured by minimising the loss function $L = E(\pi^2)$. The following simple reaction function is obtained

$$i = i^* + g^*[\lambda\theta\pi_{-1} + \theta\hat{\omega}] \equiv i^* + g^*\hat{\pi}, \tag{14}$$

where the expression in square brackets is the conditional inflation forecast for period *t*, $\hat{\pi} = E(\pi / i = i^*)$ ($\hat{\omega}$ being the central bank's forecast of the shock effects on the inflation rate) and $g^* = 1/\theta\psi$ is the optimal reaction intensity to the inflation forecast. If the parameters α, β, γ, η decrease, g^* increases. Hence, if the economy reacts more sluggishly to inflationary shocks, monetary policy must compensate for this by reacting more strongly, and vice versa.

If the central bank is able to observe the shocks in period *t* before it sets the interest rate, it has an informational advantage over the private sector (asymmetric information), enabling it to act with perfect foresight: $\hat{\omega} = \omega$.[13] If the central bank has no informational advantage (symmetric information) it forms rational expectations about the level of the shocks, i.e. it assumes. $\hat{\omega} = E(\omega) = 0$. Both cases may be combined in the formulation $\hat{\omega} = \kappa\omega$, where $\kappa = 1\ (0)$ corresponds to perfect foresight (rational expectations). Solving for the inflation rate results in $\pi = \theta(1-\kappa)\omega$. Hence, under *optimal inflation targeting*, the deviations from the inflation target are either zero or a pure random process with zero mean. The variance of the deviations from the inflation target is:

$$\sigma_{\pi}^2 = \theta^2(1-\kappa)^2\sigma_{\omega}^2 \tag{15}$$

With perfect foresight, the central bank is able to eliminate fluctuations in the inflation rate completely. Forecasting the shocks reduces the inflation variance, provided the forecasts are not too far off the mark $(0 < \kappa < 2)$.

The *Taylor rule* is a strategy in which the central bank responds both to inflation and output. To derive the optimum Taylor rule, we set $\Phi_{\mu} = \Phi_i = 0$, which is equivalent to the loss function

$$L = E(2\pi^2 + y^2)/3 \tag{16}$$

The weight of the inflation target amounts to twice the weight of the output target.[14]

Money growth targeting is a kind of intermediate targeting strategy for controlling inflation but may also serve other purposes, as mentioned above. In what follows, monetary targeting is geared solely to deviations of the monetary growth from the monetary target, i.e.

---

[13] Romer and Romer (2001) show for the Fed that asymmetry may be the relevant case in practice as far as inflation forecasts are concerned.

[14] The usual weights in Taylor rules of 3:1 are analysed in Tödter (2002). The general results are insensitive to this parameterisation.

$$L = E(\mu^2). \tag{17}$$

Since money growth is no final target, it seems natural to include the ultimate goal of monetary policy, inflation, into the loss function as well. A strategy of monetary and inflation targeting can be derived from[15]

$$L = E(\mu^2 + \pi^2)/2 \tag{18}$$

Table 2 shows the stabilisation results that emerge with these rules assuming that the central bank operates under rational expectations ($\hat{\omega} = 0$).

Table 2. Performance of alternative strategies.

	Inflation	Output	Variance of Money growth	Interest rates
Inflation targeting	0.86	2.82	42.35	5.22
Taylor rule	1.02	1.66	18.16	1.40
Monetary targeting	2.48	2.59	8.82	1.65
MIT	2.25	2.44	8.86	1.60
Meta-strategy	*1.61*	*1.77*	*9.77*	*0.69*

$\alpha = 0.5,\ \beta = 1.3,\ \gamma = 0.7,\ \eta = 0.2,\ \lambda = 2/3;\ \sigma_\varepsilon^2 = 1,\ \sigma_\upsilon^2 = 0.5,\ \sigma_u^2 = 2;\ \hat{\omega} = 0$

Optimal inflation targeting minimises the variance of inflation. However, it leads to fluctuations of the other variables which are significantly greater than in any other strategy. Especially, the variance of monetary growth rises and there are considerable interest rate fluctuations. With just a slightly higher inflation variance, the Taylor rule results in considerably smaller fluctuations of all other variables. Monetary targeting as well as MIT differ from the Taylor rule by a halving of the variance of money growth whereas the fluctuations of inflation and output are markedly greater.

Table 3 summarises the characteristics of the various strategies using loss function (8/8'). In order to be able to assess the value of information on future shocks, both perfect foresight and rational expectations are considered. In both cases and relative to the meta-strategy, monetary targeting and the MIT strategy perform best, closely followed by the Taylor rule, whereas the loss with inflation targeting is greatest. Monetary targeting and MIT yield the closest approximations to the meta-strategy. The superior performance of strategies including money is due to the fact that money acts as a 'summary statistic' in which money demand shocks, output shocks and price shocks are reflected.[16]

---

[15] The two-pillar strategy of the Eurosystem is based on both an analysis of monetary developments and a kind of inflation targeting, i.e. it may also be interpreted in terms of (18).

[16] This is a specific variant of an old monetarist argument that money is a 'summary statistic' for the monetary policy transmission process, see for a modern interpretation Nelson (2002a, b).

Table 3. Performance of alternative strategies: Total loss*.

	Perfect foresight	Rational expectations
Inflation targeting	4.80	7.08
Taylor rule	1.56	3.37
Monetary targeting	0.94	3.20
MIT	0.95	3.04
Meta-strategy	*0.72*	*2.55*

Parameters as in Table 2.* Calculated with (8').

IV Model Uncertainty

In this section we look at the performance of the different strategies if the central bank is uncertain about the true model. In particular, we investigate whether the results are sensitive to the specification of the Phillips equation (9). Assume that the central bank does not know whether inflation responds to the price gap, the output gap, or some linear combination of both. This may be stated by the following Phillips-relationship:

$$\pi = \lambda \pi_{-1} + \rho \eta q + (1-\rho)\eta y + \upsilon \qquad (10')$$

In particular, the central bank does not know whether the P-Star model *($\rho = 1$)*, the NK model *($\rho = 0$)*, or a hybrid model *($0 < \rho < 1$)* is true.[17] In what follows, we set $\rho = ½$ in the hybrid model. The general conclusions within this model are insensitive to the value of ρ. The results are shown in Table 4.

When the central bank exclusively cares about inflation, then - almost by definition - inflation targeting is the best strategy across models. Evaluated in terms of the broad loss function (8'), MIT is the best strategy in the P-Star model as well as in the hybrid model whereas the Taylor rule performs best in the NK model. In contrast, inflation targeting is the worst strategy in all three models. Actually, the differences between the Taylor rule, monetary targeting and MIT are relatively minor. Averaging across the three models shows that the Taylor rule, monetary targeting and MIT perform almost equally well, the Taylor rule having a small advantage. Hence, when there is model uncertainty, these three strategies perform well and turn out to be robust.[18]

Table 4. Model uncertainty: Total loss*.

	P-Star model	NK model	Hybrid model	Average across models
Inflation targeting	7.08	22.71	9.63	13.14
Taylor rule	3.37	**2.61**	2.95	**2.98**
Monetary targeting	3.20	3.14	2.97	3.10
MIT	**3.04**	3.10	**2.88**	3.01

Parameters as in Table 2; * Loss function (8) with weights (8'), $\hat{\omega} = 0$.

[17] Another way of analysing uncertainty about the true model within a framework incorporating the two models considered here, so-called paradigm uncertainty, may be found in Gerdesmeier et al. (2002).

[18] Demertzis and Tiemann (2003) show that the higher the degree of risk aversion, the more likely the central bank will choose to apply a robust rule under model uncertainty.

V Asymmetric Information

So far it has been assumed that, when setting interest rates, the central bank knows either the realisations of the shocks (perfect foresight) or predicts their means (rational expectations). In what follows, we analyse an intermediate case in which the central bank has perfect foresight only on monetary growth. In particular, we assume that the central bank knows the monetary growth rates before it sets interest rates but that it does not have any information on the realisations of the other endogenous variables. On the basis of the reduced form for the deviations of money growth from target, the central bank makes a conditional forecast of this deviation which turns out as

$$\tilde{\mu} = (1+\alpha\beta)\lambda\theta\pi_{-1} - q_{-1} + \zeta \tag{19}$$

where ζ is a linear combination of the shocks.[19] In other words, under these circumstances, the central bank is able to observe a linear combination of the shocks, but not the individual shocks. If the central bank sets interest rates according to

$$i = i^* + \frac{1}{\Theta}\tilde{\mu}, \tag{20}$$

where $\Theta = \alpha\beta + \gamma + \theta\psi(1+\alpha\beta)$, it can completely eliminate the deviations from the monetary target. Somewhat surprisingly, the reaction function (20) turns out to be superior to inflation targeting or to the Taylor rule even if its performance is evaluated in terms of the loss function (16), i.e. when inflation and output variability are taken into account. This comparison is provided in Table 5. The first two lines reproduce the variance of the endogenous variables from Table 2. The third line shows the performance of rule (20) where the central bank has prior information on monetary growth (MT with prior information). The final column shows the minimised value of the Taylor loss function (16). Monetary targeting stabilises inflation and output more than do inflation targeting or the Taylor rule. It may thus be prudent to use the available information on monetary developments.

Table 5. Monetary targeting and asymmetric information.

	Variance of				Broad loss+)	Taylor loss*)
	Inflation	Output	Monetary growth	Interest rates		
Inflation targeting with $\hat{\omega} = 0$	0.86	2.82	42.35	5.22	7.08	1.51
Taylor rule with $\hat{\omega} = 0$	1.02	1.66	18.16	1.40	3.37	1.24
MT with prior information	0.53	0.87	0.00	3.70	0.94	0.64
" in NK - model	*0.83*	*0.92*	*0.28*	*4.40*	*1.23*	*0.86*
" in Hybrid model	*0.61*	*0.89*	*0.06*	*3.97*	*1.03*	*0.71*

Parameters as in Table 2. +) Loss function (8') *) Loss function (16)

[19] $\zeta = \theta\left[(1+\eta)\beta\varepsilon + (1+\alpha\beta)(\upsilon + \eta u)\right] + u$.

What if the central bank follows rule (20) not knowing whether the true model is of the NK or hybrid type? Specifically, assume that inflation only responds to the output gap or to the output gap and the price gap as in (10') with $\rho = 0, \frac{1}{2}$, respectively. The final two rows of Table 5 show that the resulting loss (8') is lower than the loss shown for these two models in Table 4 under inflation targeting or under a Taylor rule (and the same holds for the Taylor loss). The value of the information on monetary growth outweighs the loss of using the wrong model.

VI Conclusion

Inflation in the long run is widely regarded as a monetary phenomenon, yet money does not play an active role in the monetary transmission process in nowadays widespread used New Keynesian models. In these models, monetary policy impulses have an impact on the development of inflation solely through the output gap. In contrast, the P-Star model assigns an active role to money such that monetary policy impulses act on inflation dynamics via two channels, output and liquidity. The P-Star model assumes that the long-run money demand function is stable and that inflation is driven by the price gap and not only by the output gap, both being supported by empirical evidence for the euro area. Compared to the New Keynesian model, the P-Star model has attractive features in terms of dynamic stability, efficiency of monetary policy and the costs of disinflation. Of course, the numerical results reported depend on the parameterisation, which was chosen in accordance with the empirical evidence for the euro area. However, the results do not appear to depend critically on the specific parameter values.

Strict inflation targeting is a strategy which is geared solely to stabilising inflation. If the central bank has a target system in which other variables – output, money growth and interest rates – play a role alongside inflation, more broadly based strategies, such as the Taylor rule, monetary targeting or a combination of monetary and inflation targeting are clearly superior to inflation targeting. This conclusion is reinforced if model uncertainty is taken into account. Even if the central bank is uncertain about the transmission channels of monetary policy these three strategies yield good and remarkably similar results. Moreover, if the central bank has information on monetary growth before setting interest rates, monetary targeting is superior to inflation targeting and to a Taylor rule, even if the central bank's loss function is geared to stabilising inflation and output.

Economic theory and empirical evidence support the view that monetary growth determines inflation in the long run. Yet, in the last decade the '*science of monetary policy*' (Clarida et al. 1999) has largely neglected money in the analysis of central bank policy. In this respect, the P-Star model provides an alternative framework that is both simple and flexible.

References

[1] Bardsen, G., E.S. Jansen, and R. Nymoen (2004): "Econometric Evaluation of the New Keynesian Phillips Curve", *Oxford Bulletin of Economics and Statistics*, **66**, Supplement, 671-686.

[2] Benhabib, J., S. Schmitt-Grohé, and M. Uribe (2001): "Monetary Policy and Multiple Equilibria", *American Economic Review* **91**, 167-186.

[3] Brand, C., H.-E. Reimers, and F. Seitz (2003): "Forecasting Real GDP: What Role for Narrow Money?", *ECB Working Paper* No. **254**, September.

[4] Calza, A., D. Gerdesmeier, and J. Levy (2001), "Euro Area Money Demand: Measuring the Opportunity Costs Appropriately", *IMF Working Paper* No. **01**/179.

[5] Calza, A., and J. Sousa (2003): "Why has Money Demand been More Stable in the Euro Area than in Other Economies? A Literature Review", *ECB Working Paper* No. **261**, September.

[6] Carstensen, K. (2003): "Is European Money Demand Still Stable?", *Kiel Working Paper* No. **1179**, August.

[7] Christiano L.J., and M. Rostagno (2001): "Money Growth Monitoring and the Taylor Rule", *NBER Working Paper* No. **8539**, October.

[8] Clarida, R., J. Gali, and M. Gertler (1998): "Monetary Policy Rules in Practice", *European Economic Review* **42**, 1033-1067.

[9] Clarida, R., J. Gali, and M. Gertler (1999): "The Science of Monetary Policy: A New Keynesian Perspective", *Journal of Economic Literature* **XXXVII**, 1661-1707.

[10] Clausen, J.R. (2003): "Inflation Forecast Targeting: A Monetary Policy Strategy without Shortcomings?", *Zeitschrift für Wirtschaftspolitik* **50**, 289-308.

[11] Coenen, G., A. Levin, and V. Wieland (2004): "Data Uncertainty and the Role of Money as an Information Variable for Monetary Policy", *European Economic Review*, forthcoming.

[12] Demertzis, M., and A.F. Tieman (2003): "Robust versus Optimal Rules in Monetary Policy: A note" De Nederlandsche Bank, Staff Reports 2003, No. 103.

[13] Deutsche Bundesbank (1992): "The Correlation Between Monetary Growth and Price Movements in the Federal Republic of Germany", *Monthly Report*, January, 20-29.

[14] Deutsche Bundesbank (2000): Macro-Econometric Multi-Country Model: MEMMOD, Frankfurt am Main, June.

[15] Estrella, A., and J. Fuhrer (2003): "Monetary Policy Shifts and the Stability of Monetary Policy Models", *The Review of Economics and Statistics* **85**, 94-104.

[16] Fase, M.M.G. (2001): "Monetary Policy Rules for EMU", in *Coordination and Growth*; Essays in Honour of Simon K. Kuipers, Dordrecht: Kluwer Academic Publishers, 181-98.

[17] Favara G., and P. Giordani (2002): "Monetary Policy without Monetary Aggregates: Some (Surprising) Evidence", April, *mimeo*.

[18] Gerberding, C., F. .Seitz, and A. Worms, (2004): "How the Bundesbank Really Conducted Monetary Policy: An Analysis Based on Real-time Data", Deutsche Bundesbank, *Discussion Paper Series* **1** 25/2004.

[19] Gerdesmeier, D., R. Motto, and H. Pill (2002): "Paradigm Uncertainty and the Role of Monetary Developments in Monetary Policy Rules", available at http://www.ecb.int/events/conf/other/mprules.

[20] Gerlach, S., and L.E.O. Svensson (2003): "Money and Inflation in the Euro Area: A Case for Monetary Indicators?" *Journal of Monetary Economics* **50**, 1649-1672.

[21] Goodhart, C. and B. Hofmann (2000): "Financial Variables and the Conduct of Monetary Policy", University of Bonn, London School of Economics and Zentrum für Europäische Integrationsforschung, *mimeo*.

[22] Gottschalk, J., and S. Bröck (2000): "Inflationsprognosen für den Euro-Raum: Wie gut sind P*-Modelle? Deutsches Institut für Wirtschaftsforschung, *Vierteljahresheft*, **69**/1, 69-89.

[23] Hallman, J.J., R.D. Porter, and D.H. Small (1991): "Is the Price Level Tied to the M2 Monetary Aggregate in the Long Run?" *American Economic Review* **81**, 841-858.

[24] Herwartz, H., and H.-E. Reimers (2001): "Long-Run Links Among Money, Prices, and Output: World-Wide Evidence", *Discussion paper* 14/01, Economic Research Centre of the Deutsche Bundesbank, September.

[25] Hoeller, P., and P. Poret (1991): "Is P-Star a Good Indicator of Inflationary Pressure in OECD Countries?" *OECD Economic Studies* **17**.

[26] Issing, O. (1992): "Theoretical and Empirical Foundations of the Deutsche Bundesbank's Monetary Targeting", *Intereconomics* **27**, 289-300.

[27] Issing, O., and K.-H. Tödter (1995): "Geldmenge und Preise im vereinigten Deutschland" in D. Duwendag (ed.), Neuere Entwicklungen in der Geldtheorie und Währungspolitik, Schriften des Vereins für Socialpolitik, Berlin: Duncker & Humblot, 97-123.

[28] Kimura, T. (2001): The Impact of Financial Anxieties on Money Demand in Japan, in Klöckers, H.-J., Willeke, C. (eds.), *Monetary Analysis: Tools and Applications*, Frankfurt, 97-116.

[29] Kole, L.S., and M.P. Leahy (1991): "The Usefulness of P* Measures for Japan and Germany", *International Finance Discussion Paper* No. **414**, Board of Governors of the Federal Reserve System.

[30] Leeper, E.M., and J.E. Roush (2003): "Putting "M" Back in Monetary Policy", *Journal of Money, Credit and Banking* **35**(6), 1217-1256.

[31] McCallum, B.T. (2001): "Monetary Policy Analysis in Models Without Money," Federal Reserve Bank of St. Louis *Review*, **83**/4, 145-160.

[32] Nelson, E. (2001): "What does the UK's Monetary Policy and Inflation Experience Tell Us About the Transmission Mechanism?" *CEPR Discussion Paper* 3047.

[33] Nelson, E. (2002): "Direct Effects of Base Money on Aggregate Demand: Theory and Evidence", *Journal of Monetary Economics* **49**, 687-708.

[34] Nelson, E. (2003): "The Future of Monetary Aggregates in Monetary Policy Analysis", *Journal of Monetary Economics* **50**, 1029-1059.

[35] Nicoletti-Altimari, S. (2001): "Does Money Lead Inflation in the Euro Area?" *ECB Working Paper* No. **63**, May.

[36] Orphanides, A., and R.D. Porter (2001): "Money and Inflation: the role of information regarding the determinants of M2 behaviour", in Klöckers, H.-J., Willeke, C. (eds.), *Monetary Analysis: Tools and Applications*, Frankfurt, 77-95.

[37] Orphanides, A., and S. van Norden (2003): "The Reliability of Inflation Forecasts Based on Output Gap Estimates in Real Time", CIRANO Working Paper 2003s-01, January.

[38] Reimers, H.-E., and K.-H. Tödter (1994): "P-Star as a Link Between Money and Prices", *Review of World Economics* **130**, 273-89.

[39] Romer, D. (2001): "Advanced Macroeconomics", 2nd ed., Boston et al..

[40] Romer, C.D., and D.H. Romer (2001): "Federal Reserve Information and the Behavior of Interest Rates", *American Economic Review* **90**, 429-457.

[41] Rotemberg, J.J. (1982): "Sticky Prices in the United States", *Journal of Political Economy* **60**, 1187-1211.

[42] Scharnagl, M. (2002): "Is there a Role for Monetary Aggregates in the Conduct of Monetary Policy for the Euro Area?", Deutsche Bundesbank, *mimeo*.

[43] Scheide, J., and M. Trabandt (2000): "Predicting Inflation in Euroland - The P-Star Approach", *Kiel Working Paper* No **1029**, December.

[44] Seitz, F., and K.-H. Tödter (2001), "How the P* Model Rationalises Monetary Targeting: A Comment on Svensson", *German Economic Review* **2**, 303-308.

[45] Smets, F. (2003): "Maintaining Price Stability: How long is the medium term?", *Journal of Monetary Economics* **50**,1293-1309.

[46] Svensson, L.E.O. (2000): "Does the P* Model Provide any Rationale for Monetary Targeting?" *German Economic Review* **1**, 69-81.

[47] Svensson, L.E.O. (2001): "Response to Seitz and Tödter, 'How the P* Model Rationalises Monetary Targeting: A Comment on Svensson'", German Economic Review **2**, 309-312

[48] Tatom, J.A. (1992): "The P-Star Model and Austrian Prices", *Empirica* **1**, 3-17.

[49] Taylor, J.B. (1999): "The Robustness and Efficiency of Monetary Policy Rules as Guidelines for the Interest Rate Setting by the European Central Bank", *Journal of Monetary Economics* **43**, 655-79.

[50] Tödter, K.-H. (2002): "Monetary Indicators and Policy Rules in the P-Star Model", *Discussion Paper* **18**/02, Economic Research Centre of the Deutsche Bundesbank, June.

[51] Trecroci C., and J.L. Vega (2002): "The Information Content of M3 for Future Inflation", *Review of World Economics* **138**, 22-53.

[52] Woodford, M. (2003): " Interest & Prices – Foundations of a Theory of Monetary Policy", Princeton and Oxford.

INDEX

A

B

D

E

I

J

K

L

M

N

O

P

Q

R

S

T